ON DUPONT CIRCLE

ON DUPONT CIRCLE

*Franklin and Eleanor Roosevelt
and the Progressives Who Shaped Our World*

JAMES SRODES

COUNTERPOINT

BERKELEY

Copyright © 2012 James Srodes

All rights reserved under International and Pan-American Copyright Conventions.

Library of Congress Cataloging-in-Publication Data is available.

ISBN 978-1-58243-716-3

Cover design by Ann Weinstock
Interior design by Erin Seaward-Hiatt

Printed in the United States of America

COUNTERPOINT
1919 Fifth Street
Berkeley, CA 94710

www.counterpointpress.com

Distributed by Publishers Group West

10 9 8 7 6 5 4 3 2 1

for Cecile
the better angel of my nature

Contents

PREFACE	I
The Characters at the Beginning	7
Chronology of Important Events	11
ONE Dinner at the House of Truth	17
TWO Avoiding an Unavoidable War	33
THREE The Dupont Circle Set at War	49
FOUR Fighting for Peace in Paris	63
FIVE Compromises and Betrayals	75
SIX Victory without Triumph	91
SEVEN Progressivism in Retreat	101
EIGHT Adrift in Smoke-Filled Rooms	115
NINE Dupont Circle Diplomats	131
TEN The Best Laid Plans	151
ELEVEN Rethinking Progressivism	165
TWELVE Who but Hoover?	179
THIRTEEN The Making of a President	195
FOURTEEN Messy Foreign Affairs	211

FIFTEEN War Clouds on the Horizon   227

SIXTEEN Looking Over the Horizon   245

SEVENTEEN Success Threatened by Scandal   261

CONCLUSIONS The Legacy of the Dupont Circle Set   281

NOTES   289

ACKNOWLEDGMENTS   315

INDEX   317

Preface

I ONCE MET A WOMAN IN HER NINETIES who had graduated from a teacher's college in Mississippi and had spent the rest of her life educating children in the rural schools of that state. As she talked about the long sweep of history she had witnessed, I asked her what had been her ambition on the day when she graduated from that college and set out on her life. She answered without hesitation, "To work for the League of Nations." Noting my surprised expression, she added, "Everyone wanted to in those days. It was such a noble idea."

Anyone who reads much history has to be struck by how there are so few really important people involved in any great event. Take any epoch, say, the Hundred Years War, the Age of Enlightenment, or the Great Depression, and it is hard to come up with a list of more than a few score—fewer than a hundred, certainly—characters who truly can be said to have been important to the outcome. What is so remarkable about our cast of a dozen young characters who assembled in the Dupont Circle neighborhood of Washington, D.C., on the eve of World War I is how important they would remain to the history of the rest of what we call the American Century.

Their story is about a time when a tectonic movement shifted the axis of the entire world. During the first half of the twentieth century, no corner of the globe was immune from the aftershocks as the rush to industrialization produced a series of tremors that toppled monarchies, reduced great capitals to rubble, and condemned millions to famine and violent death while at the same time producing an unimagined prosperity for some and dispossession and resentment for others. This cultural and political upheaval threw off a deadening past and freed millions to aspire to a civil society based on the ideal goal of equality for all under the rule of law. What had been unthinkably idealistic in the early years of the previous century would become an unquestioned standard of what a good society is today.

This is not the place to discuss the tidal shifts and adjustments of that time. Instead I have focused on the lives of a dozen individuals who were born in the late nineteenth century, who came of age in the early decades of the twentieth, and whose roles in that ultimate quest influence our lives today. Each of my twelve personalities was prominent in their own right; each has been the subject of at least one biography, and in several cases, whole shelves of books have been devoted to some of the others. Additionally, they all were outsiders. Even Franklin and Eleanor Roosevelt, despite their aristocratic lineages, were viewed by their social equals and others in their wide circle of family as being slightly exotic. Walter Lippmann, Felix Frankfurter, and Herbert Hoover stood apart from the American mainstream by virtue of their religious faiths. The three Dulles siblings, John Foster, Allen, and Eleanor, spent their youths shuttling between privilege and privation. Phillip Kerr and Eustace Percy were born into the tiny enclave of the British Catholic nobility but spent their lives in radical politics.

What binds them together is how, at an unusually young age, all of them became acquainted and how they came and went in and out of each other's lives during the twenty-year period between the two world wars. Even when they were separated by careers, private lives, and changing fortunes, they remained unified by common commitment to that ultimate quest that so engaged other young people of their age. So they are not just a group of friends who banded together, they are a metaphor for a generation who had to overcome the restraints of being born in one era and living their lives in the turmoil of another even as they struggled to create a better future.

The name they gave themselves was *Progressives*, a word that has a different meaning today. Just as today's Tea Party partisans have little in common with the revolutionaries who dumped tea in Boston harbor in 1773, our cast of characters would have been astonished at the political objectives of those who call themselves Progressives today. The enlarged role of the national government in determining social standards, for example, would have discomfited them. For that matter, many of the labels and descriptive terms in this story have changed during the more than a hundred years between their time and ours. While the two major political parties were called Democrat and Republican, they represented vastly different coalitions of interests then and in many ways were more fluid groupings; there were Progressive wings of both parties then, for example.

There were as many kinds of Progressivism as there were Progressives themselves. One reason that Progressivism never achieved the cohesiveness it needed to survive as a lasting political force lay in the single-issue zealotry of some of its adherents. For example, in his fine history of the Prohibition movement, historian Daniel Okrent shows how discord over whether or not the campaign's ultimate goal was to extend voting rights to women proved to be the crusade's undoing.[1] The movement also attracted eugenicists who believed that selective birth policies could solve many social issues; for a time there was a vogue for enforced sterilization of individuals judged to be genetically unfit to participate in the society's gene pool. Unlike Socialist dogma, most Progressives were as chary of big government as they were of an overweening corporatist state; bigness to the minds of most was suspect. Progressive advocacy ranged from those who retreated to rural communes based on Christian doctrines to those who proclaimed new economic theories from Marxism to Fascism with all of the ideological gradations in between.

WHILE THE LARGER MASS of people still could be thrilled at the sound of the drum and the sight of a flag, Progressives saw war as a bacillus that infected all of a society's tissues. The lives lost robbed families of their hold on prosperity; the materials consumed in munitions and engines of war were better and more profitably used to improve domestic infrastructure, better housing and sanitation. The increasing prospect of a major war between alliances of great powers spreading into a global conflict threatened the very existence of civilization.

Like other Great Awakenings of the past, the Progressive search for peace drew support from individuals who did not always share in the movement's broader agenda of government reform and social uplift. But perhaps no one captured the heart of Progressive peace seekers more than the bellicose hero of the Spanish-American War, President Theodore Roosevelt. It was to his banner that our cast of characters first rallied. However, as his age and intemperate judgment took its toll, the young Progressive shifted—warily at first—to the ranks of that other American Messiah of Peace, Woodrow Wilson.

Our story is about the period of profound disappointment that came after Wilson's ill-starred crusade to create a permanent world peace, which was rejected by the American people. We will follow the public careers and private lives of our youthful Progressives— the Dupont Circle set—as they mature and refine their ambitions. We will see how their search for some mechanism to win peace in a world bent on war will send them seeking another leader, and how, as warily as before, they will coalesce around Franklin Roosevelt for yet another effort. In so doing, these once-young idealists will end up giving us the world we inhabit today.

When these young people first began to arrive in Washington, D.C., to seek their fortunes, they and the far larger group of young people they represent lived in a nation and world that was vastly different than our world today. Yet they were aware that everything was changing around them and that the outcome could evolve in a hundred different ways. Over the twenty years our story covers, these young crusaders would change their own attitudes on many specific issues. But what is important to us today is how firmly they stayed constant to an overarching vision of a strong America that would guarantee social justice at home, install democracy in other nations, and, above all, try to foster a world where peace—not war—was the norm. The world as it is today is our inheritance from these ambitious, flawed pioneers for peace. They are remarkable people, and it is a remarkable story.

The Characters at the Beginning

FRANKLIN D. ROOSEVELT, 1882–1945

Born into a wealthy and socially prominent New York family, FDR was schooled in social responsibility at Groton and Harvard. He was elected to the New York State Senate in 1910 where he earned respect for fighting Tammany Hall's bosses but was generally considered a lightweight political figure until he was an early backer of Woodrow Wilson's 1912 presidential election. He came to Washington in 1913 as assistant secretary of the Navy.

ELEANOR ROOSEVELT, 1884–1962

Orphaned by age ten, Eleanor was educated at a feminist school in England until she returned to New York and became a social worker in the slums. Shy and awkward socially, she played no role in her husband's early political career and disliked the duties imposed on a government official's wife when they joined the Wilson administration.

HERBERT HOOVER, 1874–1964

Hoover was a wealthy mining engineer living in London when World War I began in 1914. He became the director of a massive relief program for Belgium and, when America entered the war, returned to Washington to head the government's successful food rationing program. He became an international celebrity and a regular guest at the House of Truth.

WALTER LIPPMANN, 1889–1965

Lippmann was born into a wealthy German-Jewish family and was educated at an elite New York prep school. He enrolled in Harvard at seventeen and graduated with honors in three years. He published his first book of political philosophy in 1913 and was among the founding editors of *The New Republic*. He was an adviser to Theodore Roosevelt. In 1916 he moved into the House of Truth in Washington as a journalist.

FELIX FRANKFURTER, 1882–1965

Frankfurter was born in Vienna and educated in the public schools of New York's Lower East Side; he graduated from the City College of New York and from Harvard Law School with honors. A supporter of Theodore Roosevelt and early contributor to *The New Republic,* he became one of the early tenants at the House of Truth until Wilson's election in 1912. He returned to Harvard Law School to teach but came back to Washington in 1916 to work in the War Department.

JOHN FOSTER DULLES, 1888–1959

Foster Dulles had lived in the Washington mansion of his grandfather, a former secretary of state, while he attended law school. He joined the powerful Wall Street law firm of Sullivan & Cromwell in 1912 but returned regularly to Washington when his uncle, Robert Lansing, became Woodrow Wilson's secretary of state.

ALLEN W. DULLES, 1893–1969

After graduating from Princeton in 1916, Allen Dulles was recruited as a diplomat-spy by his uncle Robert Lansing and was sent to Vienna.

ELEANOR LANSING DULLES, 1895–1996

After spending much of her childhood living at the Foster-Lansing mansion, Eleanor Dulles was about to graduate from Bryn Mawr and trying unsuccessfully to get a government job in Washington.

WILLIAM C. BULLITT, 1891–1967

William Bullitt's father was a wealthy Philadelphia lawyer, but after graduating from Yale, he dropped out of law school and became a widely published journalist. He came to Washington in 1916 as a correspondent and became a frequent guest at the House of Truth.

Sumner Welles, 1892–1961

As a youth, Welles was befriended by both Franklin and Eleanor Roosevelt and was a page at their wedding in 1905. He also had family connections with the Dulleses and visited the Foster-Lansing mansion regularly while applying to join the State Department in 1917.

Philip Kerr, 1882–1940

Philip Kerr was heir to a Scottish title and was educated at both Eton and Oxford. After an early diplomatic career in South Africa, Kerr in 1910 founded the *Round Table Journal,* a British political magazine. He visited Washington regularly and resided at the House of Truth. His visits increased in 1916 when he became a key foreign affairs adviser to the British prime minister, David Lloyd George.

Lord Eustace Percy, 1887–1958

A British nobleman, Percy joined the diplomatic corps after graduating from Oxford and was posted to the Embassy in Washington as a secretary. He was an early tenant of the House of Truth.

Hamilton Fish Armstrong, 1897–1973

Ham Armstrong was born to a wealthy New York society family. He was a student peace activist at Princeton and joined the staff of *The New Republic* in 1915. When Lippmann moved to the House of Truth in 1916, Armstrong was a frequent visitor.

Chronology of Important Events

1912

Woodrow Wilson defeats incumbent William Howard Taft and the Progressive Party's nominee Theodore Roosevelt for the presidency.

War in Balkans starts.

1914

World War I begins with Britain, France, Russia, Belgium, and Italy allied against Germany, Austria-Hungary, and Turkey.

U.S. Marines occupy Veracruz, Mexico.

1916

U.S. troops enter Mexico in unsuccessful pursuit of Mexican revolutionary Pancho Villa.

Eight-hour workday for railroad workers prevents nationwide strike.

1917

United States enters World War I in April.

Four women are given six-month jail sentences for picketing White House for women's suffrage.

1918

World War I ends with armistice.

Republicans win control of U.S. Congress in November elections.

Woodrow Wilson sails to France for Paris Peace Conference.

1919

Versailles Peace Treaty signed in June; rejected by U.S. Senate in December. The treaty demands Germany pay war reparations for the destruction it caused; an Allied commission in 1921 set the amount demanded at $785 billion (current).

Woodrow Wilson wins Nobel Peace Prize; suffers series of debilitating strokes.

British and American staff members at the Paris conference agree to form what will become the Council on Foreign Relations (U.S.) and the Royal Institute of International Affairs (Britain).

1920

Republican Warren Harding elected president; U.S. Senate rejects joining newly formed League of Nations. Democratic vice-presidential nominee Franklin D. Roosevelt makes more than eight hundred speeches in the campaign.

Royal Institute of International Affairs founded.

Italian anarchists Sacco and Vanzetti indicted for murder.

Prohibition begins in United States.

1921–1922

Franklin D. Roosevelt stricken with polio, which cripples his legs.

Five-nation Washington Naval Conference reduces number and size of battleships; first major disarmament conference.

Mussolini forms first Italian Fascist government.

Council on Foreign Relations formed in New York.

Inflation ravages German economy.

1928

Kellogg-Briand Pact, outlawing war, signed by sixty-five nations.

Herbert Hoover elected president; Franklin D. Roosevelt elected Governor of New York.

1929

New York Stock Exchange crash on October 28 marks start of global economic crisis; U.S. shares lose $364 billion (current) in value.

1932

Bonus Army of seventeen thousand World War I veterans demonstrate in Washington, D.C., for Congress to provide benefits promised but never funded. Led by General Douglas MacArthur, U.S. troops disperse the demonstrators by force.

Franklin D. Roosevelt defeats Herbert Hoover in landslide presidential election.

Nazi Party gains second place in German elections.

1933

FDR inauguration marks start of New Deal economic recovery program; Congress grants president wide powers.

Adolf Hitler becomes Germany's chancellor; first concentration camps set up.

U.S. goes off the gold standard.

Japan withdraws from the League of Nations after invading Manchuria. It will renounce the 1922 naval treaty limits in 1934, starting a global arms race.

Roosevelt signs diplomatic recognition and trade pact with U.S.S.R. William C. Bullitt becomes first American ambassador to Moscow.

1936

Spanish Civil War begins.

Hitler and Mussolini sign Berlin-Rome Axis pact.

FDR reelected to second term. Bullitt named Ambassador to France.

Chinese Nationalist leader Chiang Kai-shek declares war on Japan.

Italy seizes control of Ethiopia despite League of Nation protests. Will leave League in 1937.

1939

Hitler invades Poland; Britain and France declare war on Germany, marking the beginning of World War II.

On FDR's orders, Undersecretary of State Sumner Welles sets up secret postwar policy research group with Council on Foreign Relations; group later folded into a formal policy research staff inside the State Department to produce outlines of United Nations.

1940

Roosevelt elected to unprecedented third term.

1941

In August, FDR and Winston Churchill sign the Atlantic Charter that pledges to defeat Axis Powers and to set up a United Nations organization after the war to insure peace.

On December 7, Japanese airplanes attack the U.S. Naval base at Pearl Harbor; by December 10, both Germany and Italy have declared war on the United States.

1942

Naval battles at Midway Island and in the Coral Sea are U.S. victories.

In October, four hundred thousand U.S. troops land in North Africa.

1944

June 6: D-Day invasion of Nazi-held Europe by Allies.

Dumbarton Oaks conference to organize United Stations begins.

Bretton Woods conference to organize postwar World Bank and International Monetary Fund.

1945

On April 12, Franklin D. Roosevelt dies.

On May 8, Germany surrenders—VE Day.

On June 26, United Nations Charter signed in San Francisco. League of Nations ceases operations in October. World Bank begins postwar reconstruction lending.

On August 15, Japan surrenders—VJ Day.

One

DINNER AT THE HOUSE OF TRUTH

1911–1916

"It was Justice Holmes who gave the place the name, The House of Truth. It was to tease us because we were all so certain we were right. He also said we were the brightest minds and the fastest talkers in Washington. And we were."

—U.S. Supreme Court Justice Felix Frankfurter

*I*T NEVER OCCURRED TO THE young men and women at the House of Truth, as they sat arguing around a late night dinner table strewn with empty wine bottles and smoldering ashtrays, that they were the inheritors of a long tradition in American politics.

They would have laughed. They knew better. For although they all had been born in the last years of the nineteenth century, the early weeks of 1916 now found them placed very firmly in a new age. They considered themselves a generation of crusaders in a new cause—Progressivism. They came from diverse family backgrounds, but education at elite universities gave them a sense of superior judgment that entitled them—no, required them—to speak their new truths to an older age. They were unique, they thought.

In reality, these young Progressives were the advance guard of the next phase in the evolution of America into the society we have today. As they disputed and tested each other in that shabby boarding house in Washington, D.C., all of them dreamed of achieving great things. But none of them could foresee just what important lives they all would come to live or how far their legacy would reach into our own times. They hoped to create a new world. We are the inheritors of that dream as surely as they were the heirs of a tradition that began with America's founding.

America always has been in a state of tension between ideals and interests. From the first debate after the War for Independence about what kind of national government we wanted, Americans divided between those who wanted to push for a more expansive vision and those who wanted to consolidate and to conserve what had been achieved.

This tension remains constant. But the issues that dominate any moment are in perpetual flux. A party formed around an idea will, with success, become a party of interests and will grow staid and unresponsive to the next wave of change. Then another group urging idealistic goals will coalesce into a new force, and the political cycle will begin again. Traditional parties must evolve and adopt these new ideas, or they die out and vanish.

Driving all this is something in the genetic code of Americans that makes them want to reform and improve their own lives and the world around them. This irresistible urge—shared both by native-born citizens and newly arrived immigrants—lies at the heart of that other unique national trait, a boundless optimism, a conviction that the future must be better than the present.

So the Democrat-Republicans who battled the early Federalists morphed into the Democrats, who fractured in the 1840s to produce the Whig insurgents. Then the Whigs themselves splintered into heated disagreement over slavery, immigrants, and the new lands on the frontier. Out of that breakup emerged the new party of ideals known as the Republican Party.

However, by the end of the nineteenth century, both Republicans and Democrats had come to represent interests and not ideals. The land-hungry farmers and fervent abolitionists of the GOP (Abraham Lincoln's Grand Old Party) had been replaced by the Civil War's victors. Bankers and railroad builders vied with owners of factories that made mass-produced goods to squeeze more wealth out of the land. The Democrats presided over a coalition of corrupt Northern big city bosses who herded huge blocs of immigrant claimants and disaffected Southerners who were trying to climb back out of the economic wreckage of their lost rebellion.

Once again, the forces of change pushed their way into the political arena. The new movement became known as Progressivism. It took its name from theorists such as William James, John Dewey, and George Santayana, each of whom had pioneered new ways of organizing "progressive" education reforms and cultural improvement. To the vexation of the leaders of both the Republicans and Democrats, groups of Progressive advocates began to appear within their own ranks.

The Progressives were at root a hybrid of various reformist movements that had come and gone before. Campaigns for improved wages and fair labor standards, for the abolition of slavery, for a prohibition of alcohol, and for increased rights for women all had existed well before the Civil War. Indeed, there always would be as many varieties of Progressivism as there were Progressives devoted to one cause above all others. But this loose conglomeration of causes gained a unifying theme as the nineteenth century came to an end.

What united these loose strands that had existed without much impact was the revolutionary concept that a strong and active government was needed to intercede for the individual citizen as a referee and advocate in the increasingly exploitative relationships people had with big corporations and big city governments, which had agendas that too often ignored the public good.

The immediate target of the Progressives was to reform city governments, and it was here that the movement met its first successes. But the longer-term goal was a national government that imposed a nationwide standard of fairness and equality into all corners of American life. This was a novel idea that overturned the traditional notion that government's prime responsibility was to foster conditions for the benefit of the major corporations and banks and otherwise stand out of the way of prosperity.

The Progressive theorists argued that America was changing. Through their teaching and writing, they pointed to the tidal wave of industrialization and urban sprawl they saw as both the great promise and even greater threat to the nation's contract of equality of opportunity for its citizens. With so many of those citizens being swept into a mass society of cities and factories, it also was clear that a more activist national government was the third force that could protect the citizen and also harness the irresistible power of those masses for to build a better nation.

It fell to a new generation of students of these theorists to attempt to put the tenets of Progressivism to work through government policies. By the first decade of the twentieth century, a steady stream of university-trained, fiercely ambitious intellectuals began to seek careers that took them out of the academic world and into the public arena. They became missionaries who carried a new evangelism of social engineering into crowded tenements and dismal factories. For the more determined, two avenues that offered the quickest access to the power of reform were the law and advocacy journalism, and indeed, one could try both. While New York City was an obvious magnet for these young Progressives as a place to exchange ideas and publish their thoughts, increasingly, the most ambitious were drawn to the hitherto somnolent backwater seat of the national government in Washington, D.C.

By the second decade of the twentieth century, a remarkable group of these young strivers found their way to Washington and by chance found themselves clustered in a neighborhood that was both newly fashionable and handy to those government offices where they would try their hands at reforming America into the best of all possible nations. The neighborhood was identified with a small round park dedicated to an obscure Civil War admiral—Dupont Circle.

A convenient starting point for our story begins on a Sunday afternoon in January 1916 when journalist Walter Lippmann wrote a note from New York City to Franklin D. Roosevelt, then the assistant Secretary of the Navy in Washington:

Dear Mr. Roosevelt, I shall be in Washington Wednesday and Thursday and I would like to see you if it is possible for a little talk while I am there. I have to spend the afternoons at the Capitol. So if you could make it in the morning or, preferably, if you could lunch with me either day that would be fine. I shall be staying at 1727 19th Street. Could you drop me a line there about this? Sincerely, Walter Lippmann.[1]

The note marks the start of a cautious shift by Lippmann from his role as a confidential adviser for the first real hero of the Progressive movement, Republican ex-President Theodore Roosevelt, to backing the re-election campaign of the then incumbent, Democrat Woodrow Wilson. It also confirms the start of a lifelong and often contentious relationship between the thirty-four-year-old Franklin Roosevelt, a rising star in American politics, and Lippmann, who already at twenty-seven was a nationally recognized author on political philosophy and one of the founding editors of the most powerful voice of the Progressive movement, *The New Republic*. Intriguingly, this also is the first reference to the boarding house, which served as Lippmann's base for the two years he was in Washington, a nondescript row house on a tree-shaded side street just two blocks east of busy Connecticut Avenue—jocularly known to its inhabitants and many visitors as The House of Truth.

The House of Truth came into being in 1911, when Robert Grosvenor Valentine, the Taft administration's Commissioner of Indian Affairs, rented it and turned it into an informally run bachelor's boarding house. Valentine was a wealthy Harvard graduate and MIT professor in the new discipline of industrial engineering.

If one occupation symbolized the Progressive image, it was the engineer. He was the fact-driven, unassailably honest inventor whose constructions—whether a bridge, a new machine, or a social reform—were both more efficient and at the same time more moral than what had come before. If industrialization was inevitable, the engineer would make it a force for good. As Harvard historian John M. Jordan has observed, "Engineers appeared as heroes in over one hundred silent movies and in novels that sold roughly five million copies between 1897 and 1920."[2] Technocrats like Alexander

Graham Bell, Thomas Edison, and Henry Ford, who created new technologies and then turned them into commercial successes, were living proof of American intellectual and (equally important) moral superiority.

So Valentine had little trouble recruiting congenial companionship from among the growing number of Harvard alumni who were beginning their careers in the federal government.[3] The narrow three-story house featured a large living room-dining room space on the ground floor that served as a commons area; tall French windows on the front could open in the evening to catch the breeze. The furnishings there and in the six upstairs bedrooms were second-hand and a bit rump-sprung, but that added to a raffish, slightly bohemian atmosphere that made it highly attractive to the young people who were drawn there.

Another important attraction of the house was its location in the newly fashionable neighborhood of embassies and important residences that orbited the Dupont Circle intersection of the grand boulevards of Connecticut and Massachusetts Avenues. As late as the 1880s, the area had been a marshy wasteland and dumping ground at the outer limits of the city. But by 1900, the boundaries of the District of Columbia had been greatly expanded northwards in response to a building boom.[4]

The circle with its small park was less than a mile northwest of the White House and the baroque office building that housed the State, Navy, and War Departments, so government workers and high officials alike enjoyed an easy commute. Radiating out from the circle, newly paved streets crossed a recently opened bridge on P Street across Rock Creek Park to link with Georgetown; another bridge for trolleys extended Connecticut Avenue northwards and spanned the Rock Creek to reach out to the faraway farm hamlet of Chevy Chase. If one had business in downtown Washington, Dupont Circle was where one wanted to live.

The neighborhood had undergone change almost from the start of its development twenty years earlier. First, huge beaux arts mansions had been built by the wealthy and powerful. But plainer row houses then filled in what had been empty lots on either side of the major spokes off the circle. Many of the older, more ornate structures had changed hands by 1916 and now housed important embassies including those of Great Britain, Italy, Austria-Hungary, and China. But the House of Truth was in a compact enclave of row houses and small apartments that had originally served a community of affluent African American families of mid-level government employees.

Valentine was a generous host when it came to entertaining, so the House of Truth quickly became a social magnet for the influx of young men and women who had come to Washington for exciting careers. Two early visitors who became residents were a young lawyer from New York named Felix Frankfurter and a British nobleman, Lord Eustace Percy, who was the private secretary to the British ambassador. Percy later recalled,

> That household had a touch of du Maurier's Quartier Latin, with law and the erratic politics of the then infant *New Republic* taking the place of art as the focus of its endless talk and even more endless flow of casual guests. The range of our talk and our entertainment was 'extensive and peculiar'; but we hardly took ourselves or our symposia seriously enough to deserve the mocking nickname of the "House of Truth," which some humorist conferred upon us.[5]

The "humorist," of course, was Supreme Court Justice Oliver Wendell Holmes Jr., who lived nearby. Despite his age (he was seventy-five), Holmes quickly had established himself as the paterfamilias of the younger men, and he relished ruling over the dinner table debates as both referee and devil's advocate.

Most of the bachelors of the House of Truth were very young, in their twenties. They favored the new soft–collar shirts and slightly shabby suits common to the graduate students they had recently been. Their drink of choice was the newly popular daiquiri cocktail, and they pursued debutantes of suffragette convictions with the intensity of their arguments and their taste for dancing to gramophone records of that new syncopated rage known as "jass." The food served was indifferent but was available at all hours—a good thing because the fierce debates around the dinner table often lasted all night, and arguing was hungry work.

The house on Nineteenth Street was just one of several important addresses in the Dupont Circle neighborhood that were homes to prominent political names in the Progressive roster. These houses served as both debating arenas and recruiting centers for what New York socialite Mabel Dodge had dubbed as the young "movers and shakers" of the movement.

Nearby at 1323 Eighteenth Street was a vastly different place that was the focus for what might be called the Old Guard Progressives. The huge art-filled mansion of former secretary of state John Watson Foster was a base for older reformers who had come to power in the previous century, but it also drew young place-seekers from the wealthier families of the Eastern Establishment. Its lure for young visitors was enhanced by the fact that by 1915, one of Foster's sons-in-law, Robert Lansing, had just been made secretary of state for Woodrow Wilson. Lansing and his wife lived there as well.

Champagne, not cocktails, was the drink of choice for the guests in white ties and tailcoats who gathered amidst the collection of Russian and Spanish art collected during Foster's tours as U.S. ambassador. During the day, young diplomats wore the same high starched collars of their elders, and when their day jobs did not require the cutaway coat and striped trousers of officialdom, their suits were cut more formally and were newer than those of their friends at the House of Truth.

Lansing, a Democrat, and Foster, a Republican, were the two most prominent activists in what was called the arbitration movement in international affairs. For more than twenty-five years, they had participated in more negotiations to settle international disputes than anyone. The common wisdom that prevailed was that conflicts between nations could be reduced to legal issues and adjudicated peacefully if only the contending parties would concede to the judgments of impartial arbitrators. Arbitration had drawn the support of determined peace activists such as Alfred Nobel, the inventor of dynamite, who funded a prize to reward those who sought to end war. Steel baron Andrew Carnegie had donated the funds to establish a World Court in The Hague, Netherlands, as a permanent forum for international law adjudication.

The quest for peace was hardly new. After the carnage of the American Civil War, the nature of war itself had morphed from distant conflicts between professional armies to a general melee that resulted in horrifying civilian destruction without resolving the causes of the wars themselves. Whatever other issues might engage Progressive reformers, all agreed that the quest for peace was paramount. The new genre of warfare—exaggerated by new armaments of staggering firepower—threatened civilization itself. No one felt safe. So Prussia could conquer France with ease; Russia could attack the tottering Ottoman Empire and in turn be sent into near-revolution by its defeat at the hands of the upstart Japanese navy. However emotionally satisfying America's triumph over the Spanish in 1898 might have been, it nevertheless added to the growing instability of the globe.

For all his public reputation for bellicosity, no one had worked harder through arbitration to resolve disputes between nations than Theodore Roosevelt. He saw neither irony nor contradiction in this commitment despite his much-publicized role in the 1898 war with Spain and his leadership in the creation of the United States Navy as an overnight world sea power. He was not alone in this, for many Americans, Progressives included, accepted the need for U.S. global power while decrying the empire-driven conflicts of other nations in Europe and Asia. Roosevelt had supported U.S. participation in the First Hague Peace Conference held in 1899, where the twenty-five other nations failed to achieve a general disarmament pact but did set the first agreed-on constraints on modern warfare.

As president, Roosevelt used the prestige of his office to broker two important peace settlements that could have deteriorated into a world conflict. In 1904, the Japanese surprised the world and Czarist Russia by defeating the Russian fleet at Port Arthur, Manchuria. By 1905, Roosevelt brought the warring parties together to Portsmouth, New Hampshire, and used the sheer force of his personality to win an agreement to end hostilities. The treaty was internationally hailed as a triumph for peace even though it left the main parties dissatisfied. A year later, Roosevelt intervened again when Germany and France came close to war over possession of Morocco. In 1906, he became the first American president to be awarded the Nobel Peace Prize.

The high-water mark of the arbitration movement came a year later. Roosevelt had called for a second Hague conference in 1904, but it did not actually meet for three more years because of international tensions. Yet there was a mood of optimism, for by 1907, there were on the books nearly fifty bilateral treaties agreeing to arbitration among the forty-six nations that attended. The large official U.S. delegation was led by the secretary of state, Elihu Root. American prestige at the conference was boosted by the presence of John Watson Foster, who attended as the official delegate of the Imperial Chinese government. General Foster, as he preferred to be called, had been a Civil War hero chosen by presidents starting with Ulysses Grant for important ambassadorships that had taken him from Mexico to Russia and Spain, and included a brief stint as Secretary of State. Later, Foster was so successful in brokering a peace treaty between the Japanese and Chinese that both governments asked him to become their permanent legal representative. Foster chose China, and to help him at the Hague meeting, he took along his eldest nephew, a Princeton junior named John Foster Dulles, as his secretary.

The 1907 Hague meeting quickly became a nullity largely because the major powers would not halt their own rearmament programs, especially the race to build ever-bigger navies to expand their global reach. The slide to a global war began to accelerate. In 1911 and 1912, the overture to World War I began with a series of wars and temporary truces involving Turkey, Greece, Bulgaria, and Serbia. The tide of global war had become so inexorable that by the time it began in earnest in the summer of 1914, most Progressives were seized by a fear that America for the first time would be drawn into a conflict that could destroy the new nation they were trying to build.

It was this threat that was on Walter Lippmann's mind two years later when he approached Franklin Roosevelt for advice in

January 1916. Lippmann and Roosevelt had met before through Harvard connections, but they were not yet friends. Roosevelt was a cousin of the former president but had chosen to be a Democrat and an early Wilson backer. What the journalist wanted to know was whether President Wilson was in earnest when he vowed to keep the United States aloof from the horrifying carnage in Europe and to use America's undeniable influence to bring warring parties to the peace table.

Wilson was something of a mystery to most Progressives; he was a Democrat, and most of them had begun their political lives as Theodore Roosevelt Republicans. Just forty years old when the assassination of President William McKinley elevated him to the Presidency in 1900, Roosevelt had been symbolic of the young Progressives' coming of age.

Even in 1912, when Roosevelt tried a comeback, most Progressives, including Lippmann and Felix Frankfurter, had enthusiastically backed his return to the White House. Both were equally dismayed by Wilson's overwhelming win in the Electoral College. When Roosevelt returned from his near-fatal trip to the Amazon in 1914, among the first people he invited to breakfast at the Harvard Club in New York to discuss another presidential challenge in 1916 were Lippmann and Frankfurter. Lippmann continued to plot strategy with Roosevelt well into 1915.[6]

But by 1916, Roosevelt appeared old and out-of-touch. Moreover, he had dismayed many of his backers by urging an immediate American involvement in the war on the side of the British and French allies. Many of the older mentors of the young Progressives, men like Justice Holmes who owed his Supreme Court appointment to Roosevelt, were privately turning against him. Holmes, despite his age, was more than a figurehead guest at the head of the House of Truth dinner table debates. While theorists like James, Dewey, and Santayana had given the Progressives the philosophical foundation of pragmatism and social reform, Holmes had been one of a quartet of older Progressive activists who far more directly influenced the House of Truth residents and others by showing how to apply their beliefs to the real world. Along with Holmes, each of the other three—muckraking journalist Lincoln Steffens, attorney and perennial Cabinet officer Henry Stimson, and Boston lawyer Louis Brandeis—served as talent spotters, mentors, and patrons of a group of promising young Progressives who either frequented the House of Truth or lived in the immediate vicinity of Dupont Circle at this critical time.

There were other forces that impelled the Dupont Circle set into the arms of Woodrow Wilson. Not the least was the fact that Wilson had reached out in 1912 to a number of important and wealthy Jewish leaders who were among the key backers of Progressive reforms. Men like financiers Bernard Baruch, Jacob Schiff, and Henry Morgenthau all came from families who had come from Germany or Austria thirty years earlier and made their fortunes. They had succeeded despite a prevailing anti-Semitism which seemed to them to increase over the years as a flood of poor new arrivals—many of them Jews from Eastern Europe—washed into America's major cities. Like the younger Frankfurter and Lippmann, these older men were skeptical of the Zionist campaign for a Palestinian homeland; rather they wanted to be Americans who happened to have been born Jewish. The newly arrived Eastern Jews, with their foreign tongues and strange ways, were an embarrassment to their more established co-religionists.[7] What Wilson offered, which these Republicans never had, was access to political power and position.

Wilson's public image was attractive to other Progressives who were looking for an alternative to the Republicans. He was both an intellectual and a robust manly figure. He had been a recognized scholar on Congressional government and had coached college football. He had successfully transformed Princeton into a first-rank university, and it helped that he was a devoted husband and father. More compelling to the Progressives who sought a Democrat to challenge the corrupt stranglehold of the big city (and Irish dominated) political machines—like New York's Tammany Hall—Wilson, as Governor of New Jersey, had disavowed the equally corrupt local bosses there. It also helped that he was a devoutly religious man and a highly persuasive public speaker.

Wilson's great strength was the uncanny ability to guess which way the public parade was headed and to appear to lead without getting too far in front. He also was quick at bringing his new backers into useful service beyond simple campaign finance. Morgenthau was made U.S. ambassador to Turkey, and Baruch, who was regarded as Wall Street's leading expert on short selling into bear market downturns, was made an ex-officio personal economic adviser. And in the spring of 1916, with the re-election campaign looming, Wilson nominated Louis Brandeis to a vacancy on the U.S. Supreme Court, making him the first Jew to sit on the High Court bench. To welcome Brandeis to Washington, his friend Justice Holmes made a point of taking him for a celebratory dinner at the House of Truth.

While there was general pride in all the progress that was evident for much of the new century, it had been accompanied by a visible national instability that had begun to discomfit Americans. This instability had become the focus of Progressive domestic policy concerns. A rolling series of panics and recessions followed by brief booms of prosperity generated as much fear and poverty as they did opulent wealth and brash opportunism. The huge concentrations of people moving into already crowded cities threatened to drag the nation into the same spiral of class warfare that was shaking Western Europe. Newly arrived populations of African Americans from the rural South jostled for place with alarmingly exotic immigrants from Italy and the Balkans; all chafed against the more-established communities of Irish and Germans and terrified the WASP elite. Efforts to unionize labor brought a collision between the old-line craft guilds of the American Federation of Labor and new unions of heavy industry workers whose skills were confined to the machines they operated.

American culture was colliding with itself as well. Railroads and the automobile made for a more mobile and volatile population; the movie houses created national idols overnight with lurid tales that challenged previous standards of acceptable art; phonograph records created dance crazes and a new language called slang. America was becoming more homogenized and yet more fragmented at the same time. It also was becoming a more violent place. Anarchist bombs exploded in major cities, labor insurrections had to be suppressed by military force, and the number of Negro lynchings rose and spread beyond the South.

The center core of the Progressive philosophy then was to establish a new certainty in a world that seemed to be unraveling more each day. The historic myth of the village meeting where yeomen of equal worth could make public decisions had vanished. The new masses of the cities were to be both feared and led. And to do the leading on decisions of ever-growing complexity, what were needed were experts. Science became a faith that replaced religion in the Progressive mind. The engineer, the sociologist, and the economist could devise the solutions that the political specialist would use to convince the ordinary, self-absorbed, and generally ignorant citizen how to build a better life for himself and his society.

Of course, by political specialist, the Progressives meant themselves; they anointed themselves with leadership because their extraordinary academic achievements had turned them into an elite class of modern samurai—clear-eyed specialists who could speak with persuasive authority to the more self-absorbed: the worker, the corporate executive, the elected lawmaker, perhaps even the President of the United States. There was no area of human existence that could not be improved by the scientific approach. Experts could bring order and equity to the marketplace; the general health of all could be improved by imposing scientific principles to public health, and even imposing limitations on who might produce children.

What the Dupont Circle Progressives came to realize was that although Roosevelt had talked a radical reform line, the new president was proving to be far more of an activist in pushing through important policy changes that had remained stalled during the Taft years. In 1913 alone, the new administration put into effect a Federal Reserve System that both created and regulated a national banking system. Monopolies and corrupt business practices were challenged not by separate lawsuits but through administrative reforms such as the new Federal Trade Commission and the Clayton Antitrust Act. The first national income tax also came into being.

But after 1914, local peace movements began to spring up all over the country, sparked in part by groups of women who saw that by combining the suffragist demand for the vote with the prohibitionist campaign for a ban on alcohol and adding a strong pacifist platform as well, they could broaden their appeal.

While the majority of Americans in 1916 still were strongly opposed to any U.S. involvement in the European war, Secretary of State Lansing was not one of them. Nor was Colonel Edward House, who had become the president's most trusted foreign policy adviser.[8]

Both counted on Wilson's own deep distaste for all things Germanic including its culture (which he found too florid) and its philosophers (whom he found impenetrable). Both men gave Wilson advice to openly side with the British and French allies, advice which he evaded because he realized correctly that public opinion was lagging behind events. So Wilson temporized for the time being. Lansing's advice was easy to ignore since the president considered himself to be his own foreign policy expert. House was kept in check by being sent by Wilson to Europe on a series of missions to win agreement from both the Central Powers and the Allies to set up a conference where he, Wilson, could be the Arbitrator-in-Chief and dictate the terms of a general peace. Neither side ever seriously considered such a scheme even though officials of both made positive noises in order to keep America from supporting the other side.

Lansing however believed U.S. involvement in the war was inevitable and wasted no time in expanding the manpower and resources of the State Department for a greater diplomatic role in world affairs. He began to recruit likely prospects and looked first within his own family. General Foster's other son-in-law was a nationally known Presbyterian minister named Allen Macy Dulles, and three of his children routinely lodged at the Foster mansion in Washington as they tried to launch their own careers with help from their grandfather and uncle. The eldest, John Foster Dulles, was a junior lawyer at the Wall Street international law firm of Sullivan & Cromwell. His younger brother Allen Dulles had just returned to Washington from spending his first year after graduating from

Princeton teaching at a missionary school in India. Their younger sister Eleanor Lansing Dulles was just about to graduate from Bryn Mawr and was plaguing her relatives for a government job that would allow her to work on reforming labor laws for women.

Both the Foster-Lansing mansion and the House of Truth had come to symbolize the choices that faced the young strivers of Dupont Circle. One could, like Frankfurter, Lippmann, and their friends, seek places of influence within those government agencies that focused on domestic policies—Interior, Labor, and Justice. Or, like the friends of the Dulles brothers, one could try to gain entrance to the small and exclusive State Department where careers in foreign affairs were still the province of the wealthy and well connected.

But whatever the choice, all the Dupont Circle set were determined to find a place in Washington for the great adventure that they saw looming ahead.

Two

AVOIDING AN UNAVOIDABLE WAR

1916–1918

"He deserved a good time. He was married to Eleanor."

—Alice Roosevelt Longworth on FDR's affair
with Lucy Mercer

HEN WALTER LIPPMANN SOUGHT out Franklin Roosevelt in 1916, it was to be reassured that President Wilson would honor his promise to keep the United States aloof from involvement in the European war. Lippmann was disappointed if not surprised to find that the dynamic Navy assistant secretary was one of the leading war hawks within the administration.

Roosevelt saw the war as an opportunity. He firmly believed that turning the U.S. Navy into an undisputedly powerful strategic force was vital to American security. Building a bigger fleet also would bring the prospect of his gaining the White House, as it had for his cousin Theodore twenty years earlier. As the assistant navy secretary in 1897, Theodore Roosevelt was widely credited with preparing U.S. naval forces for their stunning victories in the Spanish-American War a year later. That success and his celebrated exploits in the war as head of the Rough Riders landed him in the Vice Presidency in 1900 and, a year later on the death of President William McKinley, in the White House itself.

Roosevelt's pro-war stance may have disheartened Lippmann, but the journalist was well aware that other Progressives were shifting their opinions from opposition to U.S. involvement in the Anglo-French cause to debating just what that involvement should be. At the House of Truth and elsewhere around Dupont Circle, the pressing question of the moment was what the European war meant for America, and, not least, for their own careers. The campaign for "preparedness"—which critics charged was shorthand for "involvement"—began as behind-the-scenes maneuvering among Progressives both inside and outside the government.

Nowhere had the war caused more surprise than in the editorial offices of *The New Republic*. The first edition, which appeared in November 1914, had been sent to the printers with only the cautious comment that efforts should be made to halt the conflict quickly lest it spread. Lippmann's colleagues were forced with most other Progressives to painful rethinking of their priorities as the battle casualties on both sides grew more horrible, and as the threat to America became a reality. Suddenly, domestic social issues—the vote for women, the prohibition debate, the worsening racial climate, labor unrest, urban poverty and decaying farms—receded in the face of the clear need to stop the European war, and indeed, to stop all wars forever.

American public opinion was hardly unified; citizens of German, Austrian, and Irish origin were dead set against any support for Britain and its Allies. At least through 1915 there was a consensus, which President Wilson echoed, that argued that the proper American role was as a dispassionate honest broker who could arbitrate the points of dispute between the two warring blocs without siding with either. A long-standing proposal to create some sort of formal international organization that would have the power to compel disputing governments to negotiate peacefully took on a new life; it was called a League to Enforce Peace, and the campaign was bolstered by former President Taft becoming its chairman.

So compelling was the idea of American arbitration that in December 1915, automobile maker Henry Ford financed what was called a "Peace Ship;" he and a collection of peace activists and celebrities (including Thomas Edison and William Jennings Bryan) sailed for Europe on a ship he had chartered. Ford's intention was to use his wealth and international prestige to confront personally the leaders of the warring nations and to win a peace that, he boasted, would "get the boys out of the trenches by Christmas." The voyage proved fruitless from the start, and Ford returned to ridicule in the press. But the idea would not die, and President Wilson began to muse privately that he was the one meant to succeed where the pacifists had failed.

To be young and Progressive and in Washington meant possessing a level of self-confidence that would not admit to having any opinion leader other than their own consciences. But increasingly, the Dupont Circle residents kept an eye on Franklin Roosevelt, not only for the importance of the sub-Cabinet post he held but also because he seemed to have a more acute intuition about the direction of the future.

Roosevelt was one of the more visible movers and shakers among the young Progressives, and he made it a point of being a frequent drop-in guest at both the Foster mansion and the House of Truth. He was welcome in both because he clearly was a favorite of his boss, Navy Secretary Josephus Daniels, and of President Wilson. The ebullient former New York state senator had not achieved the stellar record in Albany of his cousin Theodore, but young Roosevelt had earned praise for standing up to the Tammany Hall machine bosses of New York City. He had also taken a gamble as an early backer of Wilson's presidential campaign in 1912. His reward of a sub-Cabinet appointment at the young age of thirty-one was fortuitous. Secretary Daniels was a North Carolina newspaper publisher who had little interest in the details of administering naval affairs, and the energetic Roosevelt soon became the de facto head of the department's ambitious program of expansion and construction.

Frank Roosevelt, as he preferred to be called, was a force of nature even then. Tall, lithe, and athletic, he fit the image of the admirable

college hero that dominated popular novels and magazine advertise-
ments. He had a film star's manly profile and was a compelling public
speaker, but what most attracted people was his ability to project a dynamic personality that was both forceful and yet strangely vulnerable
at the same time. Others found themselves wanting to help Roosevelt;
they were drawn to him, and he had a great need for that devotion.
Already he was gathering supporters about him, most of who would
dedicate the rest of their lives to his service.

He and his wife Eleanor had been among the early young Progressives to settle in the Dupont Circle neighborhood. They first
rented a relative's house at 1733 N Street, just around the corner
from the Foster mansion. By 1916, the Little White House (so-
called when Theodore Roosevelt had used it as a refuge from the
family chaos of the Executive Mansion) on N Street was already
teeming with activity. In the spring, Franklin's wife Eleanor gave
birth to their sixth child in ten years (one son had died in 1909)
and moved into a separate bedroom. Also in residence was the first
FDR acolyte, Louis Howe, an emaciated, untidy New York newspaperman who was a political alter ego. While Eleanor may have
withdrawn from the marital bed, she had become adept as a public
figure in her own right. As the wife of a sub-Cabinet officer, the social and official demands on her time led her in late 1914 to hire a
twenty-three-year-old secretary named Lucy Mercer to sort out her
schedule and correspondence.[1]

Lucy lived with her mother in an apartment a few blocks away
at Twentieth and P Streets; they were from Maryland's Catholic
upper-class and so were still socially prominent in Washington
despite having fallen on hard times financially. Tall, with auburn
hair and a porcelain complexion, those who knew her agreed that
her quiet reserve masked a deeply emotional nature. Franklin was
attracted to her at once, and Lucy would remain unquestioningly
devoted to him all her life. It was this total and uncritical love
that Franklin Roosevelt required from everyone around him. Precisely when their romance started is unknown, but by that summer of 1916, when Eleanor gathered up the children to escape to
the cooler climate of their summer home on Campobello Island

in New Brunswick, the love affair was in full swing. Franklin and Lucy dined in public together that summer, and his large Stutz touring car was often spotted bringing the two of them home from lengthy trips into the Virginia countryside.[2]

The Mercer-Roosevelt affair has attracted much comment, most of it focusing on the sexual conduct, if any, of the couple. And while intimate details are always interesting, it is worth considering for a moment the emotional quadrant of their relationship. Throughout his life, Franklin Roosevelt was a psychological black hole that no amount of love and devotion could ever fill completely. Several forces made him so. Part of the genetic heritage of the entire Roosevelt clan was a history of unstable emotions and excesses. Alcoholism and depression were rife among the various uncles and brothers; Cousin Theodore, for all his upbeat outward appearance, frequently suffered mood swings that immobilized him.

FDR's mother, Sarah Delano Roosevelt, was an obsessively clinging and manipulative force through most of Franklin's adulthood. As a child, he had been infused with a poisonous combination of insecurity and an exaggerated sense of entitlement. The end result was that FDR needed huge injections of uncritical devotion from everyone around him but was unable to invest himself emotionally in others. What he thought he was doing when he married Eleanor remains a mystery, but it soon became clear that whatever it was he sought, he was not going to get it from her.

Early on, FDR built a wall about himself buttressed by hearty laughter, physical energy, and all-too-apparent charm. He also had an uncanny eye for weakness in others and turned it into a preference for supporters whose own shortcomings made them all the more dependent on his friendship. Louis Howe was merely the first to face the truth that without Roosevelt to orbit around, his own life as a failed newspaperman and indifferent husband and father would have been empty misery. Lucy Mercer, whose father had died when she was young, saw in FDR both the parental authority and physical romance that she craved. They would become separated in years to come, and both would have others in their lives, but the two of them clung to each other emotionally until his death.

Despite the spreading gossip, Roosevelt's political star continued to rise. His tireless work to expand the shipyards and the capacity to turn out the larger class of battleships of the day had won him
friends among the so-called Big Navy lobby of steel and armaments
makers and their sympathizers in the Congress. But with Wilson
campaigning for a second term on the slogan, "He kept us out of
war," there was just so much Roosevelt could do. So he stayed quiet
in his public statements on the question of whether the U.S. should
back Britain and France more directly. And he advised Lippmann,
who had been commissioned by *The New Republic* to begin regular coverage of the Washington debate on the issue, to be cautious
about criticizing the president's apparent ambivalence.

One thing Roosevelt had learned was the need for organized
support. He concentrated on building up his own network of protégés and friends to help him on his way to the White House. He
paid particular court to the same New York financial supporters
who had backed Wilson, including the president's famous *Émi-
nence grise*, Colonel Edward House.

FDR also began to recruit allies within the government itself.
In 1915, he brought to the Foster mansion for Secretary Lansing's
approval a young New York society swell named Sumner Welles.
Welles had just made an almost-perfect score on the Foreign Service entrance examinations. The young man was closely connected
with nearly everyone who mattered in New York society, especially
the Roosevelt clan. He had carried Eleanor Roosevelt's bridal train
as a page boy when she married Franklin in 1905; he had roomed
at school with her brother and had spent summers at Franklin
Roosevelt's family retreat at Campobello Island. Welles's family
had frequently crossed paths with both the Fosters and Dulleses
on their regular European summer holidays, and as a teenager in
the 1900s, he and the two Dulles brothers had gone mountain
hiking in Switzerland.

Roosevelt had a number of reasons for proposing Welles for a
diplomatic career. The Navy's offices were in the same ornate office
building as the State Department. From that vantage point and
from his frequent calls on the Foster mansion, he had observed that

the State Department no longer was the sleepy backwater it had been during Wilson's first term when perennial Democratic presidential candidate William Jennings Bryan had been given the secretary's job as a kind of sinecure. The pacifist Bryan had resigned in the summer of 1915 in protest of Wilson's diplomatic meddling in the European war. His successor Secretary Lansing had been busy adding manpower. But Roosevelt wanted loyalists inside the State as well as the Navy offices. He advanced other friends from the 1912 Wilson campaign into jobs with Lansing or elsewhere in the expanding bureaucracy. Breckinridge Long, a wealthy lawyer from Missouri, and Louis Wehle, a Kentuckian who had been FDR's co-editor on the *Harvard Crimson* student newspaper (and a nephew of Justice Brandeis), shuttled among the houses near Dupont Circle but would stay loyal activists in his cause the rest of their lives.[3]

There was also a deeply personal motive for Roosevelt's sponsorship of Welles. Despite the ten-year difference in their ages, Welles and Roosevelt had been boyhood friends during their summers on Campobello Island. There was an emotional bond between both Roosevelts and this intensely shy, somewhat priggish young man. Welles had followed Roosevelt's educational path (and that of many other of his class) first to Groton and then Harvard where he had graduated in three years of studies that concentrated on Spanish culture and history. But Welles was something of a wounded bird with exotic plumage that aroused pity in some even as it repelled others.

Sumner combined a rigid reserve with eccentric manners and dress that clashed with Harvard's strict conformist social code; he reacted to being turned down by the better clubs and class offices by drinking heavily and flaunting his patronage of Boston brothels that catered to bizarre tastes. While neither vice was unknown to Harvard undergraduates, Welles became the target of scorn when it was widely rumored that his exclusive taste was for black female prostitutes.[4] What the Roosevelts both knew, however, was that he possessed a brilliant mind and was intensely loyal to them. They could not foresee how his darker nature might be a threat to them in the future.

Having secured his Harvard degree, Welles decamped in the summer of 1913 for Paris, ostensibly to study architecture, but really as an excuse to plunge into the seedier precincts of the Left Bank's demimonde network of cabarets and brothels. He was abetted in his quests by a classmate, Nelson Slater, himself a sexual adventurer and heir to one of New England's greatest textile fortunes.[5] The duo joined other wealthy Americans in pursuit of their appetites, including a safari to Kenya where Sumner's passion for African women was given free rein. Roaming between Paris and a Thames River houseboat in London, Sumner also may have had his first homosexual experiences, although he assured his friends he was repelled by the idea.[6]

Like thousands of other well-to-do American tourists and expatriates who were sunning themselves in Europe in the summer of 1914, the abrupt spread of the war caught Welles and Slater by surprise, and it was some months before they could get back to America and the sobering need to confront their futures. Sumner's response was to pay serious court to Nelson's sister Esther, a reserved, somewhat naive girl who was noted for her charitable work among Boston's poor. Despite receiving an anonymous telegram that stated "On no account let your daughter marry Sumner Welles," Esther's mother was delighted to see ties established to an equally prominent New York family. Their wedding in the spring of 1915 was covered in the national newspapers, and thousands of onlookers crowded the street to witness the happy couple set out on their honeymoon.[7]

Roosevelt's intercession with Lansing led to Welles snaring a prize appointment to a diplomatic post in Tokyo, and everyone could breathe relief that Sumner had at last settled down into respectability.

As the year 1916 began, the debates among the Dupont Circle Progressives grew more focused on just how America could insert itself between the warring European powers and take the lead in influencing a lasting peace. At the House of Truth, the arguments took on a sense of urgency that drew Eustace Percy and Felix Frankfurter into pointed argument. Percy predictably argued that since America's long-term interests—political as well as economic—were tied to Britain, it was vital, if not inevitable, that the United States enter the war against Germany at once. Frankfurter, bolstered by Lippmann's arrival, was not so sure.

It's hard to imagine two more dissimilar personalities becoming such devoted friends, as was the case with Percy and Frankfurter. The twenty-four-year-old Percy was tall and fastidious in dress and manner to the point of being a bit prim. His ducal family had raised him in an evangelical sect of Catholic Anglicans, and, while he remained a member of the Conservative Party all his life, he had early on become committed to the social reform movement known as Fabianism that had attracted many of his Oxford classmates of that time.[8] Frankfurter by contrast was short and careless of his dress, and he was a nonstop talker who bubbled over with ideas and arguments; he was a terrier to Percy's greyhound.

For Percy, the twenty-nine-year-old Frankfurter was both exotic and impressively accomplished. Felix was born and had lived in Vienna until he was twelve and his family moved to America. He learned English and a feisty toughness in the crowded streets and public schools of New York City's Lower East Side. He graduated Phi Beta Kappa from the City College of New York and spent a brief period as a social worker among the newly arrived immigrants who jammed the city's slums. Perhaps feeling insecure due to his rough-and-tumble early life, Frankfurter was attracted to Percy's refined persona and became a fan of English manners and customs. It was a light-hearted affectation that he would joke about but cling to the rest of his life.

Just as Oxford and Cambridge had trained a new generation of Britons to government service and social improvement throughout the Empire, so many American universities had undergone a similar revolution; they no longer trained scholars and clerics but now saw their purpose to prepare young Americans to lead the way to a new society. The law had become the sharpest weapon in the Progressive reform arsenal. Judge Holmes, as both a state court and Supreme Court justice, had been in the forefront of that change.[9]

Frankfurter and Harvard Law School were made for each other. By the time he took his degree, he had been elected editor of the

Harvard Law Review and had earned a grade point average that was second only to that of the school's previous star law student of twenty years earlier, the already legendary Louis Brandeis.

The diminutive Frankfurter was a protégé of all four of the leading talent scouts of the Progressive movement. Brandeis, not surprisingly, first noticed Frankfurter while the younger man was still in law school. By that time, Brandeis had achieved a national reputation as "The People's Lawyer" for winning a series of landmark law suits he had filed against railroad and banking monopolies and for successful crusades to establish new workplace safety laws, better business practices, and, significantly, the creation of the controversial Federal Reserve System. Now approaching fifty, Brandeis was in the enviable position of being sought after by lucrative corporate clients that enabled him to take on litigation for social causes on a pro bono basis. Both law student and established attorney found they had much in common. Both were from fairly prosperous immigrant families (Brandeis was raised in Louisville, Kentucky); both were Jewish but secular in practice; both were short in stature and had problems with faulty eyesight; but both were possessed of extraordinary energy and ambition.

Frankfurter's journey to the House of Truth began shortly after his graduation from law school in 1906. He returned to New York City to join a prominent law firm, but soon afterwards, he went to work for Henry Stimson, President Roosevelt's newly appointed U.S. Attorney for the Southern District of New York. Stimson was from a wealthy family that had been among the early founders of the Republican Party. He also was a Theodore Roosevelt loyalist and an ardent Progressive. Stimson began a series of antitrust prosecutions that made him and his precocious aide national figures. Frankfurter also began his friendship with the tall, urbane Lincoln Steffens, who was at the top of his renown as one of the leading investigative journalists of that storied time.

"Muckrakers" had started out as a cautionary phrase of Theodore Roosevelt's to describe a group of Progressive writers who twenty years earlier had exposed the dangers and injustices of America's rush to become an industrial superpower. Upton

Sinclair had warned about tainted meat products that were mass-marketed staples of every household; Ida Tarbell had exposed the predations of John D. Rockefeller's stranglehold on the petroleum products that were fueling an explosion of wealth. Steffens, with the easy charm of his wealthy background and craggy good looks, had talked his way into and then exposed the corrupt city political machines of major cities such as St. Louis, Minneapolis, Chicago, and, not least, New York City.

By 1906, Steffens was freelancing profiles of celebrity Progressives to magazines and was beginning to dabble in socialist theory out of a frustration with his earlier belief that reforms were inevitable once the truth was revealed. Challenging injustice through aggressive legal action—which is what Stimson and Frankfurter were doing at Roosevelt's urging—was attractive to Steffens and drew him to these younger men and ultimately to another protégé, an even younger New Yorker who was making his name as a socialist at Harvard—Walter Lippmann.

Lippmann was the most notable member of a star-studded class of 1910 at Harvard that included the budding poet T. S. Eliot and the radical journalist John Reed. The handsome, effervescent Reed (he had been a cheerleader at Harvard football games) quickly bypassed Lippmann's commitment to socialism and became an ardent devotee of the Bolshevik Revolutions in Russia, both the one that failed in 1905 and the successful one in 1917. His zeal would earn him the singular honor of being buried in the Kremlin Wall.[10]

While the Lippmann and Frankfurter friendship began at Harvard out of their shared beliefs, there were important differences. Lippmann's family was wealthy enough to spend their summer holidays in Europe and to be prominent members of the elite Jewish congregation at New York's Temple Emanu-El. Walter had been educated at an elite Manhattan prep school where he excelled both as a scholar as well as a member of its football, hockey, and tennis teams. He entered Harvard at the age of seventeen. There he continued to win prizes for academic distinction at a pace that earned him his bachelor's degree in three years. What really engaged Lippmann was Harvard's Socialist Club, which he helped to found, and through which he quickly became a student leader in the movement's national hierarchy. Where people noted Frankfurter's explosive nervous energy, the taller, bulkier Lippmann had a stolid solemnity that was heightened by dark eyes that tended to bulge intensely whenever he was arguing a point. Where Frankfurter had opted for the newly popular soft-collared shirts, Lippmann was always carefully turned out in a dark suit and traditional high starched collar that added to his air of formality.

Despite having completed his course work, Lippmann stayed on at Harvard during the winter of 1909–1910 to study with philosopher George Santayana, but in the spring, he left to become a reporter on *The Boston Common*, a reformist newspaper edited by Ralph Albertson. A proponent of Christian Communism, Albertson had founded a series of rural communes, which were financial failures. Indeed, his perennially shaky finances forced him to edit the newspaper at the behest of its patrons, which included Brandeis and the Filene department store family. They also underwrote his latest attempt at a rural communal society. The Farm, as it was known, was near West Newbury, Massachusetts, and offered guests both a place of refuge and meditation and the opportunity to explore social reform issues with other like-minded Progressives. It was at the Farm that Lippmann first met Lincoln Steffens. Walter also flirted with Albertson's wife Helen and his teenage daughter Faye.

In what would become a pattern in his life, Lippmann quickly became disenchanted with his career on the shaky alternative newspaper and with its feckless editor. After just a few weeks, Steffens hired Lippmann as his researcher and aide on a magazine he had begun to edit. But the two parted ways after a few months as Steffens began to explore more radical political action while the younger man became more deeply involved in the socialist movement that was sweeping municipal governments throughout the country.[11] In 1912, Lippmann went to work for the newly elected socialist mayor of Schenectady, New York, but again became so disillusioned at the new government's failure to do away with city taxes that he resigned after four months.

At the same time, Lippmann and Frankfurter were involved in efforts to organize a Progressive magazine, *The New Republic*. Lippmann joined the editorial board and also published his first book, *A Preface to Politics*, which was remarkable not only because of the youth of the author (he had just turned twenty-four) but also because it was surprisingly critical of the very socialist movement that he espoused. He wrote,

> The socialists are confused who think that a new era can be-
> gin by a general strike or an electoral victory. . . . It is simply that
> the reality of a revolution is not in a political decree or the scare
> headline of a newspaper, but in the experiences, feelings, habits
> of myriads of men.[12]

In short, if socialism did not produce quick improvements in society, Lippmann was prepared to find another cause to support. In that, he and Frankfurter were like many other Progressives; what was important, essential, was that an idea had to work. Where doctrinaire socialists put their faith in strong central government to improve society, Progressives like Frankfurter and Lippmann argued a faith in the scientific certainty and expert interpretation of statistics to determine social policy. Facts, they believed, were indisputable. All one had to do was gather the facts, the data, the unassailable statistics that were transforming the industrial age in such dramatic fashion, and the way to broader improvements in any community would be virtually automatic.

In the meantime, Frankfurter had moved with his patron Stimson from Manhattan to Washington. By 1911, President William Howard Taft, in a bid to shore up his popularity with the Progressive wing of his party, had appointed Stimson to the Cabinet post of secretary of war, and Frankfurter had come along as his chief of staff. Stimson and Frankfurter faced daunting challenges. In 1911, the United States Army had an estimated 107,000 soldiers and no tactical unit larger than a regiment. Yet its manpower was stretched all over the globe from China to the Caribbean; the largest concentration outside the country was in the Philippines, where a sporadic skirmish with guerrillas was now in its second decade. Adding to

President Taft's troubles was the growing controversy on the border with Mexico. A Mexican civil war had prompted rebel leaders to conduct a series of bank raids into Texas and New Mexico that led to the killing of dozens of Americans and widespread outrage in the press. Later that year, Taft sent fourteen thousand troops to the border, and the Army began to experiment with the new technologies of modern warfare: the radio, the airplane, and the automobile. Despite the advantages that came with the new military hardware, the task of chasing Mexican revolutionaries like Emiliano Zapata and Pancho Villa turned into a logistical nightmare that would keep American troops pinned down on the border until 1917.

If Frankfurter drew support from having Lippmann in regular residence in the House of Truth, Percy was bolstered by a new visitor as well. Another British nobleman, Philip Kerr, began to arrive on official business at the Embassy and stayed at the House of Truth whenever he was in town. Kerr was heir to a Scottish title but had already achieved recognition on his own as a young diplomat destined for greatness. Ten years earlier, he had been one of a group of young Fabians who had gone to South Africa after the Boer War and united the politically and culturally divided provincial governments into a single Union of South Africa. Kerr had become a leading advocate of a movement to convert the decaying structure of the British Empire into what it would later become, a commonwealth of equal nations under the Crown.

What Kerr and Percy began to argue around the House of Truth dinner table was that American disapproval of Britain's exploitation of its colonies was out of date. A glorious English-speaking union of nations around the world could become the most powerful engine for peace and social reform imaginable. And, of course, that commonwealth would include the United States. It didn't just make sense—it was destiny that a British-led commonwealth and America, two great world powers united by language, customs, and law, could overcome the inherent tyranny of lesser nations. Frankfurter and Lippmann were naturally dubious about any venture where Britain would be the senior partner, but they had to admit it was an intriguing idea.[13]

Like Percy, Kerr had been raised in a strict Roman Catholic family and educated at Oxford. For Frankfurter, Kerr was even more of what was admirable about being British than Percy. He was tall and schoolboy handsome. Where Percy was easygoing sometimes to the point of being languid, Kerr was intense and high-strung, and early on he worked himself into periodic breakdowns. But he had an intellectual authority that impressed the House of Truth debaters. In 1910, he became the founding editor of a new journal, *The Round Table,* and turned it into an important transatlantic opinion maker, something that the editors of *The New Republic* were still struggling to achieve. Moreover, in the years before the war, Kerr had traveled widely in America, investigating labor unions in Seattle and race relations in the South.

As 1916 drew to a close, the focus of the Dupont Circle Progressives became more about the logistics of preparing the United States for an active role in the war, certainly as a major supplier of arms to the Allies, but increasingly, as an active combatant "over there." Breckinridge Long may have won praise for authoring the campaign slogan "He kept us out of war" that fueled Wilson's handy re-election that autumn. But as 1917 drew near, it was clear that the period of isolation was at an end. What was important now for the guests at the House of Truth was how each of them would find something important to do in the months ahead.

Three

The Dupont Circle Set at War

1917–1918

"This book is dedicated to the unhappy many who have lived and died lacking opportunity, because, in the starting, the world-wide social structure was wrongly begun."

—Philip Dru, Administrator, by Col. Edward M. House

FOR THOSE OF THE DUPONT CIRCLE set not already in government, Wilson's overwhelming re-election and the accelerating drift of America into the European war made getting some kind of post irresistible. If one hoped to exercise influence on a Progressive remaking of the world, one had to go where the power could be found. For the Americans in the House of Truth, the example of their British friends showed that they too could aspire to real power.

Percy had already begun to commute between London and Washington on various missions to win increased aid for Britain's war effort. Kerr's visits to the House were intermittent, but his influence in Washington actually increased when, at the end of 1916, there was a shakeup in the British government and David Lloyd George became prime minister with a mandate to prosecute the war "at all costs." Along with a number of other contributors to *The Round Table,* including the American-born newspaper owner

Waldorf Astor and novelist John Buchan, Kerr became an aide for the new prime minister. The group was called The Garden Suburb because they were housed in temporary huts built in the rear of Number 10 Downing Street, but there was no doubt about their influence or that Kerr soon became Lloyd George's main adviser on foreign policy.

Lippmann and Frankfurter were just as busy. Two years earlier, despite advice from both Holmes and Brandeis to the contrary, Frankfurter had accepted a post on the faculty of the Harvard Law School that was secretly subsidized by Jacob Schiff and other patrons. During the first years of the Wilson administration, however, he remained in constant motion, finding excuses to visit the House of Truth and to keep his voice heard in the offices of *The New Republic.* Lippmann had continued to churn out his political views in an astonishing volume. He kept writing essays for *The New Republic,* but from 1915 onward, he also composed his trademark "Today and Tomorrow" opinion column in a leftist monthly, *Metropolitan.*

But it was his books that brought Lippmann national attention and the special notice of, first, Colonel House, and then President Wilson. What Lippmann did not know at first was that House in 1912 had anonymously published a novel, *Philip Dru: Administrator,* which had uncanny echoes of many of Lippmann's own conclusions. The novel—set in the future between 1920 and 1935—centered on a hero, a West Point graduate, who led a Progressive revolution in America and ultimately a war against an unjust world regime that made him for a time an all-powerful dictator. Among the reforms he imposed by fiat were many of the items contained in Theodore Roosevelt's 1912 campaign manifesto. The book was an instant best seller, and it helped solidify his position as Woodrow Wilson's chief adviser. In the preface, House quoted Italian revolutionary Giuseppe Mazzini's credo as his own: "No war of classes, no hostility to existing wealth, no wanton or unjust violation of the rights of property, but a constant disposition to ameliorate the condition of the classes least favored by fortune."[1]

Not surprisingly, House was impressed by Lippmann's ability to tease out of the confusion of current uncertainties those new truths that seemed to offer solutions that were ahead of their time. In *A Preface to Politics*, Lippmann had in 1913 challenged the mechanical faith of nineteenth century laissez-faire economics but also questioned many of the orthodoxies of Progressivism. "Tammany has a better perception of human need, and comes nearer to being what a government should be, than any scheme yet proposed by a group of 'uptown good government reformers,'" he declared. What he rejected, he said, was the belief shared by conservatives on the Right and new radical Leftists that the basic wisdom of the average citizen could cure society's ills. A year later, in *Drift and Mastery*, Lippmann refined this argument by asserting that experts and seasoned managers grounded in science and hard facts must take control of public decisions. And by public decisions he included a vision where entire industries, related labor organizations, and a stronger national government were unified behind common social improvements. Perhaps without realizing it, Lippmann was forecasting the merging of government, unions, and industries that Woodrow Wilson directed during America's rush into World War I. He began to be a regular visitor to House's apartment in Manhattan.[2]

In 1915, Lippmann returned from a trip to Britain where he was lionized by such star Fabian socialists as H. G. Wells, George Bernard Shaw, and Beatrice and Sidney Webb, and completed his third book. In *The Stakes of Diplomacy*, he attacked nationalistic pride as the source of irresistible imperialism and inevitable wars. It was not isolated issues of dispute between the great powers that had caused the war; it was the competition for dominance over the lesser-developed parts of Asia, Africa, and the Balkans that was the driving destructive force.

"Just as strong men will weep because the second baseman fumbles at the crucial moment, so they will go into tantrums of rage because corporations of their own nationality are thwarted in a commercial ambition," he wrote. And in a foreshadowing of what would be the center core of Wilson's historic Fourteen Points, Lippmann demanded self-determination for the subject people of the world.

Earlier in the year, Wilson had sought to bolster his campaign image as an anti-militarist by naming a pacifist with no military background as the new secretary of war. Newton Baker was for many Progressives, then and for decades thereafter, the very model of what they wanted as a political leader. Unlike many other Progressives, he had been an early and influential Wilson backer in 1912. At forty-four, Baker was well educated and had been an effective reformist mayor of Cleveland, but he had no military credentials at all. He immediately stirred up controversy when he told reporters on his first day at the War Department, "I'm an innocent. I do not know anything about this job." Later, he would counter charges that his pacifism endangered national security with the quip, "I am so much of a pacifist, I'm willing to fight for it."

Naive he may have been, but Baker was shrewd enough to recruit Frankfurter to come back as his chief deputy and to turn increasingly to Lippmann for advice, knowing that through both young men he was bolstering his position with Colonel House in New York and thus to the increasingly reclusive Wilson across the street in the White House. For his part, Lippmann was understandably flattered to be sought out by Baker, House, and Wilson. He shuttled between New York (where he continued to work on issues at *The New Republic*), House's Manhattan apartment, and the House of Truth, where for the time being, he stayed while he was ostensibly reporting on the Congressional debate on the war. There also were side trips to New Jersey to Wilson's summer home for conferences and regular appointments at the White House.

Still, Lippmann was ambivalent about openly backing Wilson for re-election. While he could applaud much of what Wilson had done, it was hard for him or anyone not in the inner circle of the president's family and aides to have much affection for the man. In a letter at the end of May to Eustace Percy (who was back in London on Foreign Office business) Lippmann wrote,

> I am going out to Chicago at the end of the week, with no idea at all as to the outcome of the [Republican] convention. My preference is for Hughes although I am not sure I shall not line

up for Wilson in the end.[3] T.R. gets on my nerve so much these days that I shall become a typical anti-Roosevelt maniac if I do not look out.[4]

From July 1917 onward, the War Industries Board standardized military purchase orders, pressed for mass production, rationed raw materials, and granted wage increases to unions in exchange for accelerated work schedules. In addition to its chairman, Bernard Baruch, the board also contained two other notables: St. Louis businessman Robert S. Brookings, who later founded the Brookings Institution for economic study; and New York financier Eugene Meyer, later the owner of *The Washington Post.*

Yet in the end, and it took until October, Lippmann not only publicly endorsed Wilson's re-election, he swung the full weight of *The New Republic* editorial board as well. Many of his old more radical friends were appalled at what they perceived as Lippmann being co-opted by the establishment. In what would be a characteristic reaction, Walter angrily rejected any questioning of his motives and broke off friendships abruptly.

The sharpest break was with his old classmate John Reed who made the mistake of publicly charging that Lippmann had forsaken his radical beliefs in *The Stakes of Diplomacy* and his reporting from Washington. Since leaving Harvard, Reed had become a popular journalist with a wide following. Partly to escape an irksome love affair with Mable Dodge, the wealthy social cause groupie, Reed had fled to Mexico where his articles on the Mexican revolution and his laudatory profiles of Pancho Villa had attracted an international audience. Lippmann had been an unabashed admirer of Reed's journalism but would stand a rebuke from no one.

He fired back:

> I cannot help saying you are hardly the person to set yourself up as a judge of other people's radicalism. You may be able to create a reputation for yourself with some people, but I've known you too long and I know too much about you. I watched you at college when a few of us were taking our chances. I saw you trying to climb into clubs and hang on to a social position

by your eyelids, and to tell you the truth I have never taken your radicalism the least bit seriously. . . . And I will just make one little prophecy, which will sound to you like a boast. I got into this fight long before you ever knew it existed and you will find that I am in it long after you quit.[5]

It is a measure of the confusing tides of opinion that gripped the United States in that autumn of 1916 that Reed ended up endorsing Wilson's re-election for just the opposite reason that Lippmann did—he thought that Wilson would keep America out of the war. Reed had spent the early months of the year traveling in the Balkans and reporting on the conflict there and the early rumblings of unrest in Russia. Back home that autumn, he had met and married a young divorcée and playwright, Louise Bryant. The couple had moved to the artist colony of Provincetown, Massachusetts, where Eugene O'Neill had produced a play that Louise had written. After April 1917, Reed gave speeches that denounced the war and was dismayed when public reaction turned against him so violently. Later that year, he and Louise went to report on the Russian Revolution and both wrote best-selling books about the struggle.[6]

While the Reeds may have stopped dropping in at the House of Truth after they embarked for Russia, the place became even more of a mandatory destination for other Progressives as the countdown to American involvement in the European war got closer. Lippmann was now in permanent residence there, and in the spring of 1917, he added another tenant when he married Faye Albertson and installed her in the largest of the six bedrooms. Faye had grown into a sunny gorgeous blonde who, though disinterested in the intense politics of the house, made herself instantly at home. She briskly took charge of the chaotic finances and improved the quality of the meals. She added a note of respectability for other young women guests. She struck up a warm friendship with Justice Holmes who would play double-solitaire with her and cheat in order to tease a scolding from her. There was much laughter in the House in those days, including a running joke about Frankfurter's skills as a daiquiri maker; one Supreme Court colleague that Holmes had invited quipped that Felix made cocktails even better than he argued cases in court and would have a bright future.

Love had found Felix Frankfurter as well. Among the young women who clustered around the House of Truth's star boarders was an auburn-haired, hazel-eyed beauty named Marion Denman. Marion was the daughter of a Congregationalist minister from Massachusetts. She was a Smith College graduate and had worked as a social worker. She was described as "sharp-tongued, intelligent, coquettish, and a trifle vain."[7]

The course of their courtship was problematic in the extreme. Marion suffered from acute nervous ailments and was frankly frightened by the obsessive and sometimes suffocating professions of love that poured out of Felix in a stream of letters and personal pleas. Finally, Felix backed off. The uncertainties of the coming war and his own recently widowed mother's opposition to his marrying outside their faith caused him to rescind his proposals and agree to a romantic armistice for the time being.

In truth, Frankfurter was now much too busy to pursue Marion. He had turned down Baker's offer of a major's commission in the Army as being too limiting in the role he intended to play in the War Department. Like Lippmann, he had come late to endorsing Wilson's re-election, but his attitude toward the man and the war would change just as fundamentally, largely because the president began to voice a wider purpose to the war itself.

In December 1916, Wilson had made a public appeal to both the Allies and the Central Powers to agree to peace negotiations, with the president playing the role of arbitrator. Both sides agreed but with so many conditions that the question was moot. Yet in January 1917, Wilson changed his position on U.S. involvement in a speech to the Congress that set the goal of "peace without victory." By that, Wilson said he intended to seek an end to the war that would stop short of conquest and retribution by either side and also set the lofty goal of extending the benefits of democracy to all nations. While opposition to the war remained widespread, that speech gave the Progressives the cause they sought. As Frankfurter wrote after the war declaration in April, "When this terrible battle will have been over, the democratic forces will break out anew. . . . I'm clearer than ever that democracy—the effective guidance of the minds and spirit of peoples—and force are the two halves of the scissors and the two must cut together and in unison."[8]

With the leaders of the three main government departments— State, War, and Navy—occupying the same building, Frankfurter quickly became a major force in clearing away impediments to full wartime mobilization. Ostensibly, he was Baker's chief attorney, but his mandate ranged from the Court of Military Justice to winning changes in work rules and pay standards from labor leaders like Samuel Gompers and recalcitrant manufacturers of everything from bullets to clothing for military uniforms.

Not enough study has been devoted to the astonishing transformation of the United States to a war footing in the few months that followed; certainly German military strategists had never conceived that if America did enter on the side of the Allies that it could do so with such force and impact. A reluctant Congress had authorized a doubling of the Army's manpower to 200,000 soldiers in 1916, but even that paltry expansion seemed beyond the logistical reach of a government bureaucracy that was still primitive in the extreme. The nation's factories already had backlogs of supplies ordered by the British and French. Anti-war forces focused on blocking the mandatory draft that was enacted, and Washington responded by making it a crime to publicly urge resistance to the draft.

Yet by the early summer of 1917, just four months after the U.S. formally entered the war, an American Expeditionary Force of fourteen thousand troops landed in France, and the first division (roughly forty thousand men) of combat-ready soldiers entered the trenches alongside the French and British by October. In the first twelve months of U.S. involvement, more than one million American soldiers would be sent to Europe; ultimately more than four million Americans did military service during the nineteen months the nation was at war. General John J. Pershing was able to launch the Battle of Saint-Mihiel with a five-division force in September 1918 that ended when the Germans sued for peace a month and a half later.

Simply put, America's role in World War I could not have been possible without the Dupont Circle set, especially the residents of the House of Truth. Frankfurter had early on proposed that Lippmann be brought into government in a senior role. At first he proposed that Walter's journalism background made him the ideal candidate to head the government's censorship effort to control the press and suppress dissent. However, Wilson chose George Creel to direct the publicity campaign to win popular support and handed the Attorney General sweeping powers to silence opposition, including jailing Socialist Party candidate Eugene Debs for opposing the draft.

Instead, Lippmann became another aide without portfolio for Baker. Once he and Faye were settled in at the House of Truth, he joined Franklin Roosevelt on the task force charged with erecting scores of training camps and facilities to turn the millions of civilian conscripts into troops that could be sent to France.[9] At the same time, the three men presided over a massive ship construction program that functioned without a single labor stoppage. Without that buildup, the troops could never have gotten to France in timely fashion, let alone be supplied.

This unlikely triumvirate of FDR, Lippmann, and Frankfurter cut through bureaucratic red tape and private sector inefficiencies with an informality and energy that startled onlookers. When the hallways became jammed with crowds of civil servants and place seekers, the three young men would crawl out onto the balconies of the ornate building and climb in the windows of the officials they needed to sign off on orders. In what would be a shocking lack of security today, other decisions were taken at Secretary Lansing's Wednesday night poker party for the press corps, which was held in the State Department's code-room, or at his Thursday luncheon at the nearby Metropolitan Club. And, not surprisingly, there were no secrets at the dinner table of the House of Truth.

At least part of the urgency that gripped the government stemmed from an embarrassing interlude Frankfurter suffered at the hands of Ambassador Henry Morgenthau. To his credit, Morgenthau had been successful during his time in Constantinople and had resigned in protest over Wilson's unwillingness to intervene in the Turkish genocidal attacks on its Armenian population. But once the U.S. entered the war, Morgenthau began to argue that his personal friendship with Turkey's leader Enver Pasha offered the prospect of detaching that country from its Central Power alliance and taking it out of the war. A skeptical Wilson finally authorized Morgenthau to try, but as a precaution he sent Frankfurter, despite his vehement protests, to go along as a minder.

Morgenthau was the epitome of the newly rich that Progressives like Frankfurter and Lippmann found so embarrassing. "He wasn't my kind of person," Frankfurter later recalled. "His talk was inconsequential and not coherent, but loose and big and rhetorical. You couldn't get hold of anything, but I assumed that was just the froth of the man. I didn't realize that the froth was the man."[10]

Assured by his wealth and personal influence with Wilson (he had been the finance chairman for both Wilson campaigns), Morgenthau assumed that he had political expertise as well. It never occurred to him that the Allies, especially the British, wanted Turkey to stay a combatant. Both Britain and France had broader objectives in the Middle East once the war ended and Turkey's hold on the region was broken. So it was in June 1917 that Morgenthau and Frankfurter arrived in Gibraltar to secure a British pass to get through the tight naval blockade and reach Constantinople.

And there they stayed for several weeks. In response, a worried Lloyd George sent Chaim Weizmann, the leader of the Zionist campaign for a Jewish homeland in Palestine, to lobby the pair while they waited in vain. For three weeks, Weizmann concentrated on convincing Frankfurter of the justice in the Zionist cause and the plight of Jews throughout Europe. Another force that helped change Frankfurter's attitude was that his old mentor, Justice Brandeis, had lately become converted to the Zionist cause.

Undeterred by his inability to reach Turkey, Morgenthau moved on to Paris where he tried to interest the American Commander General Pershing in his scheme. Pershing was briefly intrigued and asked Morgenthau to provide him with detailed maps of Turkey so he could assess the tactical situation. Morgenthau promptly marched off to a Brentano's bookstore and sent the general a pocket-sized tourist guide of the region. He never heard from Pershing again.

But Frankfurter did not waste all of his time in Paris. He broke away from the Morgenthau party and set out to interview scores of American and French officials on the outlook for the war and the prospects for peace. What he learned alarmed him in the extreme. There was a growing political force in France that believed any kind of peace was preferable to continuing the war much longer. Moreover, both the British and French appeared to be pursuing separate long-term strategies to enhance their powers over events in Europe once peace was achieved. Both Allies were hard at work with separate plans for a peace conference. In the winter of 1916–1917, the Garden Suburb staff produced 167 separate handbooks of plans on key issues. The French had organized three separate study committees to frame issues for Premier Georges Clemenceau's use to back up claims against the Central Powers. If America was to have any influence in a postwar world, it had to speed up the delivery of troops to the front and put a coherent strategy in place that would influence any final settlement.[11]

Back in Washington, Frankfurter lobbied Secretary Baker to create a research staff that would give President Wilson the statistical basis for an American strategy.[12] It was Colonel House, however, who seized on the notion and made it his own fiefdom. He appointed his brother-in-law the director and saw to it that it was based in New York near his apartment.

While the effort, given the cover name The Inquiry, was quickly discovered by the press, it produced an impressive volume of data with a professional staff that never numbered above one hundred and fifty. The researchers were mostly generalists with the majority from a handful of Ivy League universities. But they compiled more than two thousand reports and twelve hundred maps that showed the geography, demographic trends, raw materials, and transportation infrastructure of not just Europe but Asia and Latin America as well.

The herculean task of coordinating the scholarly work and organizing so it could be used by President Wilson fell to

Lippmann, who was summoned to the White House in September 1917 by Colonel House and sent to New York as executive director for The Inquiry.

What is so surprising about the work product of The Inquiry team is how specific their reports were considering what a wide range of policy recommendations they covered. President Wilson had set the tone of the study group at one of his few meetings with the scholars: "Tell me what's right and I'll fight for it; give me a guaranteed position."

And so they did. Inquiry reports redrew the boundaries of Europe's old monarchies and created whole new nations out of uneasy conglomerations of different peoples; former colonies were handed over as mandates to other nations; whole industries were shifted to different economies; old constitutions were rewritten; and enough supporting data was collected that when the president sailed to Paris in the winter of 1918, an estimated five railroad cars of documents went with him.

The task of overseeing all this had been a nightmare for Lippmann. He and Faye kept their room at the House of Truth but shuttled between there and New York. Part of the problem was that while The Inquiry had a central office (first at the New York Public Library, later at the American Geographical Society's offices), most of the scholars continued to draw salaries and keep to their faculty offices at their home universities. Also, Lippmann was only twenty-eight, and most of the scholars resented his pressure to speed up their research and his blunt criticism of their work.

Lippmann also had problems with his mentor Colonel House and the security of the project. House routinely quizzed his brother-in-law about specific research details and passed the information along to William Wiseman, the senior British intelligence agent in New York.[13] Not coincidentally, both House and Wiseman lived in the same apartment building at 115 East Fifty-third Street. Wiseman not only promptly relayed what he learned of American strategy to the Garden Suburb policy drafters in London, but there also were occasions when the spy lobbied House for changes in Inquiry findings to suit British interests. One such alleged instance involved a recommendation that Wilson support creation of a Zionist state in Palestine under a British mandate.[14]

The Inquiry project underscores just how far behind Washington was in the key areas of intelligence and security. Prior to 1916, neither the State Department nor the White House had any organized source of strategic intelligence. Military officers provided information to their separate services, but there was no cross-referencing. Such information that the State did receive from embassies abroad was handled by a single, rather elderly, code clerk and was rarely circulated.

Meanwhile, everyone spied on the U.S. government. The Germans had an elaborate spy service that also successfully sabotaged docks and munitions stores. The British from 1915 on had hired a private detective agency to put agents in every major port from Seattle to Miami; they and the French routinely pilfered secrets from U.S. government agencies and even reports from the Inquiry. Lansing did succeed in centralizing intelligence from the military and other agencies in a special office that Wilson authorized, but Colonel House inserted one of his own men into the post just to keep his hand in.

Lansing responded by creating his own mini-intelligence service using his two nephews. In May 1916, he recruited twenty-three-year-old Allen Dulles into the Foreign Service and sent him off to Vienna, where the still-neutral U.S. maintained its most important embassy listening post. Ostensibly, Allen was a grade-five clerk, the lowest rank in that tiny six-officer embassy staff, and so was lumbered with all the petty details of office life that were complicated by the still-large horde of American refugees who were trying to get out of Europe. But his real duties involved providing Lansing with his own sources of information, particularly on efforts to get the Austrians to drop out of the war. He apparently was successful enough that within four months of arriving in Vienna, he had advanced two pay grades, and when the U.S. entered the war in 1917, he was transferred to the legation in Bern as the senior intelligence gatherer.[15]

Lansing had work for his other nephew. John Foster Dulles had become a rising star at the Wall Street law firm of Sullivan &

Cromwell, which was the dominant legal firm for international banking and bond financiers. Just days before the declaration of war in April 1917, Lansing borrowed Foster (as he was known) and sent him on a secret tour of Central America. Bluntly put, Foster was supposed to threaten to block access to Wall Street credit to the debt-ridden region if its governments gave way to German blandishments to threaten the security of the Straits of Florida and the Panama Canal. Vulnerable governments in Nicaragua and Costa Rica quickly fell in line, but in Panama, Foster had to engineer the success of a late entry into the presidential elections. In the end, most of the governments broke off ties with Germany, and Panama and Cuba both went so far as to declare war on the Kaiser.

Another problem began to loom on the horizon for both Lansing and House during the winter of 1917–1918. It was the question of who would lead the American delegation to the peace conference that all agreed must follow Germany's inevitable defeat. Early on, President Wilson had stated he intended to head the American effort, but no one took the notion seriously at first. No American president had ever left the country on such a mission. Both Colonel House and Secretary Lansing argued that each one should lead the delegation.

But no one could appreciate how determined Wilson was to be his own peace broker, just as no one foresaw that instead of holding the conference at the neutral site of Geneva, where American influence might be all the greater, French Premier Georges Clemenceau demanded it be held in Paris as the price for French cooperation.

All the visitors to the House of Truth knew was that each one of them was determined to play an important role in that conference, come what may. There were many toasts to "next year, over there." It was a Progressive's dream come true, the chance to remake the world. If they were overconfident, who could blame them? This small group had been instrumental in winning a tremendous military victory. Surely it was within their reach to win a lasting peace for mankind.

Four

FIGHTING FOR PEACE IN PARIS

1918

"Over there, over there.
Send the word, send the word over there,
The Yanks are coming
The drums rum-tumming everywhere.
So prepare, say a prayer,
Send the word, send the word to beware.
We're coming over, we're coming over.
And we won't come back until is over,
Over there."

—"Over There," 1917 hit song by George M. Cohan

S THE DISTANCE OF HISTORY lengthens, it is difficult to appreciate just how dramatic the change was in the attitude of the young crusaders of Dupont Circle as the spring of 1918 brought with it the certainty of victory and—most important—the unprecedented chance to help shape the peace of the world. With few exceptions, Progressives had at first recoiled from the European war as a dangerous threat to the domestic reforms being struggled for inside the United States. Then as the war in the trenches of France degenerated into wholesale slaughter, a growing number had felt some way—short of involvement—should be found to aid the Allies against German barbarism. But as the vision of a historic international peace conference emerged, the chance to set a Progressive agenda on the world stage was viewed with an enthusiasm that verged on the lighthearted.

When Lippmann could take a break from riding herd on the Inquiry scholars and return to Washington to brief Baker and Wilson, he and Faye found the House of Truth more crowded than ever. The winter and spring of 1917–1918 saw a steady procession of important visitors to Washington, each with his own agenda. It helped that the place continued to feature ample servings of food and drink and the merriment of pretty girls. With both Holmes and Brandeis frequently there, in addition to Frankfurter with his War Department contacts, the House was a virtual marketplace of information and ideas.

One of the more boisterous and opinionated was a twenty-five-year-old journalist named William C. Bullitt. Bill Bullitt had decided against a career in the Philadelphia law firm that had made his family extremely wealthy. He dropped out of Harvard Law School in 1914 and traveled across Russia and Eastern Europe, where his cheerful pushiness and gift for languages produced much-praised newspaper interviews with leading statesmen in many of the contending countries. He came to Washington as the correspondent for the *Philadelphia Public Ledger* and scored fresh notoriety for reporting Henry Ford's 1915 Peace Ship adventure. Although he married into the far-wealthier Drinker family in Philadelphia, he left his wife there most of the time and contented himself with an attempted but unsuccessful courtship of the fabulous Alice Roosevelt Longworth. Alice was the free-spirited and beautiful daughter of the former president and the wife of Nicholas Longworth, the Speaker of the U.S. House of Representatives. The couple pursued their own romantic adventures, including Alice's much-publicized extramarital affair with U.S. Senator William Borah. She had little time for a brash young newspaperman.

The talk at the House of Truth was not all politics. British author John Galsworthy and Arthur Willert, the *London Times* correspondent, came to talk about art and literature. Sculptor Gutzon Borglum ruined a tablecloth by sketching with a piece of charcoal his proposed monument for the Black Hills; his idea of including Theodore Roosevelt with the faces of Washington, Jefferson, and Lincoln created an uproar.

Eustace Percy came and went between London and Washington in those days, but Philip Kerr was in at the House of Truth most of the time overseeing the purchasing of vital weapons and supplies. Nor was the House an isolated magnet. There was much cross-meeting and involvement with the Foster mansion; Percy ruefully recalled that he had been talked into joining a morning calisthenics group—"physical jerks," he called the exercises—conducted in the garden of a prominent congressman and presided over by Franklin Roosevelt.[1]

Other new faces appeared. The star celebrity visitor of that winter season was Herbert Hoover, who at that moment may have been the most famous and respected figure of the Progressive movement, eclipsing even Woodrow Wilson. Hoover was forty-three, a man of medium height but with blunt bulldog features that he accented with high starched collars and severely tailored black suits. A contemporary characterized him as having the personality of a steam shovel. He was ill at ease in groups and would often stand off by himself looking at the ground and jingling the keys in his pocket as if he could not wait to leave the room.

His dour nature was well earned. Raised a Quaker and orphaned at an early age, Hoover never attended high school yet achieved a geology degree from Stanford University. He then gained an international reputation as a mining engineer in the remote regions of Australia, China, Burma, and Russia. He knew so much about the geography around Peking that he was able to guide the U.S. Marines who fought there during the Boxer Rebellion of 1900. Happily he had married a far more outgoing and equally accomplished woman. Lou Henry Hoover had also earned a geology degree from Stanford and had traveled to many of the primitive regions where her husband worked; she and Hoover often baffled eavesdroppers by talking to each other in Mandarin.

With Lou around, Hoover was a more genial soul. He enjoyed the kind of small groups that clustered at the House of Truth table and could be found there, a martini in hand, chewing on an unlit cigar as he expounded on the miracle he had worked in Europe when the war broke out in August 1914. Hoover had retired that year, many times a millionaire, and moved to London where he was on the board of a number of major mining companies and was helping promote interest in a world's fair to be held in San Francisco.

When the war started, an estimated 120,000 American tourists, students, and expatriates found themselves trapped and destitute.[2] On the continent, borders were suddenly sealed and railroad service interrupted; ports were jammed with frantic refugees. The thousands who poured into London daily found the banks were closed. Even those with ample funds could not access them and could not get shelter or food, let alone ship passage home. After some false starts, Hoover took charge of the relief organization that sprang up; he recruited volunteers from among the American students at Oxford and other universities, and he dragooned money and credit out of banks and the U.S. government.

But scarcely had the last refugee left Britain when Hoover was confronted with an even greater challenge. The tiny but densely packed (eight million people) nation of Belgium had been wrecked by the advance of the German Army on its way to France. What infrastructure was not destroyed was commandeered by the Germans, and that included as much of the food supply as they could seize. The prospect of the extermination of an entire country by starvation shocked even the understandably preoccupied British and French. Hoover agreed to head the nongovernmental relief agency that was created to raise the money and obtain the food and medicine, and this appeared to be the insurmountable hurdle, to get it all through German lines to the Belgians without the Germans seizing it for their own use.

All of Hoover's bulldog tenacity and fourteen-hour days were needed. He personally chivvied recalcitrant British bureaucrats for the permits and orders he needed. He made more than forty trips

behind the German lines to hector German generals to make sure
the supplies made the final trip from the ports to the people. The
Committee for Relief of Belgium (CRB) became almost a country
in itself; its staff of five hundred drew their own passports, chartered
their own flag-bearing ships, and utilized transport on the fly while
both Allies and Central Powers watched suspiciously but without
real interference. Over the next two years, Hoover presided over
an $11 million operation that got millions of metric tons of food
across the Channel to where it was needed.[3]

In September 1917, President Wilson recruited Hoover to head
the newly created Food Administration. The object was to ensure an
adequate supply of food for the troops while avoiding mandatory
rationing for civilians. Announcing "food will win the war," Hoover
launched a public campaign to set specific days—"meatless Mon-
days," and "wheatless Wednesdays"—to reduce public consumption. Much to his embarrassment—and to Wilson's irritation—his
skill at rationalizing American agriculture and consumption made
him more famous than ever. "To Hooverize," became the public's
term for the kind of Progressive, no-nonsense, efficient way to get
things done.

Whatever the demands of the war effort were, all of the Dupont Circle set kept in mind that their personal objective ultimately
was to be involved in the peace conference, which now was being
planned for Paris. Everyone, Hoover included, intended to be there.
For the young Progressives who started out around Dupont Circle,
the Paris Peace Conference of 1919 would prove to be the most important event of their lives. Far more than their university or Washington experiences, their time in Paris would be the formative force
that carried them through their long, important careers afterwards.

In Paris, nearly all of them had responsibilities far beyond their
years during the months of negotiations that followed the Armistice
in November 1918. Moreover, by the time the Treaty of Versailles
was finally signed on June 20, 1919, all had to agree that their six
months in Paris had been the time of their lives.

The fabled City of Light had taken a pounding from German
long-range artillery; much of the economy that had supported the

capital had disappeared. Parts of the city remained in ruins with unexploded bombs still being disarmed; the task of burying the dead had hardly begun. Still, the French put on a brave face, dug up champagne hidden away against the Germans, and welcomed the horde of young diplomats from Britain and America who descended on the city. Wartime laws that forbade public dancing were still in effect, so wealthy Parisians opened their homes each night for dances and banquets for all comers.

The armistice two months earlier touched off a palpable wave of relief and euphoria. That spirit of gaiety and optimism accelerated from late December on as the advance guard of the delegations began to arrive and stake out hotels and facilities. Not all of the nations had been significant contributors to the Allied cause, but all of them had demands they hoped to fulfill there. Special pleaders also rushed to Paris to try to advance their causes by having them included in any international pact. Eugenicists (who both advocated birth control and enforced laws on selective breeding) jostled with women suffragists, prohibitionists, and crusaders against the trafficking in drugs or slaves.

Felix Frankfurter (inexplicably left off the U.S. staff) arrived to help Chaim Weizmann lobby for an independent Jewish state in Palestine; they would be frustrated by two powerful claimants for Arab nationhood: archeologist Gertrude Bell wanted her Iraqis to have a government, and the fabled T. E. Lawrence (dressed in tribal robes) arrived with Saudi Prince Faisal to stake their claims. Hotel lobbies were crowded with promoters seeking funds for canals, railroads, and other schemes on every continent.

This influx of free-spending diplomats and lobbyists (as many as ten thousand by some estimates) was like a wash of fresh seawater into a tidal pool that provided a reviving injection of financial nutrients to the starving city. In the wake of the official delegations and advocates of special causes, large numbers of women arrived to work for the network of war relief agencies that had come to help. Once the conference was formally underway, added hordes of tourists from America and London came to revive an international social season that had languished during the war.

Significantly, no representatives of the Central Powers were invited and Russia (which had dropped out of the war, allowing the Germans to shift troops to the Western Front) was blacklisted by Clemenceau, who threatened to throw the conference out of the city if they showed up.

Deliberately, the biggest delegation to arrive was the American, fully sixteen hundred senior and mid-level government officials, researchers, intelligence operatives, and clerical staff; it jammed the huge Hotel de Crillon in the Place de la Concorde. Extra office space had to be found throughout the city, including the division devoted to policies for Eastern Europe and Russia, which was housed upstairs over Maxim's famed restaurant. General John J. Pershing kept his military headquarters in Chaumont on the Marne River battleground but quickly established a political base in Paris from which he strung the wires for an American telephone system and ran a secure military postal delivery system for the dispersed delegations. The French intelligence services nonetheless promptly penetrated both.

Fueled by dollars and high spirits, the American and British aides joined soldiers of both armies on leave to turn the gaiety into hilarity. Wealthy Americans and Britons, eager to renew their enjoyment of the French capital and to witness history opened their own salons to attract prominent delegates (Secretary and Mrs. Lansing and General Pershing were eagerly sought guests) to lavish catered buffets and dances. Wealthy American hostess Pearl Mesta presided over a perpetual house party at a rented mansion. William Sullivan, the flamboyant senior partner of Sullivan & Cromwell, set up a rival open house at his townhouse.

Troops of debutantes eager for romantic adventures and prospective husbands joined the whirl. No night was judged complete for the young diplomats unless they could seize one of the many captured German cannons that lined the Avenue des Champs Élysées, hook it to a taxi, and clamber aboard the gun carriage with a load of champagne and pretty girls for a jolly ride about town before turning in. City officials gamely swept up the broken glass in their wake and recovered the cannons each morning to put them back in place.

James Rives Childs, later a distinguished diplomat and author, recalled those heady days when, as a twenty-five-year-old Army radio code breaker, he was recruited by the legendary Herbert Yardley, the Army's expert cryptologist, to join the Crillon staff in the secret effort to eavesdrop on the radio traffic of both the British and French allies.[4] For a young man from Lynchburg, Virginia, it was an astonishing experience:

> Paris was dance mad in those days. . . . The "dancings" were usually aristocratic premises resembling private dwellings. They included the ultra-smart dancing around the corner from the Place de l'Etoile on the Avenue d'Iena, crowded for the most part with South Americans, kept women of bankers, editors, deputies, an occasional well-known French aviator whose tunic was covered with medals, a sprinkling of girls from the stage and the smartest of Parisian cocottes. Then there were two others on the Left Bank, one in the Rue de la Pompe, another in the Eiffel Tower district. There was another, near the Opera, with long divans at opposite ends of the room, frequented by ballet girls and young French artists, with a free and easy bohemian atmosphere which became one of our favorites. There was yet another off the Champs Elysees, a rather noisy and vulgar place where the girls who solicited in the promenades of the Folies-Bergere and the Casino went after the theater, and, as might have been supposed, expanded the oppressive atmosphere of a bawdy house. We came in time to know them all . . . when one was closed, word of its new address was passed on to its habitués. . . . Yardley and I grew tired of the Crillon and, to have greater contact with the French, decided to try out a French pension.[5]

British prime minister David Lloyd George brought a smaller support staff of five hundred with him. But other government officials could come over as needed on the overnight boat-trains that shuttled between Paris and London. They were housed in the grand Majestic on the Rue la Pérouse near the Arc de Triomphe. Because it was considered to have the better restaurant and was less crowded than the Crillon, the Majestic soon became the social center for the younger Americans as well as their new British colleagues. This is not to say the British were better organized than the Americans in their objectives. Arthur Balfour, the British foreign secretary, may have occupied a Paris apartment just above the one rented by Lloyd George, but the two men rarely met, and the prime minister rarely consulted him, or anyone for that matter. Indeed, aside from the obvious political need to be seen to squeeze the most in war damage reparations out of the Germans, Lloyd George's goals were as elusive as the man himself. Even Liberal Party allies called him the "Welsh Wizard" because he rarely made political commitments that could not be abandoned if the occasion arose. Now in Paris, he used Philip Kerr as a cut-out to keep other British officials at a distance, to their intense irritation. Eustace Percy, who had originally come to work on the committee that would draft the treaty's Covenant, was finally recruited as an aide by Balfour to keep him informed through his friendship with Kerr.

But even the prime minister's enemies conceded him one overarching strength. He could, as one described it, "look through the wall to see what was on the other side." Both he and Clemenceau knew what Wilson refused to acknowledge: that they had little time to get things done. Both governments had to get on with the business of reviving their home economies before their nations descended into political anarchy. Nor could they ignore the rest of Europe. Germany was starving, with its army still intact. Other European societies were in chaos; some like Hungary and some major cities in Germany had already fallen into Bolshevik control. So from the first day of the peace conference, America's two main allies were determined to put almost anything into place that would stabilize Germany, help themselves revive their own nations, and bring some rudimentary order to the rest of Europe. Whatever else was agreed to it would not be permanent but just the beginning of a return to the old remedies of traditional diplomacy and power politics.

So, even as President Wilson was arriving in France in mid-December to almost hysterical adulation, he was already the odd man out. One of Woodrow Wilson's key objectives, as stated in his famous Fourteen Points speech of January 1918, had been to change the culture of diplomacy and make it more transparent and more open to public scrutiny than it had been at any time in history.[6] At the Congress of Vienna of 1814–1815, the map of Europe had been redrawn in a closed room and essentially brokered out by two princes, Metternich for Austria-Hungary, and Talleyrand for France. Wilson not only believed in the ideal of transparency, but it also seemed a good political strategy for himself. At that moment he was atop a wave of almost-universal prestige and respect. If much of the world had painted its own dreams on the surface of his image, that was all the more reason to use the power it gave to create an international mechanism that would regulate the peace process. To ensure that creation, Wilson brought a tsunami of detailed studies and plans and enough staff to dominate whatever committees were formed to settle specific issues, draw new national boundaries, and transfer restive ethnic communities from one nation to another.

Of course it did not work out that way. It never could have. While Lloyd George, Clemenceau, and Orlando chafed each other over their own specific agendas, they were united in a determination that the American president was not going to run roughshod over them. Clemenceau, who in the 1880s had lived in the United States as a schoolteacher while he had been in political exile, was particularly scornful of the American penchant for moralizing about public issues; Wilson's rigid piety especially irritated him. Lloyd George thought Wilson possessed a second-rate mind and was not above appearing to agree with him for his own purposes. Italy's Orlando grew increasingly resentful about the little attention given to his country's demands for expanded territory carved out of the old Hapsburg Empire. He often had to return to Rome to shore up his political base that was eroding beneath him; in the city of Milan in the north, a disaffected army veteran and radical journalist named Benito Mussolini was organizing his first combat squad of two hundred fascisti thugs as the core of a new political party.

Against this was Wilson's conviction that he could construct a League of Nations mechanism—a self-perpetuating machine—that, once up and running, would automatically checkmate future aggression by any nation. The notion was the center core of Progressive faith in the power of experts to solve political issues. It was, however, a chimera, created at least in part out of Wilson's own fundamental disinterest in foreign affairs. In his heart he saw his main duty in transforming his own nation into a just and moral society; America's role in world affairs should only be to set the corrupt older nations of Europe (and the lesser peoples elsewhere) on a peaceful course so their future quarrels could be of no concern to the United States. Wilson is rightly considered one of America's first internationalists, but there also was a strong strain of provincialism in his character that cannot be ignored.

Wilson had come to believe at least part of his myth although privately he worried that his efforts would come to naught. It is hard to gainsay him that sense of conviction. His conduct of the war was praised at home as the key to the Allied victory. In Europe it was Wilson's promise of lasting peace and self-government that turned the early weeks of what was a victory lap through major cities into a near riot of adulation. Peasants knelt by the tracks when his railcar rolled by; boulevards and newborn children were named after him; groups of ethnic pleaders trudged to Paris from Eastern Europe to beg him to give them nationhood; a young Vietnamese named Ho Chi Minh who was washing dishes in a Paris restaurant helped draft a petition to Wilson to free his country from French rule. When the president and Mrs. Wilson finally arrived in Paris and were paraded down the Avenue de Champs Elysees, a million people blocked the carriage's passage to cheer. Hanging from a lamppost vantage point, a young American artillery captain from Missouri was awestruck by the emotional surge; years later President Harry Truman would say it was the most impressive sight he had ever seen.

But Wilson was, like the other three heads of state, dogged by political troubles back in the United States that worsened every week he was away in France. Despite the war victory, the November 1918 Congressional elections turned both the House and Senate over to Republican control. The abrupt cessation of the war had caught both the government and industry by surprise; a heroic mobilization and imposition of detailed regulations had supported the war effort, but Wilson's response to the peace had been to thoughtlessly shut down all the government agencies that had overseen that effort. Factories were stuck with undeliverable inventory, farm prices collapsed, and returning veterans were dumped back into civilian life without any means of adjustment. Not surprisingly, the onset of peace sent the economy into a free fall. Labor strikes and the first race riots began to plague American cities. Paris seemed far away to many Americans, and Wilson's absence was troubling. During February (in the wake of Premier Clemenceau's being wounded by an assassin's bullet) Wilson returned briefly to Washington, but when he returned to Paris, he was more determined than ever to push a treaty—incorporating a League—through to a quick adoption.

This meant that despite his pledge of "open covenants, openly arrived at," Wilson found himself negotiating in closed meetings with just the other three leaders. One result is that no official record survives of just how the Big Four reached various decisions, since the episodic notes taken by various secretaries who were in and out of the conference room differ widely. But this was not Vienna in 1815. While each of the Big Four played essentially a lone game, it became unavoidable that whenever any of them needed supporting data or guidance for their arguments, they had to reach out to the work provided by their young staffs. And, significantly, much of that guidance had been already digested and brokered by these young diplomats who were based in the offices of the Quai d'Orsay, or the Majestic and Crillon. No generation of young diplomats had ever had so much power given them.

Five

Compromises and Betrayals

1919

"Germany must not be allowed to win this war."

—U.S. Secretary of State Robert Lansing

THE PARIS PEACE CONFERENCE would be the formative event of the lives of all of the Dupont Circle set in that they faced an extraordinary challenge and had access to influence that was far greater than any previous generation of young people. However, not all of them came away from Paris with their reputations burnished by the experience. Paris was a time of testing, and some of our Progressives faced failure.

It is a fitting irony that the first of the Dupont Circle group of young claimants to set foot in France was the one who had been denied a place at the table because of her age and gender. It remained a point of personal pride all her exceptional life that Eleanor Lansing Dulles had gotten herself across the Atlantic to Paris before General Pershing in June 1917.

Fresh from Bryn Mawr that spring, twenty-two-old Eleanor was the fourth of the five children of the Reverend Allen and Edith Foster Dulles. All five of the Dulles siblings—John Foster Dulles (known as Foster), Mary, Allen, Eleanor, and Nataline—

had bifurcated upbringings. Raised in a financially straitened Presbyterian manse, their days began with cold baths, prayers, and Bible lessons. But then their mother regularly took them to Washington to the art- and treasure-filled mansion of General Foster and her family where they were exposed to formal dinners where other guests were the most powerful people in the capital. In the summer, their grandfather would often take the whole family on trips to European spas and Paris museums where they rubbed shoulders with the wealthiest of America's new rich aristocrats. But most summers the whole clan would retire to the family compound of modest cottages at Henderson Harbor on Lake Ontario. There, they not only became adept swimmers and sailors, but they were also exposed to tutorials on foreign policy from a stream of visitors—ranging from former President Grover Cleveland to ornately robed Chinese diplomats—who came to consult the General and Robert Lansing and stayed to fish and relax. Early on, the children were encouraged to develop opinions on great matters and be tested by their celebrity guests. Part of their inheritance was a proprietary feeling about the State Department. Eleanor became something of a pet of her grandfather's and often stayed with the Fosters in Washington during her childhood.

Unlike brothers Foster and Allen, who were tall, athletic, and charming, Eleanor was the smallest of the five and had poor eyesight, but she was, as she later described herself, "a tough little nut." In many ways she was the most ambitious of the five and was perhaps the most intellectually creative. She also shared with her brothers the strong romantic streak that was another family trait. One of the family legends has Foster, who rushed through two years of law school in Washington, going to Albany to take the tough New York state bar examination. He answered just enough questions, by his estimate, to guarantee passing and then dashed by train to Watertown to propose to his sweetheart, Janet Avery. The reason for the haste, the story goes, is that his younger brother Allen had been making overtures to Janet himself.

But in 1917, General Foster was ailing (he would die that autumn at age eighty-three) and Secretary Lansing had no inclination to help Eleanor find a place in government. Allen was already in Bern in the U.S. Legation serving as an intelligence contact with the scores of European exile groups who were camped in Switzerland awaiting the peace. And Foster was on loan from Sullivan & Cromwell to be legal counsel to the powerful War Industries Board that imposed unprecedented controls on military contractors and unions to speed the war effort.[1] Two family members on the government payroll were enough.

So Eleanor sailed for France and found work in Paris with other American women who had volunteered to aid French refugees who had fled the war to face dire conditions in the crowded slums of the capital. Later that summer, she joined another American aid group who worked just behind the battle zone of the Marne River valley trying to help peasant farmers plant enough crops to weather through the coming winter and stave off famine. The conditions were primitive and the work was both dangerous and exhausting, but Eleanor was elated. The theories of social reform and economics she had learned at Bryn Mawr were being challenged by the realities of the war zone. She later recalled:

> We learned, for example, not to give aid but to sell it. Now these farm families did not have much money so we didn't charge much, but they had to pay something. That way they learned to prioritize what they needed—tools, seeds, clothing, and so on— and we were able to make our resources go further.[2]

Proud as she was of her independence, Eleanor made free use of her family ties once the American delegation arrived in Paris. She liked to recount:

> There was no way to get really clean out in the countryside, so when I needed a break I would go to Paris, and barge into the Secretary of State's suite at the Crillon. Uncle Bert [Robert Lansing] and my Aunt Eleanor would usually be out at some function so I would run a steaming hot bath, have a delicious soak and use up all of his towels. Then I would order a fine meal from room service and fall fast asleep in Uncle Bert's bed. I don't

think he was best pleased to find me there; it meant he and Aunt had to sleep in the same bed that night, but he never rebuked me so I just assumed he didn't mind.

While Eleanor was learning the realities of aid and reconstruction, Allen was rapidly being schooled in the hard rules of spy-craft. Until the war, America had no organized method of gathering information about the intentions and capabilities of foreign forces—either nations or exile groups—who could affect either the war or the peace that followed. Allen had been a quick learner and a tireless traveler to other major Swiss cities where secretive and wary bands of plotters of all political stripes were waiting to return to their homelands and to power. His reports, especially about the group led by Czech leader Thomas Masaryk, formed an important part of The Inquiry's determination to create a single nation of Czechoslovakia at the peace conference.

Not that it was all work. Crowded with cash-rich foreigners, Switzerland was an oasis while the war raged around it. There was plenty of time for high spirited fun; Allen and Robert Craigie, a British embassy intelligence officer and new friend, were thrown out of a hotel after they had held an impromptu jazz concert on drums and piano and had refused to give way when the band returned from their break. And there were beautiful women of all nationalities to woo as well.

Indeed, romance was part of his most famous anecdote about that time. Dulles often told later intelligence training classes of how one Friday afternoon, he had been left as a junior officer to close the legation offices for the weekend. Just as he was to set off for a tennis date with "two blonde Swiss twin sisters," a telephone caller demanded to come to the offices at once and speak to an American official. Dulles refused him and said he should call again on Monday. The caller said that was impossible because he was leaving Switzerland the next day and rang off. The man had said his name was Lenin. Dulles never went so far as to say he could have stopped the Russian Revolution from occurring, but his point to the trainees was valid: an intelligence officer should be willing to hear any source of information. It is doubtful that the yarn was completely accurate, but it remained one of his favorites for years afterward.[3]

By the spring of 1918, Walter Lippmann had to face that he had come to the end of his usefulness as executive director of The Inquiry. It was mostly his fault. He had been unsparing in pressing the scholars to hurry their research and then was equally brutal in his criticism of the resulting studies. Isaiah Bowman, head of the American Geographic Society and the intellectual spirit of The Inquiry, was particularly offended at what he saw as a lack of due respect from a much younger man who was, after all, just a popular journalist. All of The Inquiry scholars also were vexed at Lippmann's role as a cut-out between their work and both Colonel House and President Wilson. This became almost open rebellion when, after the Fourteen Points speech, Lippmann crowed to Bowman, "This is the second time I have put words in the mouth of the President."[4] The words may have been Lippmann's, but the thoughts had been provided by The Inquiry scholars, and they resented it.

So when he was approached out of the blue by Army intelligence officers to go to France and direct a propaganda campaign to attract German troops to desert, Lippmann grabbed at the chance. The lure was twofold. Not only would he get a commission as an Army captain and be attached to General Pershing's headquarters, he would also carry with him a letter from Secretary Lansing appointing him a representative of the president and Colonel House to gather information preparatory to setting up the peace conference. This turned out to be a double mistake for Lippmann's career and his personal status though he could not know it at the time. All he saw was the chance to participate in important war work and at the same time be a major negotiator with Britain and France on the terms of the treaty. If he had confined himself to the propaganda campaign, he might have stayed on in France through the entire conference. Using makeshift resources and his own creativity, Lippmann and his colleagues generated millions of copies of leaflets that appealed to the Germans to surrender to the inevitable; they were scattered behind German lines by balloon and airplane and were used by thousands of German soldiers as free passes through Allied lines to safety.

When he arrived in France in late July 1918, Lippmann, instead of going directly to General Pershing's headquarters in Chaumont, abruptly set off for London. There his old House-of-Truth friend Eustace Percy arranged a round of lunches and dinners with leading press barons and government ministers, including a meeting with Sir William Tyrrell, who ran the British equivalent of The Inquiry for Prime Minister Lloyd George. Going beyond his orders to meet and listen to what the Allies were thinking, Lippmann suddenly proposed that London promptly accept the Fourteen Points as their position for the upcoming peace conference. More, he suggested an open show-and-share relationship between the two research staffs. Tyrrell was caught by surprise and promptly telegraphed spy William Wiseman in New York to find out who this young man was and whether, as he hinted, he was empowered to speak both for the Colonel and the president. When Wiseman checked with House, the Colonel was incensed that Lippmann was trying to do to him what he was trying to do to the president: edge into the front line of negotiations.

Wiseman's reply to Tyrrell reflected House's sense of self-preservation.

> I would not say that Lippmann is very closely in House's confidence. He is undoubtedly a very able young man and represents a certain section of the more intelligent radicals. House, however, has not very much confidence in his judgment and would certainly not think of letting him organize a political intelligence department on your side.[5]

Lippmann was unaware of this and so was puzzled at the cordial reticence of the British as they nudged him back to Paris.

There, matters could have rested, but Colonel House took the precaution of alerting President Wilson who predictably went ballistic. The first sin, in his mind, was that the Army appeared to be setting up a separate propaganda arm while he had specifically ordered that all government propaganda, censorship, and counteraction against dissent be the responsibility of his friend George Creel and his Committee on Public Information (CPI). Creel had been singularly effective in keeping the Wilson message and image on track, in dictating to newspapers, jailing dissenters, and creating a climate of public enthusiasm for the war that masked serious concerns about civil liberties among Wilson's Progressive supporters. It seems Wilson had never really trusted Lippmann all that much in the first place; he may have relied on the young man's brilliance with words and thoughts, but he also resented him and most of the other young Progressive (read: Jewish) intellectuals who had pushed into government. Creel and Lippmann hated each other, and the president held Walter responsible for the drumfire of criticism that poured from *The New Republic* about the CPI's crackdown on war doubters.

That Lippmann would turn up in London pretending to speak for the president was the last straw. He wrote House what clearly was a warning to him as well:

> I am very much puzzled as to who sent Lippmann over to inquire into matters of propaganda. I have found his judgment most unsound and therefore entirely unserviceable in matters of that sort because he, in common with the men of *The New Republic,* has ideas about the war and its purposes which are highly unorthodox from my own point of view. What he says about his interviews with Sir William Tyrrell interests me very much, but if he thinks that Lord Eustace Percy is equally trustworthy, he is vastly mistaken. He is one of the most slippery and untrustworthy of the men we have had to deal with over there.[6]

As soon as Creel heard of the Army's plans, he promptly had the propaganda program transferred under the CPI's wing, so that the Wilson message in Europe would be as tightly controlled as it was at home. Lippmann, not really understanding what was at work, concentrated the rest of that summer on leaflets at Chaumont.

Trust him or not, both House and Wilson had heavily depended on Lippmann often in the past and they would again, and soon. When House arrived in Europe in late October 1918, the end of the war was just days away. Germany had secretly signaled they would seek a peace settlement based on the Fourteen Points. But House, to his dismay, found both the British and French extremely suspicious about American objectives. To their surprise, what had appeared to be merely a message from the president to win support from his Congress had caught the world's imagination despite being vague about just how many of the objectives of some of the points were to be achieved or what the consequences of others might lead to. This put British prime minister Lloyd George and French premier Clemenceau in an unwanted bind. Simply saying that all ethnic groups were entitled to self-government was one thing, but the British, for one, were alarmed that Wilson might be pointing to Ireland (which was already breaking away) or India, and even the Dominions. French worries about their African and Asian colonies were equally acute. And this League of Nations; did Wilson mean, as some were proposing, the creation of a League army to enforce its rulings? House yanked Lippmann back to Paris from Chaumont and, in a marathon writing binge done overnight, he produced an explanatory memo for House to show around and with him shuttled between Paris and London trying to reassure both governments. The clear reluctance of either ally to enthusiastically endorse the plan caught Walter by surprise. Perhaps for the first time, he faced the frustration that his mastery of the details and the certainty of his convictions simply could not move someone else out of intransigence. He was not used to such refusal.

In late November 1918, the dreaded "Spanish" influenza pandemic that had started in the United States arrived in Paris and put Lippmann to bed in the Crillon for several weeks before he recovered. When Wilson arrived in late December with his entourage, both Lippmann and Colonel House were sharply disappointed. The Colonel was not even made an official member of the delegation; he was relegated to adviser status. Lippmann had no place made for him at all, and when he went to Isaiah Bowman to beg any kind of job on The Inquiry staff in Paris, he was bluntly told to go away. Depressed and still weakened by the flu, Lippmann sailed for home three days after the peace conference convened in January. His career had come to a crossroad with no clear way ahead. Reunited with Faye in New York, the couple headed for Florida for an overdue holiday. They did not bother to stop in Washington; there was no one there of interest anymore.

But if Lippmann's Paris experiences were disappointing, others of the Dupont Circle set saw their reputations vastly enhanced by the conference. Foster Dulles (along with his wife Janet) had been brought along with Wilson's economic guru Bernard Baruch to negotiate the thorny issue of how much in war damage reparations would be demanded from the Germans. But Baruch had also brought along his mistress and spent a great deal of time otherwise occupied. This left Dulles basically alone in negotiating with the British Treasury's expert, young John Maynard Keynes. The difference between the two was one of perspective. Keynes argued, with some reason, that a crushing war debt burden would stymie Germany's economic recovery and perhaps prevent the establishment of a viable democratic government; that, he concluded, would not help Britain's own revival, which depended on renewing its exports to Europe. When his recommendations were ignored, Keynes resigned in protest and went home to write a polemic, *The Economic Consequences of the Peace,* which would contribute to the conference's image of failure.

Dulles had a wider viewpoint. America, which had been a modest debtor before the war, was now the biggest creditor nation in the world. Wall Street was awash in liquidity; most of the gold reserves of both Britain and France had been shipped over to purchase war supplies.[7] While Dulles agreed with Keynes that keeping Germany bankrupt was a bad idea, he also recognized that the popular demand that Germany bear the cost of its aggression was just as powerful in America as it was in Britain or France. Together with Norman Davis, a young New York banker who also was on the committee, Dulles drafted what became notorious as the "war guilt" clause to the Versailles Treaty; it was intended to establish a legal liability for the damage to persons and property done by the German troops, but it was used by Adolf Hitler and other apologists to stir German resentment at the implied moral censure. But the Dulles committee left it to a post-conference special committee to set the final amount that was to be exacted.

What the committee put in place was a complex plan by which Germany, and other struggling European governments, would borrow the excess capital stacked up in New York to restart their own economies, thereby creating demand for surplus American food and manufactured products and (in theory) the earnings to pay their reparations debts to Britain and France. Not surprisingly, Foster would become Sullivan & Cromwell's managing director while still in his thirties at least in part because the firm would be the dominant intermediary between the borrowing governments and Wall Street's investment houses in many of those loan agreements over the next five years. Although Hitler blamed the war reparations as pretext for violating the rest of the Versailles Treaty, more recent scholarship questions whether the debts were that important a cause of German instability during the twenty years between the two world wars.[8]

While Foster could return to Wall Street with a much-enhanced reputation, his brother Allen was emerging as something of a star among the American staff. He had come to Paris from the Bern Legation to be on the delegation's special intelligence secretariat. The group's initial mission was to provide Wilson with the briefings on the latest developments throughout Europe and to keep contact with the various exile groups that were lobbying the conference. But soon, Allen and several others found themselves actually drawing national boundaries using the ethnic studies of The Inquiry in negotiations with their opposite British and French staff colleagues. By May 1919, with the time drawing near for the Treaty to be signed, Dulles found himself running the Peace Conference's steering committee that decided when each remaining question was to be taken up for a final vote; he would stay on in Paris through 1920 as the remaining treaties with the other Central Power governments were negotiated.

Of all the young strivers who left Dupont Circle for Paris, the one who should have been the most successful was the twenty-seven-year-old newspaper reporter William C. Bullitt, who had come to Washington in 1917 as the bureau chief for *The Philadelphia Public Ledger*. Bullitt had a lot more going for him than any of the other young Progressives, so perhaps it is not surprising that within a few months he had shouldered past them all into the top councils of the Wilson government. Tall, handsome, and aggressively charming, he had a polish and sophistication the others—even Franklin Roosevelt—lacked. Bullitt's father had been a wealthy Philadelphia lawyer, and the family had traveled widely in Europe, where young Bill, as he was known, became fluent in both French and German. At Yale, where he studied other languages and art, he was voted "most brilliant" by his classmates. But after his first year at Harvard Law School, he had dropped out to cast about for a career that engaged him more. In the spring of 1914, he had accompanied his recently widowed mother on a European tour that began in Russia just as the war broke out. Since Americans were still considered neutral, Bullitt and his mother took a leisurely return journey through the major capitals of the Central Powers. With the boundless confidence that would mark his later life, Bullitt managed to secure personal interviews with the leading statesmen on both sides of the conflict.

One of the first interviews he sought in Washington when he arrived there in early 1917 was with Colonel House, whom he charmed and intrigued with his authoritative analysis of the European leaders he had met. Through House, Bullitt was introduced to Secretary of State Lansing who by December had secured his appointment as assistant secretary of state to head the department's newly created bureau on Central European intelligence. Life in Washington was not all work by any means. Despite being prematurely balding, Bullitt exuded a certain aggressive sex appeal that earned him a number of romantic conquests, aside from his flirtation with Alice Roosevelt Longworth.

Of all the Dupont Circle set, Bullitt was the only one to be included in the relatively small official peace conference staff that sailed in 1918 to Paris with President Wilson, Lansing, and the other official delegates. He was named head of the delegation's division of current intelligence and thus was higher ranking than either of the Dulles brothers. From his first meeting with Colonel House, Bullitt had argued that the United States should take the lead in recognizing the Bolshevik government that had seized power that year in Russia; such a move, he argued, would at the least temper some of the violent purges that Lenin had embarked upon, and President Wilson's own influence could hasten the regime's transition into a true democracy. American public opinion, however, had been horrified by both the murder of the Czar and his family and the other evidence of repression. Wilson not only rejected the advice, but in the autumn of 1918, he also sent U.S. troops to Murmansk and later to Soviet ports in the Far East, ostensibly to reclaim war supplies that had been shipped to the Czarist Army.

But in Paris, Bullitt convinced Lansing (and by a nod, Wilson) to send him on a secret mission to Petrograd to sound Lenin out about the prospects of formal recognition. Lloyd George also was apprised of the plan, and he too gave unofficial support; the British were particularly keen to get Lenin to pledge that his government would honor the millions of pounds worth of bonds that the Czarist government had floated for railroads and other development projects. So, in mid-February 1919, Bullitt set out with Lincoln Steffens (who was serving as a press adviser to Wilson) and two military aides on an arduous journey by train, boat, and even sleigh that took them through Sweden before they could skirt the Allied blockade and reach Petrograd on March 6. Lenin saw them coming and recognized them as the kind of credulous Westerners he later would term "useful idiots."

Although Bullitt had at no time been given powers to negotiate anything, the Soviets rolled out the kind of official welcome usually reserved for accredited ambassadors. He and Steffens were immediately given interviews with senior foreign ministry officials and taken on tours of impressive sites where happy workers were well fed and living in stable conditions. Five days into this Potemkin tour, Bullitt was taken for his first of several meetings with Lenin who, Bullitt later reported, was "genial and with large humor and serenity." Lenin assured them that his fondest wish was to see Russia join the community of nations, that it would honor its obligations, and that the violence that had been reported in the Western press was really taken in self-defense against the counterrevolutionary attacks of Czarist loyalists. Once the American and British troops were removed from Russian soil, all these things could be negotiated. There were even hints that Russia might want to attend the Paris conference. He signed a preliminary peace proposal for them to take back to Paris, but it had a rather narrow time limit attached to it.

Both Bullitt and Steffens rushed back to Paris in a triumphant mood. There is some confusion as to which one said it first, but both have been credited with the famous quote, "I have been over to the future, and it works!" But French Premier Clemenceau, who had just returned to the meetings after being slightly wounded by an assassin, exploded when he got wind of the trip. He would not reward the Bolsheviks, who had betrayed the Allied cause by making a separate peace with the Kaiser, with a place at the conference table. Once again he threatened to cancel the conference, expel the delegations, and break the armistice. Wilson assured him he had had no prior knowledge of the adventure and refused Bullitt's requests for an interview to defend the report he had written on recognizing the Lenin government. Part of Wilson's about-face may have been influenced by a sternly worded report from Herbert Hoover, who was in Paris overseeing a huge program of food relief for the war-shattered regions and whose own sources of intelligence were confirming Soviet atrocities against their own people. "We cannot ever remotely recognize this murderous tyranny without stimulating reactionary radicalism in every country in Europe and without transgressing . . . every national ideal of our own," Hoover declared.[9]

House, who was already in trouble with Wilson for conceding issues while the president was in America, also began to backpedal. He suggested Bullitt take his case to Lloyd George and, briefly, the British prime minister was tempted by the notion that he could take the lead in restoring ties to Russia. At a secret meeting in Lloyd George's apartment, Bullitt made an impassioned argument for his report to a sympathetic audience that included Philip Kerr and

South African leader Jan Christian Smuts. But someone had leaked a copy of the report to the opposition Tory newspaper, *The London Daily Mail*, which accused Lloyd George of secret negotiations with the evil Bolshevik regime and thereby sparked uproar among his foes in the Parliament. Sadly, Lloyd George said, there was nothing he could do; the young man was advised to go back to America and make his report public. To shore up his own position, the prime minister assured Parliament he had never had any dealings with Bullitt and that there was no move to legitimize Lenin's government even as British and American troops were skirmishing with Soviet guards inside Russia itself.

Bullitt also was outraged at a number of the concessions the president had made to the territorial claims of the other Allies; for him the Treaty was becoming the blueprint for a future series of wars. He organized a dinner at the Crillon for the other staff of the intelligence department and tried to persuade them to resign en masse in protest; historian Samuel Eliot Morrison and economist Adolf A. Berle joined in, but others, like Allen Dulles and Christian Herter (a future secretary of state), stayed to see the Treaty through to its signing.

As a last act, Bullitt sought an interview with Secretary Lansing in early May. He poured out his frustration to his boss and, to his surprise, Lansing confided his own anger at having been left out of the negotiations by Wilson. The secretary also voiced his own deep worries and those of other delegation members that a number of key points in the Treaty being drafted—chiefly, the League's power to call on member nations to intervene to stop aggression—were creating obligations which the United States could not fulfill. On May 17, 1919, Bullitt resigned from the staff, packed up with his wife Ernesta (who had been left alone in Paris during his adventure), and set out for the Riviera

> to lie in the sand and watch the world go to hell," as he told friends. But he could not resist sending a last scathing letter to President Wilson: "Six months ago all the peoples of Europe expected you to fulfill their hopes. They believe now that you cannot. They turn, therefore, to Lenin. . . . I am sorry you did not fight our fight to the finish.[10]

If he had left it at that, Bullitt might have returned to the United States at least with his reputation for integrity intact. But he could not resist making his resignation letter public, and, when he and Ernesta docked in New York at the end of the summer, he gave a number of press interviews that fanned the opposition that had already built around President Wilson's determination to win Senate ratification of the Versailles Treaty with no changes allowed. Nor could he resist testifying before the Senate Foreign Relations Committee chaired by Senator Henry Cabot Lodge to express his own doubts about the pact; in so doing he also betrayed Secretary Lansing's confidences and concerns. Lansing was further embarrassed by being hauled before the committee and confronted with Bullitt's allegations, which he could not bring himself to completely disavow. For Wilson, who was in the middle of the exhausting eight-thousand–mile speaking tour across the nation to rally support for the Treaty, both men had stabbed him in the back; that he ultimately collapsed on the trip and later suffered a stroke merely added to the public image of betrayal he had suffered from his own aides. In what can only be explained as a last act of defiance, Bullitt had his report on Russia and testimony before the Lodge committee published as a private pamphlet. He appeared willing to burn all his bridges to ashes. Along with the other defections, Bullitt's rebellion was one more brick in the myth created in Paris that the Peace Conference and the League had been a doomed exercise from the start.

Yet with the advantage of hindsight, the despair that many of the Dupont Circle set felt as they left Paris was premature. The Versailles Treaty that emerged from the Conference was far from perfect but hardly a failure. Rather, that unwieldy document was a pretty remarkable first effort that set in motion a twenty-year quest for a stable peace in a world that remained very unstable. And while they could not know it at the time, all of our young Progressives would find themselves caught up in that quest. For the Dupont Circle set, Paris was just the beginning of the rest of their lives.

Six

Victory without Triumph

1919–1920

"If what we fought for seems not worth the fighting. And if to win seems in the end to fail. Know that the vision lives beyond all blighting. And every struggle rends another veil.

The tired hack, the cynic politician, can dim but cannot make us lose the goal. Time moves with measured step upon her mission. Knowing the slow mutations of the soul."

—Hamilton Fish Armstrong, *New York Evening Post,* 1920[1]

*W*HEN THEY SAILED FOR HOME during the summer of 1919, there was a pervasive feeling of disappointment and, in many cases, of individual betrayal among some of the Dupont Circle set. Nevertheless, what is remarkable about the period immediately following the Paris Peace Conference is that most of the young Progressives did not abandon their quest.

What followed over the next two years or so for them was a time of reassessment, both of individual ambitions and, more importantly, of how to achieve their common ideals in a political arena that had proved more complicated than most had first thought.

They had gone to France to remake the world. Along with the youthful elite of British and French intellectuals, they had been handed unprecedented power and had performed ambitious tasks. But scarcely had the conference gotten underway in January 1919 when compromises were forced upon them by the strategic ambitions of the governments they represented. Harold Nicolson, a colleague of Philip Kerr and Eustace Percy on the British staff, summed up the mood: "We came to Paris convinced that the new order was about to be established; we left it convinced that the new order had merely fouled the old."[2]

The trouble was that there was no old order left at all. The catastrophe of war had swept away three of the four great empires that had emerged after Napoleon had welded tiny European duchies into nations. Then, with shifting alliances, the nations had maintained a delicate balance of power that only occasionally broke down into war. Now Russia, even with the Bolsheviks in power in Petrograd, was engulfed in a savage civil war through much of its vast territory. Austria-Hungary had vanished and set a dozen nationalities adrift. Much of France, its giant industrial complex and fecund farmlands, had been left in smoking ruins; what had not been destroyed outright the Germans had looted during their retreat or ruined beyond use: mines had been flooded, food stocks spoiled, water sources tainted.

French Premier Georges Clemenceau recognized his nation faced an existential crisis that would take more than a treaty to cure. Although it had been victorious, the war had left France nearly destroyed as a nation. The French had lost the prime men of their next generation in the carnage; six out of ten men between eighteen and twenty-eight had been either killed or permanently maimed by the war.[3] For the next twenty years, the sight of hideously disfigured or crippled veterans was common on the streets of every big city or small village and was a constant reminder.

The fourth, the globe-straddling British Empire, was coming unstuck as well, although its leaders were only dimly aware of it as they traveled to Paris. Prime Minister David Lloyd George set out assuming he and his Cabinet would be the single voice of the Empire when the peace conference was being organized in December 1918. But the prime ministers of Canada, Australia, and

New Zealand were having none of that. Nominally they were still Dominions, but, as they reminded Lloyd George, now they were nations as well. Together they had suffered more combat deaths during the war than the United States; at the least they deserved to be seated at the table and to speak their minds about their special concerns (Japan's role in the Pacific, for one) as well as support the Empire's interests. An irritated Lloyd George prevailed on Clemenceau to seat the Dominion delegations. He could not do otherwise with Ireland (which had stayed out of the war) in open rebellion on his doorstep.

This is not the place to review the events of the six months that followed June 28, 1919, when thirty-two nations gathered in the ornate Hall of Clocks at the Quai d'Orsay to approve the more than four hundred clauses in the eighty-thousand-word Treaty of Versailles. That has already been done in historian Margaret Mac-Millan's authoritative work, *Peacemakers.*[4] But it is worth noting that that book and a number of recent reassessments by other historians have begun to challenge the textbook conclusion that the Paris Peace Conference, the pact that it brokered, and the League of Nations that was its dominant by-product were all failures and were the proximate cause of the rise of Adolf Hitler and the descent into the maelstrom of the next world war. That such a flawed view has survived this long is perhaps understandable. It had its genesis at the conference itself. A popular cartoon of the time has Clemenceau with the other Big Four conferees (Wilson, Lloyd George, and Italy's Vittorio Orlando) standing outside the meeting. The caption has the French premier saying, "Curious. I seem to hear a child weeping." Hidden from them behind a pillar is a naked, crying boy with the legend, "Class of 1940"—a prophetic reference to the conscription group of young Frenchmen who would face the war to come.

But the best current summing up comes from MacMillan. "The peacemakers of 1919 made mistakes, of course. By their offhand treatment of the non-European world, they stirred up resentments for which the West is still paying today. They took pains over the borders in Europe, even if they did not draw them to

everyone's satisfaction, but in Africa they carried on the old practice of handing out territory to suit the imperialist powers. In the
Middle East they threw together peoples, in Iraq most notably,
who still have not managed to cohere into a civil society. If they
could have done better, they certainly could have done worse."
And, in what is a central theme of our narrative, she adds, "When
war came in 1939, it was a result of twenty years of decisions taken
or not taken, not of the arrangements made in 1919."[5]

Looking back over the record, only Woodrow Wilson seemed
determined to use the Versailles Treaty and the League as an ironclad mechanism for peace. The French were never under such an
illusion. And Lloyd George and all of his ministers repeatedly reassured the British people that their assent to the accords reached in
Paris—including setting up the League—were merely the vehicles
through which the customary diplomatic maneuvering would now
take place. Britain was not going to give up any of its sovereignty
even though it would join the League.

Thus, Wilson's insistence that the Senate ratify the Treaty as
written, without appending any reservations of U.S. self-interests,
was a gamble that, as it turned out, he could never have won. It also
is true that the Lodge Committee did recommend ratification of
the Treaty, but with the fourteen reservations of U.S. self-interests,
which Wilson refused to accept. Wilson then lost the subsequent
vote in the full Senate to remove them.

But it also is clear that the failure of the Senate to ratify in that
autumn of 1919 was not the final American word of rejection of
the Paris conference. It was, in fact, the beginning of a struggle that
would actually heat up in the year to come.

Since 1920 would be a presidential election year, everyone still
in Paris or in Washington was well aware it would be a national referendum on both the Treaty document and on Woodrow Wilson,
the now disabled recluse confined to the upper floors of the White
House. Even Ohio Republican Senator Warren G. Harding, who
had been one of Bullitt's interrogators during the Lodge Committee hearings, refused to flatly reject membership in the League. It
was, Harding explained, important to make it clear that joining the

League would not infringe on American sovereignty; if that were done, the Treaty could be approved.

And the Treaty did have its champions among those of the Dupont Circle set who had achieved their own objectives in Paris. Felix Frankfurter was one of those who returned to America with a sense of achievement and, equally important, an enhanced personal reputation.

During his time at the War Department, Frankfurter had made a national reputation not only as an able administrator but also as a tireless legal advocate for workers who were being squeezed both by wartime pressures to increase production and by economic pressures that depressed wages. As lead counsel for the wartime mediation commission, he had taken up the cause of striking copper miners in Bisbee, Arizona, whose employers forcibly deported a thousand protestors into the desert of New Mexico and abandoned them. He also led the public fight to win a new trial for the radical union leader Tom Mooney,[6] who had been illegally sentenced for an anarchist bombing in San Francisco. After returning to Harvard Law School, Frankfurter had been recruited to go to Paris as a representative of the American Jewish Committee to join the international Zionist delegation headed by Chaim Weizmann and other European leaders. The Zionists wanted the Allies to honor the promises made by British Foreign Minister Lord Balfour in 1917 that "a national home for the Jewish people" be established in Palestine.

Frankfurter had become a late convert to the Zionist cause, and it was mainly due to his close ties to Louis Brandeis, who had been an early skeptic of any effort to build a Jewish nation. Like Lippmann and Frankfurter, Brandeis had considered himself to be Jewish "as an accident of birth" and to be foremost an aspiring American. But in his pro bono legal work before he became a Supreme Court justice, Brandeis represented a number of cases that challenged the barely human conditions imposed on non-union factory workers, many of them Eastern European Jews. Then in 1913, many well-to-do American Jews were jolted out of their fantasy of having achieved the protective cover of the middle class

when Leo Frank, a Jewish factory manager in Atlanta, was convict-
ed and sentenced to death in an openly flawed trial for the murder
of a teenage mill girl. When it appeared that a national outcry over
the case might lead to his sentence being commuted by the governor, a mob of prominent citizens broke into the jail in 1915 and
lynched Frank after mutilating him.

Brandeis began to be more active in organizing the American
Jewish Committee during the Great War as it became evident that
the breaking apart of the old monarchies was having the unintended
consequence that European Jews invariably became targets of persecution as contending sides fought for power in the new nations that
were forming. Once Frankfurter moved from Washington back to
Harvard, his old mentor drew him into the cause and away from
the old skeptics like Ambassador Morgenthau, whom Frankfurter
had come to despise. To the younger man, the conviction held by
Morgenthau and other older Jews that they could both keep their
faith and fully assimilate into the American culture seemed to be
arrogance in the face of a harsher reality.

In Paris, Frankfurter had a stroke of good luck. The young staff
members on the peace conference committee that was to divide up
Turkey's former Middle Eastern provinces were already predisposed
to assign Palestine to the British as a mandate while giving Syria
to the French. The two principal British negotiators on that committee turned out to be House of Truth friends Eustace Percy and
Philip Kerr. Despite having friends on the panel, the negotiations
were still a tricky matter. The Lloyd George government was committed to setting up client Arab governments for the Saudis, Iraqis,
and Egyptians to protect their own vital interest in the Suez Canal
pathway to their Indian colonies. Partisans such as the fabled T. E.
Lawrence would have openly opposed the creation of a Jewish state
in their midst. But even though the actual boundaries would not
be fixed until a year later, Frankfurter was able to leave Paris with
credit for negotiating a firm commitment for "a Jewish homeland"
under indefinite British protection.

Like nearly everyone else who had gone to Paris in that spring
of 1919, Frankfurter took side trips to England to renew friendships

with old Fabian Society allies and to enjoy the hospitality of the Astors at Cliveden. It was through the Astors's influence that he was able to realize a dream, a one-year scholarship to enhance his law studies at Oxford. He returned to America briefly to arrange a small civil wedding to Marian Denam. His mother showed her disapproval of him marrying outside his faith by boycotting the ceremony. Then as 1920 beckoned, the happy couple headed off for a year-long idyll among "the dreaming spires" of the famed university. There Frankfurter cheerfully adopted the trappings of the English gentleman scholar he had always fancied becoming; he bought a scarlet smoking jacket which he wore at home ever after, he developed a taste for vintage port and fine cigars, and he luxuriated in the sparkling conversation of the university banquet tables.

Despite the dissent from disaffected members of the Dupont Circle set like Bullitt and Lippmann, most saw the dramatic signing of the Treaty of Versailles in the Hall of Mirrors on June 28, 1919 as the continuation of the great Progressivist adventure toward a better world. Some, like Allen Dulles and Christian Herter, stayed on with the remnants of a U.S. delegation to work out the details on the remaining peace treaties that had to be concluded with the other Central Powers governments. From across Europe, other Americans who had been military observers, Hoover relief workers, and political intelligence gatherers poured into Paris as their own operations were wound down. There were celebrations to attend and job prospects to pursue.

One of the arrivals in Paris in the summer of 1919 was a young U.S. Army captain named Hamilton Fish Armstrong, who had spent the previous year and a half as a military aide to the Serbian forces, which had fought the Austrians in a particularly savage theater of the war.

Armstrong was from one of New York City's oldest families who were cloistered in the Washington Square enclave portrayed in Edith Wharton novels. As the editor of *The Daily Princetonian* college newspaper, young "Ham" Armstrong became a nationally known student leader for The League to Enforce Peace and had even turned down a personal invitation from Henry Ford to join the Peace Ship voyage in 1915. A year later, he joined *The New Republic* as a fledgling writer, doing research for Walter Lippmann and contributing articles on his own; he also continued to have some of his poetry published in daily newspapers. His intelligence reports on the Balkans during the war had been heavily relied upon by Allen Dulles and the political staff; in particular, he had developed a close personal friendship with the future King Alexander of Yugoslavia, and he arrived in Paris with a chestful of decorations from the grateful Serbs.

Tall and handsome and with a reserve that made him seem older than he was, Armstrong was in no hurry to return to the United States. Earlier, on New Year's Eve 1918, he had married a gorgeous Long Island debutante named Helen MacGregor Byrne in a Paris cathedral at a wedding that had gotten enthusiastic press coverage back home. But then he had hastened back to his Serbian post almost at once. Now he wanted to rejoin Helen in Paris and enjoy a return to civilian life; he also wanted to seek some sort of career with the League of Nations that was being formed.

He got his wish almost at once. A fellow Princetonian named Raymond B. Fosdick had been a personal aide to President Wilson in Paris and had been nominated by him to be one of two under-secretaries (or executive officers) of the League when it began operations that September in Geneva; the other undersecretary would be France's Jean Monnet, a future founder of the European Community. Armstrong accepted the offer to be Fosdick's personal assistant. It was an opportunity of a lifetime for someone as committed as Armstrong.

Both Armstrong and Fosdick were also enthusiastic about another prospect developing in Paris that summer. Through most of that spring of 1919, the British and American staff members had moved from casual social acquaintance to, in many cases, close personal friendships borne out of similar backgrounds and attitudes. This was especially true of the Americans who had come over with The Inquiry and their opposite numbers on Lloyd George's staff. As the Treaty moved toward a final draft, there was a consensus that the real work of the Conference, the promotion of peaceful settlements of international issues, was only just beginning. Some way had to be found to continue the discussions that had so engrossed them.

On May 30, with the official signing less than a month away, Lord Robert Cecil (who had led the British negotiations to set up the League) organized a dinner at the Majestic for a mixed group of thirty of the young staffers to find a way to keep their dialogue alive. He had previously sounded out Colonel House, who enthusiastically supported the idea but prudently decided to remain aloof from the actual affair. Among the British staff who gathered in the private dining room that night were Kerr, Percy, Harold Nicolson, and their mentor, Lionel Curtis, one of the founders of The Garden Suburb and Round Table groups before the war and a leading proponent of the Anglo American commonwealth idea. Among the Americans in attendance was General Tasker Bliss, the U.S. Army chief of staff and one of the official U.S. peace commissioners. Another was Ray Stannard Baker, the old muckraking editor who had been Wilson's press secretary at the conference; his presence was further evidence of official sanction. Along with other Inquiry members present was Harvard historian Archibald Cary Coolidge, who had been Armstrong's immediate superior in collecting Balkan intelligence for the Paris staff.

Curtis led the discussion and proposed founding a joint Anglo-American "Institute of Foreign Affairs" to help "men of knowledge take the lead in scientifically studying foreign affairs to furnish political leaders with the requisite facts with which to make policy and sound public opinion." In a joint statement that the group issued after the dinner, "Right public opinion was mainly produced by a small number of people in real contact with the facts who had thought out the issues involved."[7]

It was the Progressive ideal writ large. They were the experts that their faith had always held would bring the world to order. If they could only find a way to build on the Paris experience, surely they would succeed where the older politicians and statesmen had failed. That older men like Cecil and House (and by implication, Wilson and Lloyd George) supported them merely confirmed their certainty.

However disappointing the Versailles Treaty may have appeared that summer to its drafters, if they could just continue the discussion among like-minded experts, they could in time achieve their dream of a world free of war.

The future looked promising.

Seven

Progressivism in Retreat

1920

"America's present need is not heroics, but healing; not nostrums, but normalcy; not revolution, but restoration; not agitation, but adjustment; not surgery, but serenity; not the dramatic, but the dispassionate; not experiment, but equipoise; not submergence in internationality, but sustainment in triumphant nationality."

—Warren G. Harding, "Readjustment," May 14, 1920 campaign speech[1]

AMERICANS WHO CAME HOME from Paris in the summer of 1919 found a country in as deep a crisis as any country in war-torn Europe. The changes that had been underway in their society before the U.S. entry into the war two years earlier had been unsettling enough, but now many people no longer were sure what would become of them or their nation. All the recognizable security of class, gender, and race was overturning. And worse than these uncertainties, there were visible and ominous threats all around them.

Surprisingly though, the national mood did not immediately shift into isolationism shrinking from world concerns as some histories report. Even those of the Dupont Circle set who met with personal setbacks in Paris—Walter Lippmann and William Bullitt to name two—were more inclined to blame the compromises that had been forced on President Wilson than any flaws in the Versailles Treaty or the League of Nations idea. The world remained a dangerous place; the Armistice that had halted what was now being called The Great War had not halted war itself. In the period from 1919 to 1920, there were no fewer than twenty-four armed conflicts around the world: Poles battled against Czechs, Hungarians against Romanians, Turkish nationalists against forces from Britain, France, Italy and Greece; the civil wars in Ireland and throughout Russia continued unchecked; uprisings throughout Africa and China persisted. Nor had total peace come to the United States. As millions of doughboys flooded home from France, U.S. troops continued to serve in parts of Russia and on the border with Mexico. During the same period, Washington ordered forces to intervene in half a dozen disturbances throughout the Caribbean, in Turkey, in the Balkans, and (several times) in China.

So whatever questions there might be about the mandate handed the League, most Americans, despite their uncertainty, still were favorably inclined to support U.S. membership. Although opinion polling was relatively uncommon, as various political groups tested the attitudes of their memberships, they found both Wilson and his vision for the League to be attractive that summer. Economist Hamilton Holt, an executive committee member of the League to Enforce Peace, summarized a series of polls that had tested levels of support for the positions of, first, the "irreconcilables," those outright foes of League membership like Senator William Borah of Idaho; second, those, like Senator Henry Cabot Lodge of the Foreign Relations Committee, who would impose reservations that affirmed American sovereignty before joining the League; and, third, those who supported President Wilson's uncompromising demand for ratification and League membership without reservations.

Holt reported:

> Less than one-tenth of the vote favored Senator Borah and his band of "irreconcilables"; less than one-fifth favored Lodge.

President Wilson's uncompromising stand evoked more support than the Lodge and Borah proposals combined. In short, nine-tenths of the voters were in favor of ratification in some form and seven-tenths were for a League more virile than the Foreign Relations Committee would have it.[2]

Part of Wilson's support stemmed from developments related to the unsettling changes underway at home. Many formerly hostile Protestant church denominations had begun to find common cause on political issues that included peace, Prohibition (which was about to be imposed), and reaction against what was seen as a general moral threat caused by the lures of urban life. Inter-church groups like the Federal Council of Churches of Christ began to wield real political power. Another source of support had come from both the students and faculties of the major universities, which had become active supporters first of peace and later of mobilization. Women's groups, such as the League of Women Voters and the American Association of University Women, looked at the upcoming 1920 election not only as a first chance for women to vote but as an opportunity to effect real social change; peace and the League were vital parts of that chance.

But public opinion is like quicksilver in its capacity to change shape. There were truly awful forces at work against the president and his quest. One rather sharp but brief recession as the war in Europe had abruptly ended had caught U.S. factories and farms with vast overstocks that could not be sold either at home or abroad. For about seven months, into the spring of 1919, business activity had fallen by nearly 25 percent. Part of the problem stemmed from the precipitous White House move to dismantle many of the programs of rationing and regulation that had helped mobilize the economy to a war footing. The economy was cast adrift.

Worse, the roughly four million American men who had been drafted into the war effort were just as suddenly returned to the job market without any financial support or prospect of employment. As a concession, discharged soldiers were permitted to continue to wear their uniforms for a year. The sight of idle groups of out-of-work men in shabby military garb became a visible reminder in towns throughout the nation of the economic crisis. There was a brief respite of a few months, but by the autumn of 1919, the economy began to sink into a second recession that would last through the summer of 1921 and prove to be what economists now call one of the most deflationary periods in American history, losing as much as 7 percent of gross domestic product in ten months. Adding to the jobless woes, the competition for jobs was heightened by an uninterrupted flow of immigrant labor from Eastern and Southern Europe and by the migration of hundreds of thousands of African Americans who fled rural penury in the South for the prospect of work in the major urban centers. Even those who had jobs faced widespread pressure from employers to cut wages to counterbalance the fall-off in revenues.

Inevitably, the fear begat violence that soon escalated into civil chaos in many cities. Strikes by dockworkers in Seattle and policemen in Boston soon morphed into a running series of confrontations led by radical union groups like the Industrial Workers of the World (the "Wobblies"). Labor strife spread from Colorado copper miners to West Virginia's coal fields and on into textile mills in the South. Railroad workers, telephone operators, and even Western Union telegraphers walked off their jobs to protest cuts in wages. In all, there were 2,665 recorded strikes during 1919 involving as many as four million workers.[3] Owners turned to strikebreakers and enlisted thugs organized by the American Legion and other self-appointed patriotic groups; confrontations with National Guard troops turned the struggles into pitched battles.

Race relations had been under pressure for some time before that hot summer of 1919. On taking office in 1913, President Wilson had given in to demands from his postmaster general and treasury secretary to remove long-time black civil servants from those departments and then angrily rebuked African American leaders like W. E. B. Dubois when they protested. Now after the war, when thousands of black troops had fought in France with great distinction, African American community leaders found that even the most dignified public protests were hotly resented by white citizens. Lynching of African Americans (often targeting black soldiers still in uniform) spread from the Deep South to the Midwest, fed by a revival of the Ku Klux Klan. In Washington, D.C., more than a week of race riots sent mobs of uniformed white soldiers and sailors in search of blacks who were dragged off trolley cars and assaulted on the streets of their own neighborhoods while the police stood by. Lawless bands of white citizens in Chicago and Tulsa burned down whole sections of their cities where African American families lived, their anger fed by local newspapers, which reported inflammatory and false stories of black assaults on white women.

Overhanging this summer of discontent was the fear of foreign terrorism. Depending on where one stood on the political spectrum in America, the violent upheavals of the Bolshevik struggles in Russia and the radical uprisings in key cities of Europe either were exhilarating promises of an inevitable workers revolution here at home or a horrifying threat of godless anarchy. Italian immigrants, facing economic oppression here and turmoil back in their homeland, were susceptible recruits to anarchist plotters of various political stripes. Some of the more violent groups turned to bombing campaigns to protest the injustices done them and to destabilize the capitalist government that oppressed them. On April 29, 1919, a chance discovery led to the interception of no fewer than thirty-six exploding devices that had been put into the postal system addressed to mayors, judges, corporate executives, and lawmakers—Justice Holmes, John D. Rockefeller, and J. P. Morgan among them—throughout the country. Prompted by authorities, the press reported that the plotters probably had been Bolshevik agents attempting to tie their murders to the traditional May Day workers' holiday.[4]

A month later, that belief had to be revised. On the evening of June 2, a series of eight bombs exploded in several U.S. cities, including the homes of Cleveland's mayor; a manufacturer in Paterson, New Jersey; and judges and police officials in Pittsburgh, Boston, and New York City. That same night, Franklin and Eleanor Roosevelt returned home from a Capitol Hill dinner party in Washington. They had moved from the Little White House on N Street to the other side of Dupont Circle to a larger townhouse at

2131 R Street; across the way at 2132 R was the home of the newly appointed Attorney General, A. Mitchell Palmer.

After parking their car in a nearby garage, Franklin and Eleanor began to stroll home. They were suddenly shocked by an explosion that jarred the quiet street. Franklin joked that a war souvenir shell may have fallen off someone's mantle, but as they neared their block, both were horrified to realize that a bomb had destroyed the front of the Palmer residence and had shattered doors and windows at their house and others as well. Both made a dash for their home where their eleven-year-old son James was upstairs in his room studying when the blast exploded. FDR found the boy unhurt and excitedly peering out through the shattered glass of his bedroom window at the carnage below. The other four children were safely away at their grandmother's estate in Hyde Park, New York, leaving only a hysterical housekeeper to be comforted by Eleanor.

Police later tied the explosion to the other bomb blasts and speculated that the anarchist who made the attempt on the Attorney General had tripped before he could place the device on the doorstep. As it happened, the Palmers had retired to the rear of the house early that night, and the family was shaken but unhurt. In addition to the damage to houses in the neighborhood, pieces of the anarchist were splattered on both sides of the street; Eleanor later reported having to forcibly restrain James from collecting bits of bone and clothing that had landed in their front yard.

This time it was obvious that Italian anarchists had been responsible; the same pamphlets declaring the start of a "class war" were found at all the locations and were traced to specific terrorists allied with a labor agitator named Luigi Galleani. With race riots sparking cruel violence in Washington and other cities, and with continued labor unrest in most key industries, neither Palmer nor anyone else in the Wilson administration appeared inclined to split hairs—all this upheaval was part of a widespread plot, probably Bolshevik-inspired, and was being carried out by Italian anarchists.

By conflating the threats into one easy-to-grasp common enemy, the government responded to the broader public impatience and post-war doubts. The notorious Palmer Raids that followed over the next year saw more than ten thousand individuals arrested (and as many as five hundred deported); the arrests mostly targeted people deemed to be labor agitators or political dissenters. The crackdown was immensely popular. Felix Frankfurter, Walter Lippmann, and *The New Republic* might protest the violation of civil liberties, but their complaints were ignored by an America that wanted a return to order and some certainty. Neither of the two friends, however, bothered to come to the aid of John Reed, who after his return from Russia faced a series of criminal trials for his writings and public speeches urging that the Bolshevik revolution should spread to America.

One can scarcely blame Eleanor for fleeing Washington with her son James, snatching the rest of the children from her mother-in-law's grasp and decamping for the rest of the summer—not to the Roosevelt family's island retreat of Campobello off New Brunswick but to the Massachusetts seaside. And if Franklin resented being left behind to handle the repairs on the R Street house during yet another sweltering Washington summer, he was prudent enough to keep his disappointment to himself. Truth be told, FDR was in serious trouble both with his marriage and his political career, and he needed to keep a low profile.

FDR had enjoyed what the British call "a good war." At the start in 1917, he had been on the move almost constantly, overseeing construction of warships, building training camps, and inspecting naval bases all over the country. He had proved so indispensable to Navy Secretary Daniels that President Wilson had personally refused his request for a transfer to active military service. At last, in July 1918, he was able to get to Europe on an important mission that, at the least, would look good on his political resume.

Between July and September, Roosevelt was in high gear in an exhausting series of naval strategy meetings with the British Admiralty in London and inspecting the U.S. Navy's huge port facilities in France that had handled the flow of millions of men and tons of vital war armaments. He was much feted along the way; a personal audience with King George V was headline news, and his appearances at various Parliamentary dinners were widely praised in the newspaper reports sent back from London. He had time to relax and renew a friendship with two wealthy American expatriates, Waldorf and Nancy Astor, who invited him to meet still more British contacts at their huge estate, Cliveden, on the banks of the Thames. Waldorf Astor had inherited ownership of the influential London Sunday newspaper *The Observer* and was in the process of gaining control of the even more authoritative *Times;* he had given up his seat in the House of Commons to be in charge of the British food rationing program, and, to widespread surprise, his outrageously brash wife had run for and been elected to succeed him. Thus the Virginia-born native became the first woman ever to be seated in Britain's Parliament.

During his visits to Cliveden, FDR revisited many old British friendships with leading Fabians like H. G. Wells and George Bernard Shaw. Two old friends from the Dupont Circle era were there too. Eustace Percy was dividing his time between Foreign Office duties and his first campaign for Parliament. Philip Kerr also shuttled between 10 Downing Street and Cliveden, where he had formed a deeply emotional but platonic friendship with the effervescent Nancy. They both, as had a number of their other well-born friends, had become intensely attracted to the Christian Scientist philosophies of Bostonian evangelist Mary Baker Eddy. While the Christian Science churches had been organized in America in the 1880s, the inexplicable tragedies of the Great War had sent Europeans searching for new ways of understanding human existence. With its stress on positive faith, healthful living, and moral uplift, many Progressives on both sides of the Atlantic found Christian Science an attractive alternative to the inflexibilities of traditional denominations.

Once in France, Roosevelt alarmed his military escorts by refusing to confine his travels to safe areas of the ports and dockyards and instead plunging as close as he could get to the front lines. He even tried to join a couple of combat units. He was clearly desperate to be able to claim to have been in action against the Germans and, in later life, would expansively say that he had actually fired a railroad mounted cannon at the enemy, although there is no record that he actually did so. And wherever he went, the diplomatic pouches of confidential documents that followed him from Washington contained a steady stream of love letters from Lucy Mercer. He continued a hectic schedule of meetings with French military and political leaders until the pace caught up with him and he was felled by a serious pneumonia, which at first was misdiagnosed as the influenza that was ravaging Europe; he was hustled aboard a luxury liner, and on September 19, he was carried ashore in a stretcher to be met by Eleanor and an ambulance. His world was about to come unstuck.

The bitter truth about FDR's love affair with Lucy Mercer is that Eleanor almost certainly had been aware of it from early days. She could scarcely have been ignorant of the fact; Washington gossips, especially her vindictive cousin Alice Roosevelt Longworth, had delighted in hinting to her about seeing Franklin out with Lucy at public gatherings whenever Eleanor was away with the children. Alice had even added to the mischief by having Franklin and Lucy to dinner in her home during Eleanor's absences. To the point, Eleanor had dismissed Lucy as a social secretary when the U.S. entered the war in April 1917, only to have Franklin secure her a post in the women's branch of the Navy (a Yeomanette) as an enlisted secretary and have her transferred to his office.

One has to wonder what Roosevelt himself was thinking, or whether, as was more likely, he was caught up in emotions that were more compelling than he had felt before. He made no effort to conceal his affection for Lucy. He organized numerous outings on one of the presidential yachts that was available to the Navy hierarchy for cruises on the Potomac, and even on the rare occasions when Eleanor went along (she did not enjoy either the drinking or sometimes ribald conversation), Lucy also was present. Roosevelt did make the gesture of having her escorted by a young friend of Eustace Percy's on the British Embassy staff named Nigel Law. But Law, who found FDR "the most attractive American whom I was fortunate to meet during my four years in America," apparently had other interests. Law returned to London in December 1917 and never saw Lucy after that.

The relationship finally became too much for Navy Secretary Daniels who, despite being fond of FDR, would tolerate no hint of marital infidelity around him. Daniels took the remarkable step of issuing a direct order discharging Lucy from the Navy after only four months of service. Although he was hard pressed financially, it is apparent that FDR supported Lucy after that; she had moved with her mother to The Decatur, an apartment house at 2131 Florida Avenue, literally around the corner from 2131 R Street.

The obvious explanation is that Eleanor was prepared to ignore the romance as long as it did not directly threaten the marriage. She was well aware that most other women found her husband irresistibly attractive. And one of the traits of the newly liberated woman of the day was to flirt openly with men whether they were married or not. She had seen the office girls flutter around him when Franklin strode down Connecticut Avenue each morning to the State, War, and Navy Building. She had often come home early from country club dances where Franklin and his friends had stayed on with some of the more forward wives and debutantes to drink and carry on in a way that she found deeply offensive.

Eleanor put up with the situation even when it turned worse. She had never been fooled for an instant about Nigel Law's role as Lucy's escort. And when Law returned to England in 1917, she recognized at once what her husband was doing when he summoned Livingston Davis, a wealthy Bostonian and old Harvard chum, to the Navy Department as a special assistant.

"Livy" Davis was handsome, hearty, and a compulsive serial philanderer and heavy drinker. And like many other of the flawed acolytes who gathered around FDR, he was deeply devoted to the man. He left his wife and family behind in Boston and assumed the full-time role as Franklin's court jester. He joined Roosevelt early each morning for a strenuous round of golf, and then busied himself at the Navy Department with various make-work projects, like rounding up voluntary contributions of binoculars for the Navy's use. Whenever Eleanor and the children were away from Washington, he organized the nighttime pursuits of poker parties and not-so-discreet dalliances with available women whom he was happy to share with Franklin. Eleanor made no secret that she found Livy "disgusting."[5]

But as she unpacked her husband's bags from his European mission in September 1918, the packet of letters she discovered from Lucy must have made it unavoidably clear that the marriage was under a very real threat. What happened next is confused by conflicting versions passed on secondhand. Partisans of Lucy Mercer maintain that Eleanor confronted Franklin with the letters, refused to give him a divorce, and enlisted his mother to threaten to withhold her considerable financial subsidies unless he abandoned his mistress. Roosevelt family members, including some of FDR's children, maintained that Eleanor at least offered a divorce, and only when Franklin declined did she demand an end to the romance. It is also likely that family pressures— from mother Sara to collateral cousins—were adamant that any divorce would both be a family scandal and wreck FDR's political future forever. One also had to consider whether Lucy, a devout Catholic whose own mother and father had been estranged, would have really considered marrying a divorced man who was not of her faith.[6]

In any event, Franklin agreed to give Lucy up, or at least to stop seeing her openly. She soon left Washington and in early 1920 married Winthrop Rutherfurd, a wealthy widower who was both a devout Catholic and twenty-nine years older than she. She divided her time between her husband's lavish homes in New Jersey and in the posh horse-country around Aiken, South Carolina. That of course was not the end of the affair by any means; Livy Davis, among others, made regular journeys between the two carrying messages—very guarded correspondence between Franklin and Lucy has been found among his papers dating as early as 1926. Small wonder then that Eleanor, who "could forgive, but never forget," found it impossible to completely get over her husband's betrayal, and it marked her transformation from the dutiful, insecure wife to the public figure she would become in her own right. She had to become something, and becoming his political partner would have to do.

Life of course was not that simple. A seemingly chastened Franklin devoted more time to his family and abandoned some but not all of his outings with Livy Davis and other merrymakers. And when in December 1918 he was chosen to be part of the official U.S. delegation to the Paris conference, he lobbied for an exception to the president's "no wives" rule and got Eleanor included in the trip. Even then, his roving eye remained a cause of disquiet for her. On the trip over and throughout their stay in Paris, women flirted openly (brazenly, in her mind) with her husband. She wrote from Paris to Franklin's mother," We have nothing like some of their women or some of their men. The scandals going on would make many a woman at home unhappy."

So, in that summer of 1919 with Eleanor and the children gone, Franklin had to contemplate a future that appeared bleak both personally and politically. He well might wonder whether it was time for him to leave Washington and return to the tedium of private life in New York. President Wilson's campaign to win Senate ratification of the Treaty of Versailles and League of Nations membership had run into an unexpectedly stiff backlash in the U.S. Senate. Rather than seek a compromise with the rebellious senators, Wilson decided to go over their heads in a direct appeal for popular support. On September 3, he embarked on a carefully organized campaign of speeches throughout the Western states that took him more than eight thousand miles into the very heart of where his opponents thought they had the strongest public support. Traveling without respite in a chartered railroad train loaded with newsreel cameras and the national press, Wilson, who had suffered a number of bouts of illness (and possible minor cerebral accidents) while in Paris that spring, pushed himself with numerous appearances and speeches each day regardless of the weather. Exhausting as it was, Wilson was buoyed up by the huge and enthusiastic crowds he drew, and there was a palpable sense that he was winning the public debate. His collapse after a particularly stirring speech in Pueblo, Colorado, on September 26 was all the more shocking because he had appeared to be so close to political victory.

Even when he suffered a near-fatal stoke several weeks later back in Washington, few Progressives believed Wilson's disability meant certain defeat for the cause. For one thing, the president's wife and his closest aides kept the full seriousness of his physical condition a closely guarded secret. Wilson loyalists even hinted that with a full recovery likely (it wasn't), the president might try for his party's nomination to an unheard-of third term in the 1920 election that loomed ahead. At the worst, someone else would have to be found to pick up the fallen torch. But who would that be?

At that moment, only Franklin Roosevelt (and his acolyte Louis Howe) nurtured an ambition for him to be that leader. It was a premature hope, and he knew that. He was just thirty-eight, four years younger than cousin Theodore when he became president, so he could wait. But he would not be idle. He began the methodical task of positioning himself as a national political figure within the Democratic Party, a task that required delicate balancing if he was to appear as Woodrow Wilson's heir without any of the negative backlash against the Versailles Treaty. He would continue to support the treaty publicly, but in the final analysis, he would be his own cause. He had every confidence he could pull it off somehow.

Eight
ADRIFT IN SMOKE-FILLED ROOMS

1920–1921

"You can go to it so far as I am concerned. Good luck!"

—Franklin D. Roosevelt's response to a plan to recruit Herbert
Hoover to run for president as a Democrat, with FDR as
vice-presidential nominee[1]

ALTER LIPPMANN WAS NOT so pleased with himself. On
his return from Paris and his brief holiday, he and Faye had
moved to a small village on Long Island. He was tired of the some-
times-pointless disputes that sprang up at *The New Republic* editorial
meetings. The country was reeling from labor disputes, race riots, and
anarchist bombings, but Lippmann, perhaps more than Frankfurter,
had been appalled at the violent counter-reaction of Palmer, the Attorney General; the wholesale arrests and deportations; and the shift
in the public mood to general intolerance. He blamed Woodrow Wilson for choosing to ignore these developments in his single-minded
zeal to win Treaty ratification. He feared the kind of nation America
would become with a Republican in the White House. Nothing he
had believed seemed relevant, but what did he believe now?

One thing he did realize was he no longer had much faith in any
inherent wisdom in the general public to ultimately reach sound

decisions. The hated George Creel, Wilson's director of propaganda, had shown how easy it was to get control of public opinion, to shape it to a specific system of beliefs, and to stifle any questioning or dissent. Nor had the disbanding of Creel's Committee on Public Information apparatus offered any solace. While President Wilson might have been about to succeed in winning popular support for his policies with his dramatic train campaign, another compelling speaker might have done just the opposite.

To earn some extra money, he began work with the newly formed publishing house of Harcourt Brace, recruiting new authors for the editors; he lured John Maynard Keynes into licensing an edition of *The Economic Consequences of the Peace*, which became a best seller in the U.S. and added fuel to the anti-Treaty campaign. He began to write regular commentary on issues other than politics for the leading culture and literary magazine of the day, *Vanity Fair*. But looking around for some new topic to study, he wrote to Ellery Sedgwick, the editor of *Atlantic Monthly*, who was trying to tempt him away from *The New Republic*:

> I have started to write a longish article around the general idea that freedom of thought and speech present themselves in a new light and raise new problems because of the discovery that opinion can be manufactured. The idea has come to me gradually as a result of certain experiences with the official propaganda machines, and my hope is to attempt a restatement of the problem of freedom of thought as it presents itself in modern society under modern conditions of government and with a modern knowledge of how to manipulate the human mind. Could you say whether you might be interested in such a discussion? I don't believe it could be done well under ten to fifteen thousand words, though the discussion might fall into two or three parts. It will probably take me a month to finish it.[2]

During that autumn of 1919 and into the spring of 1920, Lippmann provided Sedgwick with three lengthy essays on the topic and they provided the core for his next book, *Liberty and the News,* which was published later that year. As he explained in a letter to his old mentor Justice Holmes,

> It is really a bit of a book on which I have been working for five years and am nowhere near the end of. I'm examining how "public opinion" is made, and am deeply troubled by the effect of the tentative conclusions on our current theories of popular government. You say, "truth is the over ground, etc., etc." But the difficulty is that in addition to men's natural limitation in apprehending truth about society, there have grown up institutions such as the press, propaganda, and censorship which block the road to truth. At best these institutions put truth second to what they think is morality or patriotism; at worst they are downright liars. How is popular government to exist when 'the ground upon which their wishes' are to be carried out is what it now is?[3]

While Lippmann had the time and the means to ponder this broad question at leisure, he, like other Progressives in that winter of 1919–1920, was forced to face the need to move quickly to find a new national leader if everything they had worked for so far was not to be lost to the reactionary fear that gripped the nation. Many Progressives, Lippmann included, would later claim to have first come up with the idea, but the truth is that his old House of Truth companion Herbert Hoover was such an obvious symbol of all they stood for. The movement to draft him to run for president can be said to have spontaneously generated.

Keynes, who had dismissed the American delegation at the Paris Conference as "broken reeds," nonetheless allowed that Hoover was "the only man who emerged from the ordeal of Paris with an enhanced reputation."[4]

At forty-six, Herbert Hoover was at that moment an even more prominent and beloved American figure both at home and abroad than Wilson had been when he had landed in France a year earlier. Wilson was admired for his high ideals. Hoover had become iconic as the embodiment of the more admirable virtue of brilliant efficiency. Hoover had saved Belgium from extermination at the start of the war. As the food supplies czar at home, he had made his program of doing without certain items on given days a popular symbol of wartime solidarity. Back in Paris for the Conference, he had administered a European-wide program of food and medical relief that had saved millions of lives even as he had skillfully worked as a negotiator on the Treaty itself. More than anyone, he had proved that an American could skillfully maneuver in the dangerous currents of foreign affairs and still keep his sturdy American values unsullied; he was an engineer who used solid facts to achieve Progressive goals. To "Hooverize" had become a common phrase not only for efficiency but for sound judgment and fairness. He would make the ideal Democratic Party standard-bearer in 1920 to take up the fight for the old Wilsonian ideals but with none of the handicaps of the ailing president.

Whether or not Lippmann was the first Progressive to consider Hoover as a presidential candidate, it was he who took the first and most important sounding of the idea when he went to Colonel Edward House and found the now-exiled former adviser excited by the notion. It is also certain that the next progression in the scheme's evolution—to recruit Franklin Roosevelt to run as Hoover's vice-presidential nominee—came from FDR's old friend and co-editor of *The Harvard Crimson* newspaper, Louis Wehle.

In early January, after testing the idea with other party leaders, Wehle went directly to Roosevelt at the Navy Department. During the war, Wehle had been chief counsel of the War Finance Corporation (which Baruch had chaired) and had worked closely with both Lippmann and Roosevelt finding ways to pay for the hasty construction of training camps and the ordering of vast stocks of munitions. He found his friend in a low and dispirited mood. Roosevelt was actually contemplating having to leave public life altogether; just the idea was suffocating. While his reputation as a successful Navy official was still bright, the political tide appeared to have ebbed, as far as he was concerned.

There had been a brief bright spot of opportunity nine months earlier. In May 1919, after having come back from the Paris Conference with praise in the press for efficiently dismantling the Navy's costly infrastructure in France, he had been asked to be the keynote speaker at a Democratic National Committee banquet in Chicago. Roosevelt had delivered a stem-winder of a speech that many judged to be the party's battle cry for 1920. Until recently, he said, there had been a struggle between liberal and conservative wings in both major political parties, but now the forces of conservatism and reaction had captured the Republican Party while the Democratic Party had evolved into the movement for those motivated by liberal and progressive impulses. The Republicans, he told the cheering party leaders, advocated "the principles of little Americanism and jingo bluff." The current Congress, he charged, was preoccupied with cutting taxes "for those unfortunate individuals with incomes of one million dollars a year or more," and with raising trade tariffs to benefit their "pet groups of manufacturers." The speech was a foreshadowing of the Roosevelt oratory style in the making, a mix of high thoughts and biting humor. There was a brief boomlet that Roosevelt return to New York to run for the Senate in 1920 (if Tammany boss Al Smith ran again for governor) or for governor (if Smith did not). There had even been suggestions that he might be a favorite son candidate for president at the party's convention in San Francisco in 1920. But the return of the economic downturn, the violent upheavals across the nation, and Wilson's collapse had put Roosevelt's prospects on hold; he also had to face the hard fact that Tammany boss Smith would not especially welcome his homecoming.

Early in the new year, Roosevelt had gone so far as to agree to form a law partnership back on Wall Street and to cast about for financial investment opportunities that might free him of his mother's financial control. Consequently, Wehle's suggestion was terribly exciting to him, and he told his friend to first check with Colonel House who still had important sources of campaign finance and organization under his control. With House's enthusiastic endorsement, other friends of Roosevelt began to push the idea, and, along with Lippmann and Frankfurter, several of them contacted Hoover directly. Lippmann even jumped the gun by suggesting Hoover run as a Democrat in a winter issue of *The New Republic*.

Bert and Lou Hoover had known Franklin and Eleanor from their early days in Dupont Circle, and the two couples had gone on joint picnic outings in nearby Rock Creek Park with their children during the early war years. Hoover had been impressed by FDR's energy and skill as an administrator, and they shared many of the same beliefs on social issues. But part of Hoover's initial hesitancy when the idea was put to him by Wehle, Lippmann, and others stemmed from the fact that he did not particularly like Frank Roosevelt. Roosevelt's heartiness seemed artificial and forced to the dour Quaker engineer, and he could not have been unaware of the rumors of the younger man's extramarital entanglements. But more than that, Hoover, in his inner soul, despised the grubby but necessary demands of political life. While he could fantasize about accepting the Presidency by acclamation, he recoiled from the notion of having to deal personally with coarse political bosses or their clamoring constituencies.

Yet a Hoover-Roosevelt ticket had a certain attraction. Hoover could claim California as his home state, and he had widespread mining and ranching contacts throughout other western states. With Roosevelt carrying New York and much of the Eastern vote, it seemed to offer the party a good chance of retaining the White House and possibly even regaining the Congress. But was Hoover a Democrat? No one could say for sure. Well into the early weeks of 1920, his only public response to press questions about his political affiliation was that he saw himself as "an independent progressive" who disdained both the reactionaries among the Republicans and the radicals on the Democrat left.

One of the Democratic loyalists pushing the nomination was Breckinridge Long, an assistant secretary of state who had worked on the reparations finance issues with Hoover; in February he heard rumors that a faction known as the Republican Old Guard was determined to prevent Hoover from declaring as a Democrat although they had no intention of nominating him themselves.

It should not surprise that the Republicans were perhaps more divided than the Democrats in the diversity of their membership and ideas. Theodore Roosevelt had been dead for a year, but there was still a hardy band of his ex-Bull Moose Republican Progressives who were determined to push through a more reformist agenda;

there also were vestiges of the old East Coast wealthy party founders of the Civil War era who were more conservative but just as internationalist in their attitudes.

But America was changing demographically and so were its major political parties. The nation was just on the verge of having more people living in cities than in rural areas. The geographical center of the GOP had shifted westward so that hitherto overlooked states like California now held the balance of power, and these western Republicans were suspicious, to say the least, of all things Progressive. This view was concentrated among the so-called irreconcilables who held the balance of power in the Senate. They meant to use that power, and they were not going to back Hoover or any heir of Theodore Roosevelt's legacy. They wanted a president who would reflect the mood of conservative reaction that had been under attack from Progressives of both parties for most of the new century. In other words, they wanted a senator like themselves whom they could influence once he was safely in the White House.

Once he had Colonel House's assent, Wehle went to Hoover's office in New York to try to push him into firmly committing to the Democrats. The interview was frustrating, for Hoover was deliberately noncommittal:

> I had a long conversation with Hoover. He professes an indifference about the presidency—which is becoming—and a disdain for political organizations, as now constituted, which is likely to lead into trouble. I told him an effort is being made by certain persons, friends of his and Republicans, to have him make a statement which by its terms would disqualify him as a Democrat, and that I did not want him to make that statement; that I was moved from loyalty to my party as I felt he had a utility to my party. He railed a bit at the essential similarity between Republicans and Democrats today, and the political bankruptcy of both parties. . . . I told him organization was essential to success in any field. He had demonstrated his implicit belief in organization; that political organization under proper leadership could be used to effect real results as an agency to an end to carry out real ideas.[5]

But Hoover was being less than candid with Wehle or any other of the suitors. He had agents scouring the country testing his popularity and the election prospects of both parties. While his disdain for the scrimmage of politics was real enough, he was shrewd enough to try to strike the best bargain he could. His agents reported back that nationally, the Hoover name was the best known and far and away most popular of any of the potential candidates he might be matched up against. This information led him to make a beginner's mistake in judgment. Hoover convinced himself he could dictate the terms of his nomination to the party of his choice. He didn't need a Franklin Roosevelt or any other running mate to win nationwide, nor, he concluded, did he need to bother seeking the nomination from the interconnected network of party professionals who did the hard retail political organizing in the widely separated regions of the country.

After dithering for weeks, Hoover finally made his choice. He allowed a group of friends from Chicago to form a Hoover-for-President committee to run for the Republican nomination and shortly afterwards declared himself to be a "progressive Republican" without going into too many details about what that meant. What he intended, he told Colonel House later, was to return the Republican Party to the Progressive roots it had put down in 1900 with Theodore Roosevelt. He had counted on Progressives who had moved to support Wilson and the Democrats to shift back again. That way he could avoid having to strike deals with the big city Tammany-style machine bosses. It was an impossible fantasy. Almost at once, Democrats who had backed him melted away to find a new standard-bearer. The Republican Old Guard went ahead with plans to nominate their choice from a menu of safe alternatives.

In April, Lippmann wrote to Frankfurter in disgust:

> Very much between ourselves, yesterday I had a telephone call from Hoover to come and see him. I found him in a bewildered state of mind at the political snarl in which he finds himself. He really wants to take only a liberal line, but he does not know how to take hold. He knows that the liberal people and the

Progressives generally are slipping away from him and that his statements so far have done nothing to hold them. . . .

I am more and more convinced myself that Hoover is now pocketed because the Republicans have nothing further to fear from him and the Democrats nothing to hope. . . . House was here last night for dinner. He says Hoover's one chance now is to bolt the Republican Party, if they nominate a reactionary, in such a way as to make himself the inevitable choice of the Democrats three weeks later. What do you think of that? Please keep this entirely under your own hat.[6]

In the few states that had party primary elections for convention delegates in those days, Hoover polled well enough. But the Republicans who gathered in Chicago in June 1920 were intent on choosing their nominee as one leader described it, "at two o'clock in the morning in a smoke-filled room." In what was certainly a humiliating rebuke, Hoover never received more than six delegate votes in the series of ballots it took to pick the slate of Senator Warren Harding, a former Ohio newspaper publisher, and Massachusetts Governor Calvin Coolidge.[7]

Of course, three weeks later when the Democrats convened in San Francisco for their convention, Hoover was a dead issue. But Hoover's collapse had the unforeseen consequence that Franklin Roosevelt's name was still very much on the mind of delegates as they cast about for a new leader. At thirty-eight he was still considered too young to be president, but he stood a good chance of securing the second spot on the ticket. And for a change, Roosevelt's luck appeared to be holding firm. After having a dismal year in 1919, he had survived three separate controversies in the early months of 1920, any one of which might have sealed his fate politically.

First, in February, FDR was collateral damage in the fallout when President Wilson finally got around to demanding the resignation of Secretary of State Robert Lansing. Lansing had compounded his embarrassments from his indiscreet talk with William Bullitt by calling a series of Cabinet meetings on his own initiative at a time when President Wilson was still recovering from his stroke. To the president, his wife, and other White House loyalists, this appeared to be a usurping of presidential powers and an act of supreme disloyalty. Since Roosevelt was known to frequent the old Foster-Lansing mansion in the pre-war days, he became suspect too. Worse, Roosevelt had gone out of his way to be cordial to Sir Edward Grey, the British ambassador who finally had to leave Washington under a cloud when he refused to send home an aide who had made a ribald joke about Mr. and Mrs. Wilson that had reached the First Lady's hearing.

But later in the spring, Roosevelt was caught in a far more serious scandal. A bitter argument over Navy administrative policy had simmered for some time between Secretary Daniels and Roosevelt with Admiral William S. Sims, who had commanded naval operations in the North Atlantic during the Great War. Sims, now head of the Naval War College in Newport, Rhode Island, was unsparing in blaming the Navy Department bureaucracy for delays that he charged extended the war by six months; the Republican Senate sensed an election year issue and began hearings. In a series of public statements defending the department, Roosevelt made himself a target, and a direct hit was not long coming.

Newport, as it turns out, had more than the usual run of opportunities for vice available to sailors on leave than most port cities. Among the seedier establishments were a number of brothels that catered to homosexuals, which drew both Navy personnel as well as some of the better respected members of Newport's elite society. Secretary Daniels, who was a rigid moralist, was outraged at reports from the naval base, especially when a Navy chaplain was accused of being a regular patron. In those days of course, homosexuality was not a matter of personal identity, and there was no distinction—in the public mind or in the law's penalties—about consensual acts between adults or the nature of the acts themselves. Whatever the act, it was classed as sodomy, and sodomy was both a sin and, in the laws of all forty-eight states, a felony carrying long prison sentences.

In 1917, Daniels had ordered Roosevelt to rid Newport of the brothels and bars that catered to homosexuals, but the anti-vice drive had merely driven the culture deeper underground. Also, local police had proved reluctant to prosecute. So in 1919, Roosevelt signed an order to create a secret vice squad recruited from among Navy enlisted personnel. To his horror, he learned that a number of young sailors who went underground to gather evidence about the brothels found themselves pressed to participate in homosexual acts themselves, thus tainting any evidence they might have gathered. Despite a quick move to shut down the squad and bury the details, Admiral Sims or someone close to him saw to it that the sordid story was leaked to a Republican newspaper, and for a time that spring, it appeared that Roosevelt might be called before a hostile Senate committee and perhaps even dismissed from the Navy Department in disgrace.

Rather than appear to be guilty, Roosevelt went on a public relations offensive with a series of speeches and press statements that coupled a ringing defense of Secretary Daniels and the Navy's enlisted men with not-so-veiled criticism of the Navy's tradition-ridden officer corps. He essentially dared the Senate Naval Affairs Committee to summon him, and when they decided not to, he emerged from the controversy with his reputation untouched and with wide public sympathy for having been caught up in what to most minds was politics at its most sordid.

As Franklin traveled to San Francisco with the New York delegation, he needed some last push to put his name into serious contention before the convention. Again, the Roosevelt luck stepped in. The antipathy the Wilsons had for him had morphed into a real hatred (Mrs. Wilson had barred him from the White House even on official business) that was public knowledge. But that worked to FDR's advantage because the president made one last ill-considered gamble at securing the nomination for himself. The leading Democratic contender for the nomination had been William McAdoo, the president's own son-in-law and a popular Secretary of the Treasury.[8] But McAdoo was a prominent New York City attorney, and his nomination would have automatically barred Roosevelt from the ticket (Article II of the U.S. Constitution forbids a president and vice president from the same state). But Wilson refused to endorse his son-in-law, and his loyalists at the convention stalled enough that the power brokers began to look elsewhere.

It was at this point that a moment of high theater occurred, and Roosevelt made the most of it. While the opening ceremonies droned on, a huge oil portrait of President Wilson was unveiled and touched off an unexpectedly fervent demonstration of affection among the delegates. Delegation banners were seized, and an impromptu parade around the convention hall erupted, fed by the martial music of the band that had been provided for just such enthusiasm. New York's delegation—dominated by Tammany political boss Al Smith—sat stolidly in their seats until Roosevelt jumped up, grabbed the New York ensign, and, after a brief scuffle, pulled the delegation to their feet and touched off a second round of parading and cheering. Franklin Roosevelt had arrived at the convention. But he was far from done.

Smith, who had been elected New York's governor in 1918, had always harbored a grudge for Roosevelt's ill-fated crusade against the New York City machine nearly twenty years earlier. He had turned against Wilson as well and was nurturing his own ambitions for the White House. He was, after all, the undisputed boss of a powerful network of big city political organizations that used discipline, patronage, corruption, and occasional violence to give an unavoidable voice to millions of new Americans—Irish, Italians, and Jews—who were the most important element in the changing American political landscape. Progressives might come up with the great schemes for improving society, but Tammany controlled the votes. To gain an acknowledgement of that power and to test the political waters as well, Smith had his minions put his name forward as a "favorite son" candidate for the presidential nomination.

To Smith's surprise, Roosevelt demanded platform access to make a seconding speech for Smith's candidacy. He vaulted over rows of chairs in his haste to get to the platform. The convention was captivated by this lithe, handsome young celebrity. His brief but spirited praise for his old foe was interrupted by applause five times, and he then bustled about the convention floor urging support for Smith through the succeeding series of ballots until the Governor, now mollified, withdrew his name. In the end, the Democrats tried to counter the nomination of Harding with another Ohio politician named James M. Cox, whose principal qualification it seemed was having the backing of Smith and the other city machines. In the meantime, Roosevelt had brought with him enough friends to busy themselves on the convention floor advocating his selection. And in the end, the geographical balance, his charisma, and the grudging acquiescence of Al Smith were enough. Roosevelt had a reason to go on fighting, this time for the vice presidency, and even if the prospects for victory appeared dim, he knew the nomination gave him the national platform he needed if he ever were to reach beyond to the White House itself.

This was not the time, however. Cox, a shrewd and successful Progressive governor in a Republican state, liked Roosevelt's energy. Together they made an emotional pilgrimage to the White House to pledge to the still-resentful Woodrow Wilson that they would do as he would have done, use the election campaign as a national referendum on American membership in the League of Nations. Then, essentially, they ran two separate campaigns and did not appear together that often. Roosevelt immediately began to assemble the final members of the political family who would stay with him the rest of his life.

He already had Louis Howe at hand at the Navy Department; he was eager to set up Roosevelt's campaign headquarters in New York and to get back into the game. Roosevelt had early on decided that unlike past election campaigns where the candidate stayed aloof from the public, he would embark on a national speaking tour much like the ill-fated but nonetheless successful one President Wilson had undertaken nine months earlier. He leased a private railroad car, The Westboro, to carry his entourage across the country. In addition to Howe, who soon would resign from the Navy Department, FDR also recruited Marvin McIntyre, a Washington newspaper reporter who had been the Navy Department's public relations director. For an advance man, he picked Stephen Early, an Associated Press veteran who had covered the Navy. Perhaps most important, his office manager spotted a twenty-two-year-old secretary at the Democratic National Committee offices in Washington and had her transferred to Roosevelt's campaign. Marguerite

"Missy" LeHand was an immediate convert to the Roosevelt cause and in time would be known as his "other wife."

For the moment though, this was the founding of the fabled "Cufflinks Gang" of FDR devotees who would serve the man and his various causes all the way to the White House.[9] That each of them had a personal need to fix their fortunes on his star obscures the fact that Roosevelt gained the security of having totally loyal and talented aides working solely in his behalf. They would have no other agendas, or indeed any private ambitions, beyond serving him and his needs.

Eleanor, on the other hand, was something of a problem. She had remained with the children up north in Campobello when he went to San Francisco to win the nomination and had to be begged to come back to Washington to oversee the closing of the house on R Street and transfer to their new home in Manhattan, a townhouse adjoining the home of her dreaded mother-in-law, Sara. Worse, from her standpoint, she was expected to join the campaign train on the exhausting trip across the nation and to appear on the rear platform of The Westboro for photographers to snap her standing by the candidate, and not much more.

There were in fact two Roosevelt campaign trips that dwarfed Wilson's foray in distance covered and speeches given. In an era where newsreels were in their infancy and broadcast media was unknown, Franklin Roosevelt set out to make his face, his sonorous voice, and his impassioned beliefs known to as many individual Americans as was humanly possible. Starting on August 11, the first campaign trip took him throughout the middle and far western states; a second was a two-week tour of New England. In all, he passed through thirty-eight states and by one estimate gave one thousand speeches at whistle-stops and major venues in every region except the Deep South. Newsreels and newspaper photographers chronicled the campaign for eager readers, and Roosevelt's huge audiences, who voted for Warren Harding anyway, came away impressed with the fervor of this young dynamic figure. Eleanor joined The Westboro on the final month-long push but found, with the coaching of Louis Howe, that she began to enjoy the excitement and that she had something to contribute to strategy discussions along the way. The start of the evolution of their relationship into a political partnership began with that trip.

While the campaign was a personal triumph for Franklin Roosevelt's political future, the results of the November 2 election were surprisingly disappointing. Harding and Coolidge trounced the Cox-Roosevelt ticket, winning 61 percent of the popular vote (16,152,200 to 9,147,353), carrying thirty-seven states, and swamping the Electoral College vote by four to one.[10] Congress remained firmly in the hands of the Republicans, and the prospects of finally winning official ratification of the Treaty and League membership appeared dim indeed.

For the Progressives who had begun their youthful quest around Dupont Circle before the Great War, it was an unmistakable repudiation. Walter Lippmann summed up the mood in a post-election letter to an old Harvard mentor, "I feel we shall not have much immediate influence on America for perhaps a decade, but I'm not discouraged because we can use that time well to reexamine our ideas."[11] Earlier, he had sent a telegram to FDR that read, "When cynics ask what is the use we can answer that when parties can pick a man like Frank Roosevelt there is a decent future in politics."[12]

The Dupont Circle set was chastened by the immediate setback but had kept enough faith in its cause to launch itself into the Jazz Age with a cautious determination. They could not foresee just how long it would take them to come back together again.

Nine

DUPONT CIRCLE DIPLOMATS

1922

"More battleships have been sunk by this treaty than have been lost by all the admirals of history."

—British comment on the Washington Naval Conference of 1921–1922

WALTER LIPPMANN WAS WRONG when he predicted a decade of political exile for the Progressives of Dupont Circle after the 1920 presidential election. The eight years in which Warren G. Harding and then Calvin Coolidge occupied the White House certainly marked the end of the period of youthful certainty for the alumni of the House of Truth and their neighbors. But it also brought them all to a new maturity, a time to hone their thoughts and advance their own personal careers toward the day when they all would once again play an important role in American affairs.

As so often happens in American politics, when one faction turns a rival out of power, the victors continue many of the old policies despite vocal promises of restoring some ancient régime of virtues. So while President Harding promised a revival of "normalcy," there really was no prospect of turning back America's clock to the imagined security of the years before the Great War. Indeed, in that same standard campaign oration, he sounded a note that would echo in later presidential exhortations. He urged "a popular government under which a citizenship seeks what it can do for the government and country rather than what the country can do for the individual."[1] The call resonated with the public as it would forty years later when it was repeated by John F. Kennedy.

One unexpected result was that while Lippmann, Frankfurter, and Roosevelt left Washington, others of their friends found their careers and influence enhanced by the return of the conservative Republicans to power. Despite the boasts of the "irreconcilables" that American membership in the League of Nations was a dead issue, in 1921, the bulk of the Republican establishment acknowledged that the United States was now a world power with global strategic interests that could not be ignored. A foreign policy had to be fashioned that differed from what they saw as naive Wilsonianism, and that meant that there were opportunities for the young Progressives who had made their marks during the Great War and at the Paris Conference.

Two who looked to promising futures in the new political environment might have first appeared the least likely. Sumner Welles had been Franklin Roosevelt's protégé and remained a closely identified friend both of FDR and especially of Eleanor. Allen Dulles too was closely identified with his uncle Robert Lansing, who now was being excoriated by the Republicans for being a Woodrow Wilson loyalist and by friends of the ex-president for being a betrayer. However, both young men had made international reputations for themselves as experts in areas of diplomacy that now were in short supply when the new secretary of state, Charles Evans Hughes, took office. Divisions devoted to closely analyzing the flow of information from various key regions of the world were to be staffed by Foreign Service officers who had served in those regions. A new mission to provide intelligence and aid to American corporations who were venturing into foreign markets was a prime objective.

Welles had received widespread praise for his work as a junior officer in Tokyo during the two years he and Esther were posted there; he advanced two grades on the promotion scale and was especially commended for his tireless efforts to establish personal friendships within the closed Japanese diplomatic community. It had been a rewarding time for Welles, who enthusiastically threw himself into studying Japanese culture and amassing a large collection of art works. But then the first signs of trouble in his marriage appeared. While he had plenty of work to occupy himself, Esther found the life of a diplomatic wife in a strange country to be confining and boring. When his first tour of duty came to an end in 1917, Welles requested a transfer. The U.S. was now in the war, so many of the European posts he might have claimed were not available. Since he had studied Spanish culture as an undergraduate, he opted for Latin America. It was to be a fateful decision.

Welles was just twenty-five when he and Esther returned to Washington in the summer of 1917 and, resisting advice to the contrary, pressed his request for a Latin American assignment. His time in Tokyo had convinced him that Japan would emerge from the Great War more determined than before to expand its power in the Pacific. What that told Welles was that Latin America, long a political and commercial backwater in Yankee minds, would assume a new importance in U.S. economic and political strategy. Already, Argentina and other South American nations were growing wealthy and at the same time being eyed covetously by both British and German purchasers of their raw materials and food exports.

With a disappointed Esther in tow (she had hoped he would stay in Washington), Sumner arrived in Buenos Aires in November. Nominally, he was a junior secretary, but he had been given an important task. Now that America was in the war, President Wilson had joined the British in trying to stymie the large German-Austrian commercial presence in Argentina from supplying the Central Powers with important war materials. A formal blacklist was ordered that would ban any Argentine exporter who violated it from doing business in the U.S. market. Since the Argentine government was fiercely maintaining the pose of strict neutrality, Welles had to tread carefully by offering expanded commercial access to U.S. sales while threatening exporters who tried to evade the embargo.

In many ways, Argentina and Welles were made for each other. Buenos Aires was a fabulously wealthy, opulent city, and its people considered themselves both the most cosmopolitan in the entire Western Hemisphere and the proudest inheritors of Spanish culture. Welles, with his good looks and formal manner, quickly perfected his Spanish language skills and showed a remarkable sensitivity to the punctilious formality of dealing with Argentine government officials and business leaders.

But there was a dark side to the Argentine culture of the time that resonated with Welles's own vulnerability to alcohol and to exploitative sexual escapades. A rigidly enforced public moral code relegated wives to an almost monastic life of social events, child-bearing, and gossip about the amorous misadventures of other women's husbands. The men, jaded by new wealth and stultified of other outlets, turned to drink and to homosexual dalliances as diversions in their private lives, all the while maintaining the starched formality of respectability that their public reputations depended upon. For Sumner Welles, the slide into adventures with lovers of both sexes was irresistible.

He continued a hectic professional life and earned regular commendations from his ambassador for his success in winning commercial business away from the Central Powers and, it must be noted, from the competing British as well. But he soon found himself in a love affair with a handsome, dissolute Argentine playboy (named in Esther's diary as "Carlos A") as well as involved in public flirtations with some of the more sophisticated wives of Buenos Aires society. Then there were reports of periodic benders, which sent Welles into the upholstered bordellos of the city where his penchant for dominating his lower-caste sexual providers could be more conveniently obtained. From her diaries, Esther emerges as a naive, somewhat shallow woman who yearned to return to the Boston-New York social whirl of parties, fashions, and theater. Bored with the rigid routines of diplomatic life, she had sometimes embarrassed her husband with ill-timed silly pranks, such as unscrewing the tops of salt shakers at dinner tables and short-sheeting the beds of houseguests. Still, as this second two-year tour of duty neared an end, she was very much in love (and expecting a second child) despite the early suspicions that he might be straying with other women.[2]

The Welleses returned to the United States in the autumn of 1919 and went on three months sick leave (Sumner had been seriously ill after being bitten by a dog), which they spent in Paris. Arriving back in Washington in early 1920, Sumner was surprised when an unexpected vacancy led to his appointment as acting head of the Latin American Affairs Department at State, which oversaw relations with eighteen nations of the Caribbean, Central America, and South America. He was just twenty-eight. America's standing in the hemisphere was in a perilous state. Under the banner of the Monroe Doctrine, the United States in the previous hundred years prevented most efforts by European powers to gain a presence in the region. But successive presidents had exercised an imperious disregard for the sovereignty of what were assumed to be lesser nations. Whenever American interests were involved, American intervention had been inevitable. During the Great War, the Wilson administration had dragooned the rest of the hemisphere into either outright support for the Allies or grudging neutrality. De facto Yankee control was imposed on the governments of Panama (to protect the Canal), the Dominican Republic (to protect U.S. business interests), and Nicaragua (to stymie a popular revolt), while U.S. Marines had landed in Haiti, Mexico, and Cuba (twice).

But with the war's end, and President Wilson's promises of self-government for all people of the world on the record, popular movements to remove the restraints of Yankee rule were alive throughout the southern part of the hemisphere. As a candidate, Senator Harding had repudiated the previous policies of American interference, but even before the election, Welles had been tasked to begin the delicate surgery of removing the U.S. hegemony over three of the most contentious, and arguably least stable, of its neighbors—Cuba, Haiti, and the Dominican Republic.

The extent to which senior State Department officials were aware of Welles's sexual vagaries remains unclear. They could not have been totally unaware, however, since Esther and her friends had begun to talk openly of her unhappiness and suspicions. But two points are important to remember about those times: A man's private life was considered no one else's business unless it caused a public scandal or interfered with his professional career, and, equally important, the State Department had come to depend on Sumner Welles's expertise on Latin American affairs and his growing reputation among the top echelons of those restive governments.

The end result was that Welles led a bifurcated existence balancing between the disciplined and committed career of diplomacy and lapses into the darker side of his sexuality. He was not the only one of the Dupont Circle set to attempt such an emotional highwire act. But as we shall see, when scandal finally did reach him, the repercussions were catastrophic.

The lure of international diplomacy and increasing demands of government service could strain the happiest of marriages. Allen Dulles had won kudos for his intelligence work during the war and for his skill as the chief American staff member on the steering committee, which scheduled the key decisions to be reached at the Paris Peace Conference and in the four other peace treaties that were brokered out with the other defeated Central Powers in 1920.[3] But he was able to break free of his bureaucratic responsibilities in early January 1920 and return to his first love, spying. He was transferred to Berlin, which was the central observation post for the chaos that was threatening most of Europe as war-shattered societies faced a severe winter, scarce food and fuel, a ruined infrastructure, and governments that were toppled whenever mobs took to the streets. Berlin was an open city in the midst of an open struggle between Bolsheviks and right-wing bands of demobilized soldiers called Freikorps, which refused to be disarmed until their demands had been met. He later joked that the anarchy was so great that his intelligence work consisted mainly of keeping current telephone numbers of the various factions and shifting casts of characters since the streets were so often barricaded by rival factions.

Into the midst of this maelstrom came brother Foster Dulles a few weeks later. While the United States was not a signatory to the Versailles Treaty, or to the reparations committee it had established to exact payments from the Germans and other defeated governments, it was Wall Street that held the key to any hope of European economic recovery, and even critics like Keynes had faced up to that truth. Certainly William Cromwell, the colorful head of Sullivan & Cromwell, had recognized this fact sooner than most. He had moved permanently from New York to his palatial Paris mansion, ostensibly to direct a number of French charities he had founded, but he was there to oversee a complicated program of matching needy European manufacturers and governments with American suppliers and financiers, and brokering the transactions that allowed billions of dollars of capital to flow back into the Continent—all at hefty commissions from both sides for the law firm, now Wall Street's largest and most powerful.

The point man for this matchmaking was John Foster Dulles, who celebrated his thirty-second birthday in Berlin with his brother, as they picked their way through the violent streets with the sound of machine gun fire in the distance. He was just seven years out of law school and already the firm's rising star and its founder's chosen deal-maker. Foster's ability to rise so far and so fast lay in the then-blurred line between government service and private enterprise. While he was busy pursuing deals for Sullivan & Cromwell's clients abroad, he also served as the legal counsel to the U.S. government corporation that made export financing loans to American firms so they could sell their products overseas. An unprecedented $400 million of these short-term credits were made to commodities and machinery exporters including such giants as International Harvester, Babcock & Wilcox, International Nickel, and a combine of textile manufacturers that wanted to sell both their products and their machinery; he even represented U.S. firms that printed engraved currency and bond documents to facilitate the deals that took place.[4]

Foster, and Allen to a lesser degree, benefited greatly when, as they roamed through empty official hallways in government buildings, they made contact and a friendship with a Brooklyn-born German economist and banker with the improbable name of Hjalmar Horace Greeley Schacht. A member of the German Democratic Party at the time, Schacht urged the Dulles brothers to do all they could to draw American capital into Germany. Only economic growth, he argued, would enable Germany's well-intentioned middle class to become strong enough to thwart the forces arrayed against it on the right and left. Schacht soon became the currency commissioner for the just-formed Weimar Republic, and later would head its central bank, the Reichsbank, during the tumultuous decade ahead in which Germany skillfully played off the reparations burdens, mainly through a systematic inflation of its currency which made debt payments easier but stoked ruinous inflation for the German people. Schacht was able to keep new loans coming from abroad through his close personal relations with the heads of the central banks of the U.S., Britain, and France.[5]

The Dulles brothers also had time during their travels outside Berlin to other European cities to discuss their future prospects. Whatever sibling rivalries there had been when they were younger, Foster had been impressed with Allen's ability to analyze complex political situations. There would be a place for him at Sullivan & Cromwell if he would consider leaving government service. But Allen was still enjoying his intelligence ventures too much, and there was so much more he could learn from taking on new assignments. That being the case, Foster advised his brother to seek a posting in the Middle East, preferably to the U.S. embassy in Constantinople. His argument was a prescient one. The Great War may have spelled the end of colonial empires for the European powers, but it did not signal the end of the scramble for control of sources of raw materials, which modern industry needed but which many countries lacked domestically. And of all those industrial commodities, the one emerging as most important was petroleum. The events in Berlin might seem the more dramatic, but the real action would be over who controlled the vast oil fields of Persia and the still-to-be-developed fields of the Arabian Peninsula.

When Allen returned on leave to Washington in May, he found his superiors shared Foster's view. Oil, gasoline, and other petroleum products had assumed an enormous importance during the war that no general or economist could have predicted in 1914.

Airplanes, tanks, and automobiles had been exciting innovations in the war arsenal, but the conversion of most of the world's navies from coal-fired power to fuel oil suddenly had made petroleum crucial to all the great powers. While America had mature oil fields in Pennsylvania, the vast reserves of the western states were still some years from discovery and development. Besides, the U.S. Navy needed oil reservoirs around the world if it was to be an all-ocean force. American oilmen had convinced President Wilson and the State Department that it was important for U.S. producers to stake a claim to a share of the easily exploitable fields of the collapsing Ottoman Empire. In addition to the expanding U.S. appetite for petroleum supplies, it was just as important to ensure that other powers—Britain for one, but also the newly threatening competitor, Soviet Russia—not be in a position to control Middle Eastern oil supplies and thus wield enormous military advantage.

To his surprise, Allen was told to hurriedly take some of the leave time due him but to get to Turkey as quickly as possible. He was chosen both because he had worked on the Paris Conference staff drafts of the peace agreement being worked out with the new Turkish government and he had, early in 1919, been involved in planning for the failed effort by the Allies to bring the rival factions in the Russian civil war to a conference on the Turkish island resort of Prinkipo. Even though the Treaty of Sevres was still being negotiated, representatives of Britain, France, and Russia all were busy in Constantinople trying to bribe, bargain, and otherwise secure the lion's share of the Turkish National Oil Company's undeveloped leases as well as leases that were being offered by the newly installed Shah of Persia. There were problems facing American efforts to get into the game. The United States had never officially been at war with the Turks even though they had fought on the German side. So the Americans could not simply force their way into oil leases the way the British and French were trying to do. Worse, The U.S. commissioner who was on the scene was a brusque admiral named Mark Bristol who hated the British worse than he had hated the Germans, and he had so angered his diplomatic colleagues that London had officially ordered their negotiators to block American access at all costs. So Allen would first have to placate the British diplomats on the scene and then proceed to win Turkish approval of a share of the leases for American oil exploration companies.

While specific marching orders were being drafted, Allen went on leave to spend some days sailing and relaxing with the rest of the Dulles-Lansing clan at their collection of cottages at Henderson Harbor on Lake Ontario. It was during a weekend visit to friends at a lakeside resort farther north in the Thousand Islands that he was introduced to a young lady visiting from New York City named Martha Clover Todd. Clover (a family surname) Todd was a golden American girl of those days. She had light auburn hair, blue eyes set above high cheekbones, and a charming face that was heart-stoppingly pretty in repose. She was an avid horsewoman but not at all an athletic hearty like Allen or other Dulleses; sports like golf and tennis bored her. Instead she had a mind drawn to the mysterious and exotic, and she preferred to wander alone along the wooded paths of the resort. Travel was an abiding passion, especially if it involved both a physical challenge and an intellectual quest. She had worked at a soldier's canteen in Paris during the conference (they had not met then) and earlier in 1920 had undertaken an ambitious exploration of Aztec ruins in southern Mexico and Guatemala.

They fell in love at first sight. She was attracted to his quick mind and ready humor, he to her curious nature and aura of self-assuredness. He later joked he had shown enormous restraint and had not proposed marriage until the third day of the visit. She had accepted at once. She had found a man she admired and who offered to share in the exciting life he planned to pursue; he would have a good and loving companion who accepted him, flaws and all. The engagement announcement delayed Allen's departure for Turkey. It was not until October that his father, the Reverend Allen Macy Dulles, would perform the marriage service.

On Election Day in November, Clover and Allen finally sailed for his new assignment with a promotion to first secretary and a boost in salary from the $2,000 per year he had earned to the princely sum of $3,625. The newly married couple broke their journey in London where, with their newfound prosperity, Clover went on a shopping spree and Allen invested in the formal attire of a young diplomat headed for his first important post abroad. While they were there, a round of dinners was hosted by Lady Astor and Harold Nicolson, Allen's friend from the Paris conference. He also renewed a friendship from his time in Bern with Robert Craigie, a British intelligence officer who was now a rising diplomat. There also was an important first meeting with Sir John Tilley, the British Foreign Office undersecretary responsible for Turkey and the Middle East. Without undercutting his new boss, Admiral Bristol, Allen tried to assure Tilley that Britain had nothing to fear and much to gain by allowing U.S. oilmen to join in the search for petroleum resources in the region.

The Dulles-Tilley negotiations (Craigie would later be included) were the first of a series of discussions that would last through 1922 and result in Standard Oil and other U.S. producers ultimately gaining an important foothold in the region.[6] When today one contemplates America's tangled involvement in turmoil of the Middle East, it is important to remember that it began with these talks. The immediate impetus was to gain access to oil, but in a larger sense, Dulles was responding to a decision by a succession of U.S. administrations to expand the nation's presence in the region for the first time. And once that foothold was gained, there was no turning back.

When Allen and Clover reached Constantinople, they found themselves hurled into a whirlpool of luxurious white-tie social affairs amidst almost medieval poverty and political chaos. Thousands of refugees, including whole regiments of White Russian troops that had been driven out of the war by the Red Army, were clustered in primitive camps around the city. Clover at once joined a group of volunteers to provide food and medicine to the camps. Allen became engrossed in the dark undercurrents of gathering intelligence on everyone and everything from Turkish oil leases to Soviet efforts to sow mistrust among the French, British, and American diplomats. His early success as a spy also brought the first test of his marriage.

Bertha Karp was the daughter of an Austrian-born Jewish merchant of Constantinople who had died at the outbreak of the war in 1914. She was left without money, but she was well educated, fluent in at least six languages, and well connected within that Byzantine web of highly placed Jewish families whose alliances crossed ethnic, religious, and political boundaries in the old Ottoman Empire capital. She had been hired by Ambassador Henry Morgenthau early in the war, as her first job description stated, "as a type-writing machine operator," but she had proved invaluable in making contacts for him with the beleaguered Armenian and Jewish communities that were his concern. By 1920, she had changed her name to Betty Carp and had become such an indispensable figure of the U.S. Embassy staff that Morgenthau had helped her acquire American citizenship as a protection. She soon became the "fixer" for the American envoys in Constantinople and would still be on the job more than forty years and a thousand grateful American diplomats later. Shorter than five feet, she was a dark, plain, exuberant woman with the fierce energy of a hummingbird. Betty Carp, it was said, could round up a scarce apartment (she had found the Dulleses a house and staff) or arrange a meeting with a spy with equal ease.

She also fell in love with Allen Dulles, and there is some evidence that he may briefly have succumbed. But in the hermetically closed world of an embassy family, the romance would have been spotted immediately. Whatever she knew or suspected, Clover's response was one she would adopt with unhappy regularity the rest of her married life with Allen; she made friends with Betty herself. The result was that Betty became a lifelong family friend of Clover's and an invaluable source of intelligence for Allen throughout his career. In later years, she would often boast of having had a love affair with Allen, sometimes even asserting that the child she had adopted was really his "love child," a chronological impossibility that was nonetheless taken at face value by credulous newcomers to Turkey, and it became institutionalized in the Dulles sexual mythology.[7]

Myth aside, Allen Dulles from his earliest days was a sexual adventurer. His hearty humor, robust spirit, and athletic sexuality attracted women from the start of his career. He had been teased by other staff in the Bern legation in 1918 for the mash notes he received from a Mrs. Vera Whitehouse, a New York society lady who was directing a public relations campaign among the Swiss. Paris had been something of a bachelor's paradise for him. And Betty Carp was not the only woman in Constantinople to make a pass at him; an American missionary named Fanny Billings felt the need to confess her crush on Allen so often that Clover finally had to threaten to have her sent home unless she backed off.

Instead, early in 1922, it was Clover and Allen who returned to America. Clover was pregnant, and Allen had just been appointed head of the Middle Eastern division of State; he was just twenty-nine. The State Department under President Harding's administration was still racing to catch up with its responsibilities. The entire senior staff of officers of the rank of second secretary or higher numbered fewer than fifty. When he took command of the Middle East office, Dulles found himself with only five clerks who were responsible for tracking events in a region encompassing Afghanistan, Albania, and all of the Balkans including Yugoslavia, plus Persia, Syria, Palestine, and Egypt. More, it was a region in turmoil. Starting with the Treaty of Sevres in 1920, a series of tense negotiations between the victorious Allied governments (excluding the United States) and the crumbling Ottoman government had resulted in parts of the old Empire being partitioned off, and that had the consequence of forcing the expulsion and the transplanting of millions of Greeks and Turks from their historic homes back to their native lands. Inevitably, war broke out between Greece and the Turks. An attempt to achieve yet another treaty—this one in Lausanne, Switzerland—in late 1922 was stymied in part because of American insistence on a fair share of oil leases for Standard Oil. To break the logjam, the British sent Robert Craigie to Washington to negotiate directly with his old friend Allen Dulles. The result was that Standard Oil was assured of a firm foothold in the region at last.

At least part of the sudden willingness on the part of the British to share the prospects of the vast Middle Eastern oil bonanza with the Americans can be traced to a rather remarkable foreign policy triumph that President Harding and Secretary Hughes had pulled off earlier in 1922. Like the young Progressives, most foreign observers of American politics had interpreted the election of Harding and the Republican majority in the Congress as a clear signal that the United States was headed into a period of stark isolationism in foreign affairs and self-absorption at home. They had some reason for this belief at first, for while Harding had not specifically pledged himself against U.S. membership in the League, others among his key supporters in the right wing of the Republican Party had been more outspoken.

And there had been plenty of domestic problems to absorb the public's interest in the future of America now that the Great War had been won. The persecution of political dissenters continued, fueled by fear of Bolshevik subversion that came to be known as the Red Scare. Labor unrest threatened to drag the economic recovery back into recession. Race riots fueled by a rising Ku Klux Klan erupted across the nation. One of the first acts of the new Republican Congress was to enact the first stringent anti-immigration laws. The new quota limits were aimed mainly at the large Japanese population on the West Coast but also choked off the unrestricted flow of new arrivals from Europe.

The immigration laws were widely applauded; Progressives who advocated eugenicist policies on racial miscegenation endorsed the quotas as helping preserve white Anglo-Saxon genetic dominance. The eugenicist sub-group within Progressivism would ultimately fracture in disagreement between those who advocated birth-control to empower the control of women over their own lives and those who during the 1920s pursued new state laws that banned interracial marriage and authorized enforced sterilization of individuals judged to be mentally defective. Clover Todd Dulles's father, a prominent Columbia University scholar, had led a movement to win legislation that forbade immigrants from changing their often unpronounceable surnames to more familiar "American names" in their effort to blend in. Everywhere Americans looked, life was changing around them, and much appeared threatening. There was an upheaval in sexual mores, and often, ludicrous attempts to reverse the trend led the morally outraged to impose dress codes on young women and to impose censorship on salacious movies; the literary periodical *The Little Review* was prosecuted for running excerpts of the scandalous new novel *Ulysses* by James Joyce. The civil liberties struggle over attempts to impose moral standards on a rapidly transforming society would be one of the dominant issues of the next fifty years of American culture and would ultimately yield to the powerful impact of mass media such as the movies, the wave of new magazines of news and political comment, and, not least, the new medium of radio.

Harding, not surprisingly, had run true to form upon his inauguration in March 1921. He had given the most visible and, at the time, most politically powerful Cabinet level appointments—postmaster general, secretary of the interior, attorney general—to friends from the notorious "Ohio Gang" of cronies since those posts had the most patronage to dole out to supporters. As consolation to the East Coast liberal Republicans, he named Charles Evans Hughes (the party's presidential nominee in the 1916 campaign) to the still-skeletal Department of State, which consisted of a mere seven hundred or so diplomats, consuls, and support staff spread across the globe. And perhaps out of guilt for having snookered him so badly, Herbert Hoover was offered the post of secretary of commerce, a backwater agency that was lower on the prestige totem pole than the Department of Labor in the best of times. To everyone's surprise, Hoover accepted at once.

Of all the problems Harding inherited, the most vexing was the worsening economic recession that gripped the country. America's factories were jammed with unsold inventory, and the average price of the nation's ten leading farm crops had declined about 67 percent through the spring of 1921. Cotton prices, which had averaged forty cents a pound a year earlier, had dropped to ten cents, a 75 percent contraction. Moreover, both farmers and industrialists had borrowed heavily during the rapid buildup of the war economy in order to expand production when prices had been higher. Many of these loans, particularly on expanded farm properties, were now under water; that is, the debt owed was far higher than the asset upon which the loan had been based. Five million men, about 12 percent of the workforce, were jobless.

An alliance within the Harding Cabinet between Old Guard Republican internationalists (led by Hughes) and younger Progressives (led by Hoover) presented the president with a plan that offered to solve a number of problems at once. Since American exports of capital, machines, and commodities needed a prompt revival of the European economies, Wall Street's banks would be encouraged by a new round of government loan guarantees so they could begin to finance those transactions. A key stumbling block to that idea lay in the fact that all of the Allied governments owed the United States billions of dollars of war loans already, and since Harding firmly rejected the idea of cancelling those debts, the only way to pay was to extract the reparations demanded of Germany and the other Central Power losers. Worse, Britain, France, and Japan were showing signs of starting a fresh round of arms buildup, and that was causing many of the newly created European states—Poland, Czechoslovakia, and Hungary, to name just three—to begin to add to their weapons arsenals too.

Through most of April, Hoover and Hughes began to refine their argument that only a dramatic reductions in arms spending by the European nations—victor and vanquished alike—would produce the balanced budgets, the stable currency rates, and the revived economic activity that would lead to a renewed demand for American capital and goods. And only when Europe had revived and stabilized could Washington with reasonable assurance enact added financial incentives for a reluctant Wall Street to extend the necessary new credits to European borrowers to spark that demand. In a letter to Harding dated May 11, 1921, Hoover put disarmament at the top of a list of policy recommendations for solving what by now was a full blown depression in America. Hughes quickly followed suit with more detailed recommendations to call for an ambitious international conference of all the major nations to agree to a massive reduction in both naval and land weapons and to abstain from building more. Harding, it was suggested, could even call for the conference to be held under the auspices of the League of Nations without committing the United States to membership.[8] The main object of the conference, it was agreed early, would be to suggest a general disarmament pact, but to push hardest to check the headlong rush among nations to add to the arsenal of battleships.

For any nation that sought to extend its influence beyond its borders, the battleship was the atomic weapon of that time. Since the 1870s, these armored warships with their heavy caliber cannons were the dominating instrument for governments that wanted to project their national force elsewhere in the world; they could go anywhere, push past most land-based protection, and put troops ashore wherever that nation's interests or desires indicated. Despite a consensus among naval experts that the few classic Great War battles between these capital ships pointed to the growing importance of other naval weapons—the submarine and the aircraft carrier—the increased speed and range of the new Dreadnought class (thanks to fuel oil) and the increasing firepower of the cannons made them a dangerous strategic weapon in the wrong hands. Japanese plans for a massive expansion of its Pacific Fleet was viewed as a threat to the British Empire, the business interests of the United States, and the security of both China and Russia.

When diplomats for the great powers (Britain, France, Italy, and Japan) gathered in Washington in November 1921, Secretary Hughes gave a perfunctory nod to the League of Nations process, but all the delegations were aware that this was an American effort, and there was much curiosity about Harding's motives and objectives. The British came most willingly. Having the first major postwar peace conference in the United States gave them the excuse they needed to treat the League in Geneva as merely a forum for debate. Cooperating on arms reductions also earned them the assurances that U.S. participation in Middle Eastern oil development would be cooperative and not competitive. Most important, the government of David Lloyd George was determined to protect Britain's dominance of the oceans through the supremacy of the Royal Navy. France came more grudgingly and only after insisting that the question of reducing the land weapons of armies be scrapped unless the United States would agree to the same kind of secret treaty Paris had just reached with Poland for mutual defense if Germany should attack either. Since that was out of the question, the conference agenda was quickly reduced to naval weapons and soon thereafter circumscribed further to deal only with battleships, which were described as warships of greater displacement than thirty-five thousand tons and carrying guns of no greater than sixteen inches in diameter.

The agreement finally reached in February 1922 is often derided as having satisfied no one and is therefore considered a failure that is invariably listed as one of the foreseeable, avoidable, and tragic causes of World War II. But considering the objectives of the Harding-Hughes-Hoover strategy—to jump-start the European economic recovery and to checkmate Japanese expansion in the Pacific—it was a remarkable success for a neophyte administration. The formal naval agreement established parity for the first time between the U.S. Navy and the Royal Navy and sharply restricted the number and size of Japanese battleships, to its ultimate cost twenty years later when its attempts to dominate the Pacific were defeated at the Battle of Midway. The treaty did neglect to deal with other naval war vessels—cruisers, destroyers, and submarines—but it was also tacitly agreed to deal with those kinds of weapons at future disarmament negotiations, and those talks continued with great regularity at meetings in London and Geneva for the next twenty years.

More to the immediate point were the other agreements that also were signed at Washington in the spring of 1922. In addition to the Five-Power Naval Treaty on battleship reduction, Britain, France, Japan, and the United States signed a separate pact to respect each other's interests in the Pacific. A broader agreement was signed that included the governments of Belgium, the Netherlands, China, and Portugal in guaranteeing the sovereignty of China and the Open Door policy that allowed the westerners to continue commercial exploitation of that vast, unstable land. In short, Japan found itself checkmated at almost every turn and forced to make pledges not to carry out its plans to expand its power and control throughout the Pacific, a pledge that it would grudgingly honor until 1933. What no one would know until much later was that Herbert Yardley, who had been General Pershing's code breaker during the war, had set up his famed Black Chamber code deciphering office after the war as a joint operation of the Army and the State Department. Even before the conference had convened, Hughes was fully briefed on the minimum terms the Japanese negotiators would accept, and the minimum is precisely what they got.[9]

One can debate without conclusion whether the Washington Conference of 1921–1922 failed to prevent World War II. But two successes must be conceded: It did at least delay a dangerous naval weapons race that could have sparked another global conflagration through the rest of the 1920s. And it showed the other great power governments a way to deal with the threat of a major international weapons race outside the public glare and the inflexibility of the League forum; deals could be made in private, and understandings could be reached.

For the Progressives who had begun their journey on Dupont Circle a dozen years earlier, the conference provided them with the motivation to revive the transatlantic conversations about peace, which had begun in the Hotel Majestic but had dropped off into silence after they left Paris. Now the conversation would begin again in a different forum altogether.

The conference had provided encouraging evidence that there was more than one road to peaceful settlement of the world's conflicts. Many of the Dupont Circle set had come to realize that it might be a more effective strategy to pursue peace on a regional basis. Rather than attempt another single, overarching world peace organization, both Dulles and Welles had shown that America could be an effective advocate of its goals by focusing on the instabilities that threatened important arenas such as Latin America and the Middle East. So too, it became clear that U.S. influence could be brought to bear on vital single issues. The 1922 Naval Treaty had not only reduced the race to build great power battleships, it had also pointed the way to beginning discussions about lessening the threat of land-based armaments in future talks.

While the United States would never join the League of Nations, American diplomats entered a new phase of active participation—albeit on an unofficial basis—in a decade of almost nonstop negotiating on a host of issues that ranged from disarmament to postal regulations and commercial aviation. Increasingly, the Council on Foreign Relations members found themselves as first-responders in debating and planning the government's policy responses. For most of the Dupont Circle set, this was an opportunity to get back into the game, and they made the most of it.

Ten

The Best Laid Plans

1921–1925

"You will be glad to know that the doctors consider me a prize patient and are much gratified at my progress toward recovery."

—FDR commenting on his polio, 1921

THE EARLY YEARS OF THE 1920S saw the Dupont Circle set, and indeed most Progressives, scrambling to seek new career opportunities and to figure out what to do next about their sense of disappointment over the results of the Paris conference.

Franklin Roosevelt had to face the hard task of stepping away from national office and returning to New York, both to start making a living but also, more importantly for him, to build a political base in his home state that could be a springboard back to Washington and the White House. An important component of that base would prove to be the new organization that had to be created to continue the transatlantic dialogue on foreign policy that was pledged by the British and American staffers in Paris at the Hotel Majestic. FDR, through his friendship with Morgan banker Thomas Lamont, played an early role in helping to organize the American side of that conversation in what came to be known as the Council on Foreign Relations (CFR).

The British were able to get their policy study group up and running first. Named the British Institute of International Affairs (BIIA), the group, which included Percy and Kerr, was organized in July 1920 and was soon moved into the quarters that would give the group its public name; Chatham House had been the home of the famed prime minister William Pitt, and its location in St. James's Square was close to government offices. Important funding, however, came from America, where the Rockefeller Foundation provided an initial grant, and from the ubiquitous internationalist Thomas Lamont, who donated money to produce an authoritative history of the Paris conference.

The BIIA would receive a royal charter in 1926 and thereafter be the Royal Institute of International Affairs, but from its founding, the group's membership entered into a close relationship with whichever government was in power as an informal—and thus deniable—source of information on foreign policy concerns of that moment. Indeed, each year the foreign secretary currently in office would outline a series of official concerns for the Chatham House scholars to address, to gather data on, and to recommend policy alternatives for, which then would be circulated throughout the government and, through the half dozen leading London newspapers, to the general British public.

In New York, a foreign policy discussion group known as the Council on Foreign Relations made up largely of Wall Street lawyers and bankers had already held sporadic meetings on America's post-League future but had lapsed into inactivity because it lacked the funds to continue.

Spurred by BIIA's formal launch and by the excitement of the upcoming Naval Conference, the old Council on Foreign Relations agreed to reorganize and merge with another foreign policy group in the autumn of 1921 under a newly chartered Council on Foreign Relations banner. Again, as with the Chatham House institute, seed money came from both the Rockefeller Foundation and Thomas Lamont.

CFR's first officers were emblematic of the organizers' intentions: the honorary president was Elihu Root, the former

Franklin Roosevelt (front row, center) leads a morning exercise group of Congressmen and officials on a hike in a campaign to promote physical fitness for the war effort. Copyright International Film Service, 1917 (permission sought). Franklin D. Roosevelt Presidential Library.

Walter Lippmann, special assistant to the Secretary of War, and Assistant Secretary Roosevelt in 1917 oversaw the construction of scores of camps where the U.S. army and navy trained for World War I. Walter Lippmann Papers Collection at the Sterling Library of Yale University.

Lady Cynthia Mosley her husband Oswald (the future British Fascist Party leader) were among FDR's visitors on board his Florida yacht the Larooco, 1924. Franklin D. Roosevelt Presidential Library.

From left: Missy LeHand, FDR, and Dutchess County neighbors Maunselle S. Crosby and Frances DeRham, on a Florida beach, 1924. This is the only known photo showing the damage to FDR's legs by his bout of polio. Franklin D. Roosevelt Presidential Library.

FDR, Missy Lehand and Eleanor Roosevelt, 1928. Franklin D. Roosevelt Presidential Library.

Lucy Mercer Rutherfurd, ca. 1933 when she began to visit FDR in the White House. Corbis.

Eleanor, FDR, Missy LeHand and bodyguard Earl Miller at the Val-Kill swimming pool, 1932. Franklin D. Roosevelt Presidential Library.

The Dulles clan, ca. 1925. Back row (left to right): Edith Foster Dulles, Rev. Allen Macy Dulles, Eleanor Foster Lansing, Robert Lansing. Middle row: Allen W. Dulles, Margaret Dulles Edwards, John Foster Dulles, Eleanor Lansing Dulles, Nataline Dulles. Front row: Rev. Deane Edwards, Mary Parke Edwards, Edith Edwards, Joan Dulles, Toddie Dulles, Clover Todd Dulles. Eleanor Lansing Dulles Papers, Dwight D. Eisenhower Presidential Library.

Lord Eustace Percy, ca 1920s, as Master of Hounds at a fox hunt in Aldershot, England. U.S. Library of Congress.

Philip Kerr, now Lord Lothian, dressed in the full regalia as British Ambassador to attend a White House reception. December 1939. Harris & Ewing Collection, U.S. Library of Congress.

Felix Frankfurter, in Harvard Law School classroom, 1939. Harris & Ewing Collection, U.S. Library of Congress.

Allen Dulles (right), head of State Department Middle Eastern Division, seated with Minister Peter Jay (left), September 1924. National Photo Collection, U.S. Library of Congress.

William C. Bullitt with wife Louise Bryant and daughter Anne Moen Bullitt, Paris, 1924. William C. Bullitt Papers, Sterling Library, Yale University.

Walter Lippmann and Faye Lippmann at their home in Wading River, before their divorce, ca. 1935. Walter Lippmann Papers, Sterling Library, Yale University.

Walter Lippmann, Helen Armstrong and Faye Lippmann in a café during the 1933 tour the two couples made of the Middle East. Snapshot taken by Hamilton Fish Armstrong. Walter Lippmann Papers, Sterling Library, Yale University.

Walter and Helen Lippmann on trip to Europe after their marriage, 1939.
Walter Lippmann Papers, Sterling Library, Yale University.

Princess Marie Bonaparte, French author and psychoanalyst (left), and U.S. Ambassador to France William Bullitt escort Sigmund Freud, who has fled the Nazi occupation of Vienna, through Paris train station enroute to England, 1938. Acme News Photo Collection, U.S. Library of Congress.

Bullitt and aide Carmel Offie on voyage to United States, ca. 1939. William C. Bullitt Papers, Sterling Library, Yale University.

President Roosevelt's ambassadors to major European countries leave White House after conference. Left to right: William C. Bullitt, envoy to France; Acting Secretary of State Sumner Welles; U.S. Ambassador to Germany Hugh R. Wilson; and William Phillips, ambassador to Italy. December 6, 1938. Acme News Photo Collection, U.S. Library of Congress.

FDR confers with Winston Churchill on board HMS Prince of Wales at start of Atlantic Charter conference, August 10, 1941. New York World-Telegram and Sun Newspaper Collection, U.S. Library of Congress.

Sumner Welles exits railroad car, 1940. Harris & Ewing Collection, U.S. Library of Congress.

secretary of state and Republican presidential candidate; the president was John W. Davis, the wartime U.S. ambassador to Britain.[1] Wall Street power lawyer Paul D. Cravath and Edwin F. Gay, editor of the traditionally liberal *New York Post* newspaper, were named officers.

Gay's appointment as the CFR's secretary-treasurer is especially significant. He had been dean of the Harvard Business School before accepting various wartime posts in the Wilson administration's agencies that centrally controlled the mobilization effort. In 1920, he had headed a group of reform-minded investors that included Franklin Roosevelt, which took over the ownership of the *Post* from Lamont.

Unlike its British counterpart, the new CFR pointed itself away from a direct relationship with either the White House or the State Department. Instead it focused its efforts on building an internationalist consensus among, first, the East Coast elite of law and finance, and through that network's contacts, among other banking and professional leaders around the nation. Using the modus operandi of the old Inquiry, special studies were to be undertaken of regions and issues of international concern.

But the CFR would also provide a forum for leading statesmen and foreign policy advocates to publicly present their views on the issues of the moment. And finally, the CFR would regularly publish a journal that would report the findings of its studies but also present the views of experts on specific international questions. Gay was also the sponsor of two new members of the council, Raymond Fosdick, who returned from Paris to become secretary of the Rockefeller Foundation, and Hamilton Fish Armstrong, who had been reporting news from the Balkans for the *Post*. Armstrong was made assistant editor of the CFR's new quarterly journal, *Foreign Affairs*.

The CFR and *Foreign Affairs* would prove an important asset for Roosevelt. He would use the quarterly as a sounding board over the years as he formed his broad policy beliefs, and the CFR membership would be the center core of his network of advisers and supporters as he planned what for him was an inevitable run for the Presidency. And the Progressives, especially the Dupont Circle veterans, were willing to oblige. They had come to realize they had no strong personality who could serve as a rallying point for their internationalist viewpoint. Woodrow Wilson was too discredited among his former acolytes, and his failing health (he would die in February 1924) kept him from any political activity.

Wilson's heir, by virtue of his stellar performance during the 1920 campaign, should have been FDR. Roosevelt was certainly alive to his future in politics when he moved back to New York City after Harding's inauguration in March 1921 and joined a law partnership (which he found boring). He also joined a company that underwrote performance bonds for business contracts and used his many contacts at the Navy Department to steer new business to the firm. For the first time, he was free of the financial tyranny imposed by his mother.

Roosevelt also continued to keep the key members of his 1920 campaign staff close at hand. He also found jobs for many of the Cufflinks Gang of campaign workers, keeping both Louis Howe and Missy LeHand on his personal payroll. During the 1920 campaign, FDR had compiled a set of index cards listing the name, address, and personal data of every Democratic Party activist he met during his travels. Now that list was organized and augmented by new names of New York state party leaders. When the time was right to re-enter the political arena, that list would be an invaluable resource.

But just as suddenly, all those dreams and preparations became horribly irrelevant. That August, the Roosevelts decamped as usual for Campobello Island in New Brunswick, Canada. Once he joined the family, FDR embarked on a strenuous holiday round of sailing and hiking that ended abruptly when he was stricken with a paralysis of his legs that doctors diagnosed as polio.[2]

Most of the standard biographies of Roosevelt deal at length with the horror of that illness and the pain he suffered as the paralysis progressively robbed him of the muscles in his legs and lower torso. Much attention is paid to how the Roosevelt family and his close aides like Louis Howe went to enormous lengths to keep the public unaware of just how seriously ill he was during the first months of his convalescence. When newspapers finally did report the story, there was a universal interpretation that the illness was not serious and that Roosevelt would quickly regain his full mobility.

One of the results of this carefully managed affair was that it gave rise to the myth that Roosevelt's illness somehow changed his character from that of the facile, superficial playboy to one of more mature compassion; in a word, his polio made FDR more of a politically liberal activist. This was a myth that had its beginnings in the hopeful psyches of many who were closest to him, Eleanor chiefly, but also acolytes like Frances Perkins, a Democratic activist friend of Eleanor's who later would be the first woman secretary of labor. Perkins reported after seeing FDR in the summer of 1922 that she "was instantly struck by his growth. He was young, he was crippled, he was physically weak, but he had a firmer grip on his life and himself than ever before. He was serious, not playing now. He had become conscious of other people. . . ." Eleanor privately told friends the paralysis had "proved a blessing in disguise."[3]

A perhaps more sober interpretation might be that the tremendous strength of character, the sheer persistence, the unquenchable public optimism that Franklin Roosevelt displayed during the early years of his effort to recover his mobility had always been there beneath the carefree facade that had caused many outsiders to dismiss him as a lightweight. Whatever else Roosevelt might have been, he remained a classic gentleman of the previous century, and part of that code was to never appear to flinch in the face of adversity.

Perhaps more to the point is the fact that neither Roosevelt, nor Howe or any of the Cufflink Gang, ever for a moment gave up the certainty that FDR one day would gain the White House. So the inevitable waves of despair and self-doubt were carefully suppressed, and the forty-year-old Roosevelt embarked on an arduous and painful regimen of treatments and exercises that not only produced a tremendous gain in upper body strength, but also began to allow him to stand with the aid of uncomfortable leg braces and ultimately to develop a kind of swinging motion that allowed him to traverse short distances. As word of this remarkable progress spread through the Roosevelt network of friends and into the press accounts, it was generally accepted at the time that—as he enthusiastically predicted—he would make a full recovery.

Whatever his innermost thoughts, Roosevelt himself gave clear indications that his recovery was just a matter of time. He returned to his law practice and bond selling within a few weeks of returning to New York City and remained hectically active in public causes ranging from the Boy Scout movement to the foundation set up to honor Woodrow Wilson. He also began to patch up his differences with his old nemesis from the Tammany Hall machine, Alfred E. Smith.

At that time in the early 1920s, Smith was the only nationally recognizable political figure who advocated the kind of social policies that Progressives favored. Raised on the Lower East Side, he never went to high school but, instead, at an early age worked his way up through the ranks of the Tammany Hall political machine that ran New York City and influenced the politics of the state. He had ascended from the chairmanship of New York's board of aldermen to the governor's mansion in Albany in 1918. New York in those days limited the governor's term of office to two years, and Smith was swept back out of office in the 1920 Harding landslide. But by the summer of 1922, Smith was in the running to recover the governorship and was locked in a contest for the Democratic nomination with the press baron William Randolph Hearst.

Roosevelt not only published an open letter urging Smith to run for governor but, at Louis Howe's prompting, Eleanor also began to openly court Democratic women who were on Smith's campaign staff, including strategist Belle Moskowitz and Frances Perkins, and to involve herself in the campaign. Howe had already encouraged Eleanor to participate in organizing the new women's division of the party now that women could vote. But working on the Smith campaign took her into the new territory of street-level politicking. Smith for his part welcomed the Roosevelt endorsement while still reserving his doubts about FDR's seriousness. Although he was never tainted by the corruption that permeated Tammany Hall, he never forgot FDR's pre-war attacks on the machine; Smith also had the self-made man's scorn for the upper classes that Roosevelt embodied.

The evolution in the political career of Eleanor Roosevelt is usually interpreted as her liberation and the transformation of her marriage into a political partnership of equals. But there is a darker, lonelier dimension to that change. Essentially, Eleanor was transformed into another member of the Cufflink Gang, valued and depended upon without doubt, but much in the same way that Louis Howe and Missy LeHand were. Perhaps there never had been a chance for Franklin and Eleanor to recapture the intimacy and affection that had existed before Lucy Mercer. But by becoming FDR's political surrogate—his "eyes and ears," as he said—and then a political force in her own right, she gave up her role as his wife. Thereafter, Roosevelt would fill that vacuum with a succession of emotional—and potentially sexual—relationships with a parade of other women.

Marguerite "Missy" LeHand would be the first and, for the rest of her life, the most important of these "other" women. One could not compare Missy with Lucy Mercer Rutherfurd, who would remain Roosevelt's true romantic love. Twenty-two-year-old Missy was slender and fair with startling blue eyes, but her elongated jaw kept her from the kind of classic beauty that Lucy possessed. Missy also was very firmly of the working class. Raised in Somerville, Massachusetts, she had gone from secretarial school to the Democratic Party campaign headquarters as a stenographer during the 1920 campaign and had found herself detailed to Roosevelt's vice presidential effort. Once he had moved to New York to plan his re-entry into politics, it was Eleanor who invited Missy to come to Hyde Park to help with a backlog of correspondence. By 1922, she had a room set aside for her at Hyde Park as well as one in the cramped Roosevelt townhouse at 47 East Sixty-fifth Street, a perquisite she shared with Louis Howe.

Did Missy and FDR have a sexual relationship? It certainly was possible physically even after the bout of polio. Most of Roosevelt's family, with the exception of his son Elliott, doubted it. What is demonstrably clear is that their ties became emotionally intense over time. For Missy, as with so many other Roosevelt acolytes, he offered not only his own considerable charm and vitality, but also the opportunity to have a more exciting and engrossing personal career than she could ordinarily have aspired to on her own. For FDR, Missy provided the uncritical devotion one usually receives from a spouse. She would share his innermost thoughts and emotional tidal currents even as she attended to the mundane chores of correspondence, appointments, and the increasingly important card index of future Democratic contacts. Sex may have been involved, but what bound them together was stronger than that.

It was Missy and not Eleanor who accompanied Roosevelt on a series of winter Florida boating excursions that began in 1923 and were repeated each year through 1926. The stated purpose of the trips was for FDR to further his therapy with swimming in the warm waters of the Florida Keys. On the first trip, he rented a houseboat, but from 1924 onward, he and a friend from his Harvard days were joint owners of a large yacht rechristened *Larooco* (an amalgam of the owners' names).

While swimming and fishing were certainly on his daily routine, Roosevelt essentially wanted to avoid the turmoil—political and domestic—that stifled him in New York and to surround himself with congenial company where cocktails and often ribald banter was the order of the day. Eleanor and other family members would make periodic brief appearances during these four-month sojourns, but she especially disliked life aboard the yacht, and she disapproved of many of the companions her husband had chosen. The usual guest list featured a procession of wealthy Dutchess County neighbors like Henry Morgenthau Jr., old Harvard drinking buddies like Livingston Davis, and occasional tourist celebrities like Lady Cynthia Mosley and her husband (and future British Fascist leader) Sir Oswald, who arrived with letters from Nancy Astor. FDR recorded in *Larooco*'s log that the Mosleys "are a most delightful couple."[4]

But it was Missy who was most in evidence. It was she who stayed with him in his stateroom on those mornings when he sank into temporary despair; it was she who mixed the cocktails and organized the board games and other entertainments that kept the shipboard mood upbeat and amusing. And it was Missy who went with FDR in 1926 when he sold his share in the *Larooco* and invested heavily in the decayed mountain resort that would come to be more closely identified with Franklin Roosevelt than Hyde Park itself—Warms Springs, Georgia.

The state-of-the-art hydrotherapy facility that Roosevelt developed at Warm Springs engaged his attention and sympathies more fully than any other quest had before. He had a genuine concern for the polio victims for whom the spa represented a last hope of help; he also firmly believed that the hot, mineral-rich water in combination with the pioneering exercises he personally supervised would produce results. And indeed they had worked for him. At the 1924 Democratic convention in New York's Madison Square Garden, the delegates were transfixed by Roosevelt, propped up on crutches as he made his painful way to the lectern to nominate Al Smith for president, calling him "the Happy Warrior of the political battlefield," a description that was forever used to identify Smith.

That speech, plus a number of political addresses Roosevelt made over the new medium of radio in Smith's behalf, served a number of purposes. No one, perhaps with the exception of Smith himself, and certainly not FDR, expected the governor to be a successful presidential candidate in 1924; Smith took the precaution of running for re-election as governor at the same time. In 1923, the Harding administration had been rocked by a pervasive corruption scandal that involved his closest friends in the Cabinet. But fortuitously, Harding had suddenly died in September, and successor Calvin Coolidge had such a reputation for personal rectitude that Republican prospects, buoyed by an economic boom, seemed unassailable.

While Smith had instituted a wide range of Progressive social reforms in the New York state government, he had many personal as well as political handicaps. He was a Roman Catholic and a staunch "wet," an advocate of repealing the Prohibition laws. Moreover, his coarse persona and absence of any foreign policy interest gave pause to more intellectual Progressives like Lippmann and Frankfurter. In the final analysis, the question for the Democrats was whether to stick to a Progressive policy line or to try to field a candidate more acceptable to the conservative mood of the country.

The mood had become increasingly reactionary on social issues even as optimism about prosperity continued to grow. Legal challenges and corporate strikebreaking had succeeded in reducing membership in labor unions to prewar levels. At the same time, hate groups like the Ku Klux Klan numbered as many as five million active members. So many of the delegates arriving for the 1924 Democratic convention were Klansmen that the press dubbed the meeting "the Klanbake."

Smith to his credit openly repudiated the Klan while the leading contender for the nomination, President Wilson's son-in-law William Gibbs McAdoo, privately sought its support. The fight that followed produced such a wearying deadlock that after one hundred roll call votes, the Democrats turned to an inoffensive compromise ticket of John W. Davis for president, paired with the brother of that old party favorite William Jennings Bryan. The election was viewed as so much of a foregone conclusion that fewer than half of the eligible citizens bothered to vote, and those that did gave the Republicans an overwhelming majority.

The 1924 election had served to keep Franklin Roosevelt's name alive among Progressives and to earn the grudging gratitude of Smith, who secured re-election as governor without much trouble. There had been some talk of nominating FDR to run for one of New York's U.S. Senate seats, but he quickly begged off, pleading the need to devote more time to his therapy.

In truth, Roosevelt was playing for time. To read his public pronouncements and privately expressed opinions during this time is to see a man unwilling to commit himself on many policy issues because of an instinct that the public mood could shift overnight. He and Howe agreed that by 1928, even with continued prosperity, Americans would have tired of the Harding-Coolidge brand of parochial conservatism and would have an appetite for a new Progressive alternative. As for the details of what that alternative would be, he was prepared to wait and see.

So during this time, he drew back on his advocacy of United States membership in the League. He temporized about supporting Smith's pro-repeal stance on Prohibition even as he kept a well-stocked bar wherever he went. As someone who had done so much to build up the U.S. Navy before the war, he now defied his Big Navy constituency and cautiously endorsed the Naval Treaty limitations.

There was one policy area, however, where Roosevelt did take a strong stance. He began to urge the Coolidge administration to reduce if not outright cancel demands that Britain, France, and other nations repay the billions in war credits they had borrowed from Wall Street and the Treasury. In this he had been prompted by Herbert Hoover, with whom he still kept in cordial contact even though the older man was now secretary of commerce.

It had been clear to nearly everyone present at the Paris Peace Conference that the financial demands imposed on Germany were too heavy to be borne unless that nation were to be kept as a vassal state for the victors. But the shocking devastation that the Kaiser's army had wreaked on Belgium and France plus the horrible losses among the other Allied forces produced such an angry backlash among the populace that Germany "be made to pay" that it overwhelmed political leaders who knew better. Worse, even though in theory the reparations demanded of the Germans were a separate issue, in fact there was little prospect that the British and French could repay the billions borrowed from Wall Street and the U.S. Treasury that financed their wartime purchases unless the Germans paid them first.

As early as 1921, the reparations authority set up by the Treaty of Versailles reduced the original 269 billion gold marks demanded of the Germans to 226 billion, but even that amount was problematical.[5] From the start, the leaders of the Weimar Republic tried to stabilize their political control over radical efforts to turn Germany into the next Soviet-style nation by increasing the money supply. While this made Germany's war debts cheaper to finance, it prompted a spiral of inflation for the German people that quickly got out of control. As personal savings were spent to meet skyrocketing prices, a wave of business bankruptcies followed. When in 1923 a shipment of coal and steel that was part of the reparations payments was not forthcoming, French and Belgian troops occupied the German industrial centers of the Ruhr valley; outraged German workers promptly went on strike, and industrial output contracted sharply. By the end of 1923, it took 4.2 trillion marks to buy a single U.S. dollar.

Even before that crisis, Roosevelt, Hoover, and others had faced up to the fact that waiting until every nation on either side of the Great War could settle its accounts jeopardized any hopes for a global postwar economic recovery. In the very first issue of *Foreign Affairs,* published by CFR in the autumn of 1922, no less an authority than Foster Dulles appealed to Washington to at least reduce some of its debt demands on Britain and France so that they, in turn, could allow further reductions in the payments demanded from a tottering German government. He wrote:

> Great Britain and France are both, on paper, creditor nations. There is owed to them far more than they owe. They would desire nothing more than to collect what is owing them and pay what they owe. But four years have shown that these paper credits are illusory. . . . It is true that the Allies will expect us to contribute to the general settlement, which is now becoming possible, by cancellation of so much of their debts as reason and experience show to be uncollectable. They do not desire this as an escape from payment. They only ask that we cancel that which in no event will be paid. But this they do ask, and regard as an essential. For the big objective, political and financial stability, will be jeopardized if one great creditor nation holds aloof and asserts the intention of repeating the experiments in collection which have, for four years past, disturbed the economic peace of the world.[6]

But in Washington, both President Harding, and later, President Coolidge were captives to a public mood that wanted to prolong the illusions of the postwar recovery and boom that were just underway. European events were far away, and, for the time being at least, there was no Progressive voice that could catch their attention. That would soon change, however, and in ways not even the Dupont Circle set could imagine.

Eleven
RETHINKING PROGRESSIVISM

1925–1928

"I do not choose to run for President in 1928."

—President Coolidge, August 25, 1927

BY THE MIDDLE OF THE 1920S, what it meant to be a Progressive was evolving at an accelerated and bewildering speed.

The once-youthful Dupont Circle set may have been the first of their generation to experience the anxiety of having events around them move faster than they could absorb. Certainties that had propelled them into the public arena ten years earlier seemed as quaint and irrelevant as high starched collars and horse-drawn carriages in this new Jazz Age of exaggerated flapper fashions and automobiles.

They had been drawn to Washington by Woodrow Wilson's pronouncement that the old faith, in arbitration to settle international disputes, should be translated into a broader framework—a League of Nations. In such a forum, diplomats could work out solutions that would influence even the most bellicose governments to adhere to peace; in that way, the more important work of domestic reforms could move forward to provide honest local government, better services, more uplifting education, and health programs that would improve the lives of all people everywhere.

From its early days, Progressivism had been an inward-looking faith. The various reform movements first began at the local level with crusades to improve housing in slums and to bring better health and education services to the American working class. The Great War had forced them to raise their sights to the world around them, but even then, Wilson's League of Nations was supposed to be set in motion to attend to the disputes between other nations so that Americans could return to the more important task of perfecting their potentially ideal society.

But now there was a creeping suspicion, even if the United States had become a member of the League in 1919, that there were existential issues—of access to oil and other raw materials, of restrictive trade patterns, and, perhaps most important, of the free flow of capital—that were beyond the reach of diplomats to solve. If that was the case, then the focus on disarmament that occupied most of the international conferences of the decade began to appear to some to be merely treating one of the symptoms of a far more serious malady. But as so often is the case in political reality, leaders of the major powers concentrated on the problems that they could comprehend. Reducing the number of battleships meant more money for economic development.

Except that it did no such thing. Almost from the day the delegates packed up to leave Washington after the Naval Conference in the spring of 1922, Japan and other signatories to the treaty had quickly shifted their construction programs away from battleships to building a new class of cruisers as well as submarines and aircraft carriers, none of which had been covered by the treaty. And while the League in Geneva did score notable successes in brokering agreements on many boundary disputes, as well as new international crackdowns on slavery and drug trafficking, it spent most of its time on issues left over from the Paris Peace Conference and had little success in addressing the new problems that were piling up on its doorstep.

This ambivalence about what it meant to be a Progressive came at an awkward time in the lives of many of the Dupont Circle set. The most adrift during this time was Sumner Welles. He and Esther had returned from his post in Buenos Aires in 1920 to praise for his diplomatic successes and with a serious commitment to improving America's troubled status among other nations in the hemisphere. Two years later, he had been confirmed as the head of the State Department's Latin American Affairs division; at twenty-nine he was the youngest man to ever be chief of a division and was being marked as a future secretary. He had been the de facto chairman of yet another Harding administration international conference; this one brokered a treaty of friendship between the U.S. and five Central American governments. At the same time, he had made headway in the tedious business of withdrawing American military occupation forces from Haiti, the Dominican Republic, and Cuba while installing stable democratic governments in the vacuum that would be created in those countries.

In the midst of all of this professional success, his private life was unraveling disturbingly. He resigned at least once only to be called back by Secretary of State Charles Evans Hughes for special assignments to one Caribbean hot spot or another. In the meantime, his marriage to Esther deteriorated beyond saving. What had been her taste for girlish pranks and eccentric outbursts at dinner parties when she was younger was now a silly affectation that angered Welles intensely; in turn, his own outward appearance grew more dignified and solemn. He often left her behind when he went suddenly off to Latin America during this time, and when he returned to Washington, she would often leave to stay with family in New York.

During all this time, Sumner continued to bounce from torrid romances with married women in whichever foreign capital he found himself to alcohol-fueled foraging for sex among the lower classes of both races and genders. There was one reported episode in the spring of 1921 that involved the wreck of a taxi and a brawl involving the driver and Welles that took place early one morning in front of the Washington's landmark Mayflower Hotel.[1]

Earlier that same year, Welles had been in the midst of an affair with a Washington socialite who was married to an Englishman. She had returned to London with Sumner's promise to join her there in the spring. But at a New Year's holiday dinner that Welles attended while Esther was away, he met and immediately became obsessed with the woman whom he would truly and deeply love the rest of his life.

Mathilde Townsend Gerry was one of the wealthiest and most beautiful women in Washington, wealthier even than the family of Esther Slater Welles. She was tall and fair and fine featured with a face set off by remarkably large dark eyes. But what attracted Welles apparently was the instinctive ease with which she greeted life with an assumed aristocracy. Where Esther had been capricious and embarrassing, Mathilde glided through life cushioned by her wealth, but also more by her inner certainty that she belonged wherever she wanted to go. At thirty-seven, she was eight years older than Welles, but she too felt the spark of attraction at once for this tall, fastidious man who was commanding such attention in the political arena.

Like Sumner, Mathilde was in an unhappy marriage. The Townsends were firmly in the Washington establishment, a rigidly exclusive society of wealth and influence that had come to the capital city after the Civil War. Taking an inheritance that has been estimated to be worth $315 million in today's terms, Mathilde's mother built a French Renaissance mansion at 2121 Massachusetts Avenue NW, just a block off Dupont Circle, which was modeled after Versailles' Petit Trianon.[2] In such splendor, Mathilde had grown up intellectually idle, with a taste for jewelry and pet dogs and a sense of boredom with the flattery and adoration she received from the world around her. As much to placate her mother, she had married Peter Gerry, a dull scion of a Rhode Island political dynasty (one of his ancestors had signed the Declaration of Independence) who held a safe seat in the U.S. Senate. Like everyone else, the well-meaning Gerry doted on Mathilde despite her growing disdain. But Sumner Welles, dignified to the point of being imperious and clearly a man on the make, offered her stimulation as well as love. For her part, she became something of an enabler, willing to dismiss signs of Sumner's darker nature as long as she remained sure of his devotion to her.

She addressed her dilemma by commencing an affair with Sumner even as she dithered over whether to leave her husband or stay. While Welles came and went from Washington on various missions—sometimes with Esther and his sons in tow, sometimes alone—he and Mathilde would break away for clandestine interludes, and there is some evidence that drink-fueled emotions could erupt into violent quarreling.[3]

But it was also clear that the two could not bring themselves to separate, and their romance soon became a scandal that kept tongues wagging both in Washington and New York and caused distress to both Esther Welles and Peter Gerry. Most onlookers at first condemned Mathilde as a shameless home wrecker until it became known that Welles had borrowed $100,000 from Esther's trust fund, ostensibly for an investment, only to use the money to buy more jewelry for his new love.[4]

Even Welles's father ended up rebuking him for his disgraceful conduct, and the two men never spoke again. Esther finally obtained a divorce decree in the autumn of 1923; still Mathilde could not quite bring herself to break free of Gerry, but she remained equally unwilling to do without Welles either. Whenever Welles would head off to the Caribbean on one of the many diplomatic missions, she would sooth her anxiety by splurging on more jewelry, in one headline-grabbing instance spending $400,000 (more than $3 million today) on a string of black pearls owned by Prince Felix Youssoupoff, one of the assassins of Rasputin.[5]

Ultimately, a political gaffe led to Welles's final dismissal from government. In the sweltering summer of 1924, Mathilde tired of Washington and decided she wanted to attend the Democratic nominating convention in New York, something the wife of a Senator could not do on her own. Welles agreed to escort her in part because his patron Franklin Roosevelt would be making his dramatic first appearance on the political stage since his polio attack. For the two weeks the convention dragged on until it nominated John Davis, Sumner and Mathilde were scandalously in evidence in the VIP section during the day and at various fashionable nightspots in the evening. Even before the convention, Welles had renewed his friendship with Roosevelt and had provided him with briefing papers on his plans to improve America's standing in Latin America; FDR duly passed them on to Al Smith who, in turn, made no secret where he had obtained his information.

For the time being, there was no repercussion since Welles was not officially a State Department officer at that moment. In the early summer of 1925, Welles and Mathilde finally married, and he prepared to take her and his two sons on an important assignment to the Dominican Republic. He was tapped by the new secretary of state, Frank Kellogg, to direct a restructuring of the newly elected government there. But just before he was to leave, disaster struck. President Coolidge, who had silently resented the embarrassment of his close friend Senator Gerry, abruptly vetoed the Welles appointment and further ordered in a handwritten note to Kellogg, "If he [Welles] is in the government service, let him be dismissed at once."[6]

Like others of their generation, Sumner and Mathilde sought refuge in Paris where they could find a life free of the unhappiness they had left behind in America. In 1919, Paris had just been climbing out of the national disaster that had engulfed France during nearly five years of war. But now the city had recaptured its old glitter, nourished at least in part by a wave of disaffected American expatriates—the fabled Lost Generation of Cole Porter songs, novels by Fitzgerald and Hemingway, and the carrying on of wealthy pleasure seekers like Gerald and Sara Murphy. At eight francs to the dollar, an American could afford to indulge almost any appetite, and Paris, ever tolerant of human desires, was happy to provide anything asked. While Mathilde and her mother exhausted themselves shopping for the latest fashions during the day, Sumner, accompanied by the tutor they had hired for his sons, would disappear at night into his old haunts in the demimonde of the Left Bank where one could move from private parties in artists' apartments to even more private establishments that catered to his needs.

At the nightly parties of the artist colony, he certainly would have come across an old Dupont Circle figure, now something of a celebrity among that raffish crowd. William Bullitt and his even more celebrated new wife, Louise Bryant, the widow of John Reed, were among the most prominent members of that colorful American community in their self-exile.

After having burned his political bridges by denouncing President Wilson's conduct at the Paris Conference, Bullitt cast about for work away from Washington and in 1921 landed a job as a script editor for the silent movie producers Famous Players-Lasky in New York. He went alone, for Ernesta had tired of his roving eye and had filed for divorce. One day in September 1923, Louise Bryant came to his office with a proposal to make a documentary film version of John Reed's dramatic eyewitness account of the Russian Revolution titled *Ten Days That Shook the World*. Since Reed's death from typhus in 1920, Bryant had become a star journalist abroad for the powerful Hearst newspaper chain and had scored the first interview with Mussolini when he came to power a year earlier. She also had a four-part series of interviews with Lenin and other top Soviet leaders that was syndicated by Hearst to all the major U.S. newspapers.

Louise was six years older than the thirty-two-year-old Bullitt, but she was still darkly beautiful and had a vibrant, dramatic persona (enhanced by the aura of her late husband's heroic image). She also was an avowed Marxist, which added to her celebrity among the same fashionable radicals of New York's Greenwich Village that Bullitt courted. In Bullitt, Louise found an urbane, forceful man who already had paid a price for the convictions they both shared.

Both agreed that America had become too stifling. Bullitt had recently come into a comfortable inheritance on the death of his mother, so they traveled first to Turkey and then settled in Paris where she could resume her journalism and he could finally come to grips with a novel he had been working on without much progress back in New York. Early in 1924, Louise discovered she was pregnant, and they married; later that year their daughter Anne was born. Bullitt's novel, *It's Not Done,* was generally panned by critics, but because it was a roman à clef that reported on the various sex scandals of thinly disguised Philadelphia society figures, it sold more than 150 thousand copies.[7] The book sales made him financially secure at last and allowed the couple to keep pace with other well-to-do American expatriates. Ever restless, Bullitt began other writing projects but spent most of his time using his gift for languages and cheerful pushiness to keep personal contacts alive with leading financiers and statesmen throughout Europe. Periodically, the couple would take holidays at a farm Bullitt had purchased in Massachusetts, but they always returned to Paris.[8]

To an outsider, the Bullitt-Bryant relationship gives the appearance of two people who had every reason to be deeply in love with each other, but something stood in their way. In Bryant's case, it may have been the ghost of John Reed and her own self-image as an intellectually superior free spirit. Bullitt for his part was always on the move, taking up projects that often were put aside unfinished. Yet he had the energy and self-confidence to keep evolving. After a year or so of marriage, he became fascinated with the insights he might acquire through the newly fashionable science of psychoanalysis—it might help him unravel his malignant anger at Woodrow Wilson and lead to a book on the subject—so he blithely traveled to Vienna and put himself (and later Louise) into the care of no less than Sigmund Freud. The extent to which Freud contributed to Bullitt's subsequent book attacking Wilson's mental stability continues to be debated, and, in any event, it was held back from publication until 1966.[9] But it is clear that a friendship grew between the famous psychoanalyst and the urbane, charismatic younger writer.

However, by 1926, the Bryant-Bullitt marriage came under a dangerous strain. Louise, like many others of the Lost Generation, used alcohol as a badge of her free spirited liberation. In a lengthy memo Bullitt prepared as part of his divorce suit in 1930, Bullitt recounted how increasing bouts of heavy drinking would send Louise into hallucinations that terrified her. Yet when he attempted to get her to stop drinking, she would fly into a rage of defiance that would spark another bender.[10]

Over the next two years the two would reconcile, and Louise would spend time in various spas and clinics in Europe, including a brief time consulting with Freud, and the result would be periods of sobriety. But she began to gain considerable weight in the form of painful fatty tissue growths throughout her body, and she would seek to ease the pain with alcohol. Finally, she was diagnosed with a rare malady known as Decrum's disease, or adiposis dolorosa, whose agonizing symptoms included pronounced feelings of paranoia.

Louise deteriorated into an increasingly disturbing pattern of behavior. When she got drunk, she would become abusive of Bullitt, often in public, denouncing him as a "dirty bourgeois Jew"—a scathing jab since Bullitt prided himself on family ties to the Langhorne and other first families of Virginia and tried to gloss over the fact that his mother was from a wealthy Jewish family of Philadelphia physicians. Louise also blamed Bullitt for preventing her from resuming her career as a writer. With some cause, she also accused him of being unfaithful when she was away at a spa.[11]

Early in 1928, she embarked on an affair with the English sculptress Gwen Le Gallienne, and the two often spent weeks away from Bullitt and his daughter as they delved into the darker regions of the Paris underworld where drugs and sex of all persuasions were fashionable.[12] At one point, she and Le Gallienne took Bullitt's car and disappeared to Marseilles for two weeks before he found them in a drunken stupor in a hotel. According to Bullitt's memo, the breaking point came when Louise took her young daughter Anne and Le Gallienne on a drunken tour of the Left Bank that did not end until Louise passed out on the floor of the Café de Paris and they were thrown out. Bullitt's reaction to Louise's lesbian adventures ("notorious pervert" was one of his descriptions of Le Gallienne) quickly moved from distaste to disgust even though he steadfastly denied that she actually had any homosexual feelings that were not generated by her alcoholism.

Through it all, Bullitt continued to travel to the major capitals of Europe and kept his astonishingly diverse political contacts alive. He took a special pride in his book of private telephone numbers that ranged from Lenin to Winston Churchill and from Thomas Masaryk, president of Czechoslovakia, to Leon Blum, head of the French Socialist Party.

Like many other Progressives during this time, Bullitt clung to a positive fascination with the evolution of Russian Bolshevism into

Soviet statism. Like many American Progressives and especially like most British Fabians such as George Bernard Shaw and the Webbs, Bullitt excused reports of Stalin's murderous repressions as regrettable but unavoidable in the struggle to build an industrial and more egalitarian society. There were many favorable comparisons between Stalin and Mussolini's brand of fascism in Italy. This was a point the Soviet officials themselves made to Bullitt and other foreign visitors to the U.S.S.R. during that time, and everyone agreed that the physical changes in Russia were most impressive. On his frequent visits to Moscow, Bullitt always placed a wreath for John Reed at his burial place of honor in the Kremlin Wall.

Yet Bullitt saw no contradiction between his political faith and his determination to live the life of a wealthy gentleman. His house in Paris was always staffed with servants and fully stocked with champagne and other vintages. He also became an avid horseman and a fan of thoroughbred racing, and he kept up a running correspondence with Waldorf and Nancy Astor who kept one of Europe's leading race stables. Since Nancy was a Langhorne, the two pretended a close family tie and called each other "Cuz" in their voluminous correspondence over the years.[13]

Bullitt was equally careful to keep his contacts firm with the one man back in the United States who was serving as a clearinghouse for the scattered Progressive forces—Colonel Edward M. House. Like Bullitt, House had a taste for political gossip as well as for hard analysis, and the younger man made his reports as breezy and amusing as they were insightful. One point he repeated throughout his correspondence with House during this period is what a fundamental mistake it had been to exclude the Soviet Union from the Paris Peace talks, and how, now that Britain, France, and other nations had formally recognized the Soviet government, the United States must follow suit. House, looking ahead to the future, sent many of Bullitt's missives on to the convalescent Franklin Roosevelt.[14] When they had first met a decade earlier at the House of Truth, FDR had derided "Billy Bullitt" as a lightweight poseur. In part relying on House's judgment, Roosevelt began to take Bullitt more seriously.

To a casual observer of the 1920s, it may have seemed that the American Progressives had shifted their base of operations from Dupont Circle in Washington into exile in Paris. At one time or another, nearly all of them passed through the fabled French capital as they embarked on the next stages of their careers and political development.

Not surprisingly, one of the first to reach Paris was Eleanor Lansing Dulles, the feisty younger sister of Foster and Allen. When she returned home from France in 1920, Eleanor had worked for a time at a metal-stamping factory in Bridgeport, Connecticut, so she could observe labor conditions for the women employed there. That led her to enroll in a joint economic research facility at Harvard and Radcliffe, and from there she and a friend, Emily Huntington, spent 1921 and 1922 at the London School of Economics, where they studied under Sir William Beveridge, the author of the British Social Security system. With the enthusiastic confidence that was common among young Progressives of that age, the two young women on their own set out to secure interviews with the chief executives of the sixty largest British manufacturing firms about the wage and work conditions in their factories. They traveled the length of Britain touring steel factories in Sheffield, shipyards in Newcastle, and textile mills in Bradford, and were surprisingly welcomed wherever they went.

But when she returned to Harvard and Radcliffe to work on her master's degree, her tutor, the economist Allyn Young, encouraged her to shift her area of studies to international finance.[15] Since she already had a command of French, she set out for Paris early in 1925 and for the next three years labored over a statistical research project that was the first study of the circulation volatility of a major currency, a hitherto unnoticed factor in how a supply of money and its value can change depending on how rapidly the money supply is moved from one purchase to the next. The study, published later by Harvard, was widely praised by no less a figure than John Maynard Keynes as being the first important work on the topic, and it made Eleanor, not yet thirty, an international name as an up-and-coming economist.[16]

Eleanor's time in Paris was far less opulent than the life enjoyed by other Americans abroad. She had a small stipend from Harvard that she augmented with her own savings. She later recalled that her tiny rented room was often too cold to work in, so she would take the research she had gathered from various government agencies and find a congenial café where she could spread out her work sheets, keep warm, and pay only a few centimes for an occasional cup of coffee to keep the waiters at bay.

And there were new friends to make among other scholars from London and America who were either studying at the Sorbonne or doing research at one library or other. It was through these friends that she met a balding, thirty-ish scholar of the philology of Romance languages named David Blondheim, who was on leave from Johns Hopkins. To her surprise, he began to court her with inexpensive bouquets of flowers and long conversational dinners at neighborhood restaurants. Their first attempts at making love were not particularly successful, she later recalled with some humor. The daughters of Presbyterian ministers were hardly schooled in the arts of love in those days.[17]

She might have consulted her brother Allen who had begun to roam further afield romantically as his career path took him into an exciting—and profitable—new arena. He had become the head of the State Department's division on Middle Eastern Affairs when he and Clover returned from Constantinople in 1922 and had been instrumental in the accord reached with the British to allow Standard Oil and other American petroleum explorers to gain access to Turkish and Persian oil fields. He also had won praise for various missions that sent him to international conferences sponsored by the League where the United States was an unofficial negotiator. When the League began preliminary planning in 1926 for the next big round of disarmament negotiations, which would begin in Geneva the next year, it was Dulles who was sent to oversee U.S. interests.[18]

In the midst of it all, Allen attended George Washington University's law school in the evening, earning his degree in 1926, even as he and Clover kept pace with the busy Washington social round of country club dances and white-tie dinners with the city's power elite. He then faced a painful choice. Secretary of State Kellogg wanted to send him to the U.S. Embassy in Peking, a prestige post but one that was prohibitively expensive for someone trying to live on a government salary, especially now that the couple had recently had a second daughter. He was thirty-three and was young by the standards of diplomacy but not if he was going to enter the private practice of law, which is what his brother Foster had been urging for some time. So in September 1926, his resignation from the State Department was handed in—amid widespread press comment about the handicaps imposed by government service—and he and Clover moved to New York to join Foster at Sullivan & Cromwell.

What that meant, however, was that Allen Dulles would continue to devote most of his energies gathering intelligence for the State Department at various international conferences, but the powerful Wall Street law firm would foot the bill. No one saw any conflict of interest in this relationship, and, in the sense that both Sullivan & Cromwell and the State Department worked in a common cause, there was none.

So in 1927 when the next big round of naval disarmament negotiations convened in Geneva, the U.S. negotiators included Norman Davis, the Morgan banker, and Allen Dulles, nominally as legal observer but in reality a gatherer of intelligence who reported directly to Secretary Kellogg.

One can only imagine the excitement and high hopes invested in the 1927 Geneva Disarmament Conference. It was certain to address the troubling buildup in cruisers, submarines, and aircraft carriers that the big power navies had resorted to in their race to supplement the limits on the huge battleships imposed by the 1922 Washington treaty.

The abrupt announcement by President Coolidge in the summer that he would not seek re-election in 1928 merely ramped up the level of anticipation among Republicans and Progressives alike. For once it became certain that Coolidge meant what his laconic statement said; it also was certain that his successor was inevitably going to be the first habitué of the House of Truth to make it to the White House—Herbert Hoover.

Twelve

WHO BUT HOOVER?

❧

1928–1932

"Who but Hoover?"
—Herbert Hoover campaign slogan, 1928

*T*HE FORCEFUL CHARACTER THAT had made Herbert Hoover so successful in directing the humanitarian aid programs in Europe during World War I would serve to make him the very model of a modern Progressive Cabinet officer for Presidents Harding and Coolidge. But that same inflexible belief in his ability to depend on efficient voluntarism in response to social and economic problems would destroy his Presidency.

When he was considering a run for the Presidency, Hoover was well aware that there was a possible disaster looming that was eerily similar to the euphoric period just before today's global financial crisis. The Roaring Twenties had seen a level of prosperity that Americans were convinced would never end. He knew better but was at a loss as to how to respond. A housing shortage had sent U.S. home prices soaring and touched off a bubble of bogus real estate schemes that roiled the markets first in Florida and California before spreading to other parts of the nation. Lax rules on Wall Street permitted shaky share offerings to credulous investors who borrowed heavily in the hopes of instant fortunes. Commodity prices began to fall, and banks began to seize farms in foreclosure. In Europe, debt-heavy governments reacted to shrinking export markets with trade barriers on imports and by devaluing their currencies. Particularly in Germany, Britain, and France, factory closures and horrendous inflation drove the middle classes and the poor into the ranks of radical political movements.

But in the methodical mind of Herbert Hoover, the best thing to do was concentrate on problems that looked as if they could be more immediately addressed. This was a view admittedly shared by most of the other major statesmen of the day. So the focus of most public debate and Hoover's own public concerns were centered on the international debt stalemate and the need to further empty the armories of war weapons that were being stockpiled around the globe. He had reason to feel optimistic, for this time, the White House appeared within his reach without his having to face the distasteful obligation of engaging in political maneuvering to get there.

Hoover had shown no ill will when the Republican Old Guard had outmaneuvered his own presidential chances in 1920. He had gamely supported Harding. He then surprised everyone by agreeing to be the next secretary of commerce, a department with no discernible mandate or programs. Hoover intended to change all that. He saw the chance to apply his faith that experts could both make government more cost effective and free up a modernizing American economy by applying efficient standards and practices.

With President Harding's bemused consent, Hoover "coordinated" new economic policies that ranged throughout the jurisdictions of nearly every other Cabinet bureaucracy—earning him the nickname of "Secretary of Commerce and Undersecretary of Everything Else." He wrung voluntary agreements from a host of industrial groups for nationwide standards and self-imposed regulation. He used government controls and licensing as a way to help business achieve a more orderly marketplace, in effect ending cutthroat competition and assuring secure market shares for innovators in radio broadcasting, air travel, manufacturing standardization and even a national pact that unified highway traffic signals.

While Coolidge came to resent the constant flow of unsolicited advice he received from Hoover ("Wonder Boy" was one of Coolidge's nicknames for him), he could not ignore the heavy support the secretary was getting from business groups who prospered under this self-regulatory environment, especially since Hoover also insisted on aggressively promoting expansion of American goods into the European export market.

But just as he had been one of the prime movers in the 1922 Washington naval limits treaty, Hoover continued to press the White House to remain a major player in the ongoing efforts to disarm the world through further cutbacks in naval power and then, hopefully, to reduce the need for land-based weapons and even of armies. Disarmament for Hoover, as for most Progressives, remained the key to both restoring political and economic stability in Europe and ensuring continued prosperity for American exporters of farm and manufactured products. Hoover economics also saw the rise of de facto cartels, first in an Anglo-American oil pact (the forerunner of the OPEC cartel today), then for major industrial materials such as nickel, copper, and textiles.

However, where Harding had been receptive to the disarmament movement, Coolidge was both indifferent and skeptical. Moreover, Coolidge was weary of the Presidency; the sudden death of his younger son, sixteen-year-old Calvin Jr., in 1924 sent him into periodic bouts of depression during the rest of his time in office. In the end, Coolidge was forced to acknowledge the reality that other nations had resumed an arms buildup of significance and that the United States either had to join that race or find a way to halt it. By 1926, Britain had three times as many cruisers either in service or under construction as did the U.S. Navy; Japan already had twice as many. France and Italy were engaged in their own naval rivalry in the Mediterranean, and even the Weimar government of Germany had begun to expand its military beyond the Versailles Treaty limits—a program that began in earnest in 1928.[1]

Bowing to pressure in February 1927, Coolidge issued a call for a five-power meeting to further reduce naval weaponry; significantly, he recommended the meeting take place in Geneva but outside the framework of the League of Nations. Neither France nor Italy (both felt cheated by the 1922 pact) agreed to participate. Predictably, the British and Japanese delegations that did attend the six weeks of wrangling found plenty of technical reasons why they could refuse specific reductions in their planned construction of the various naval craft; any agreement was made more doubtful by the active interference of lobbyists for the major steel producers who crowded the conference hallways.

The only success to come out of the conference was to the reputation of Allen Dulles as an international negotiator. The final weeks of the negotiations came to center on what became known as The Dulles Clause, a compromise proposal that he advanced to enable Britain and Japan to pledge to halt their construction plans through 1936, with the option that any of the signatories could alter its plans for specific types of ships from 1931 onward. The Japanese, who secretly had no intentions of halting their expansion plans, publicly agreed, but the British, firmly unwilling to share naval supremacy of the seas with the U.S. Navy, flatly refused, and the conferees gave up.[2]

The collapse of the Geneva talks did have another consequence. The French, realizing the dangers in a revived global warship race, suggested a bilateral security treaty with the United States. Coolidge, having taken himself out of contention for the Presidency in the coming year, tossed the question to a doubting Secretary of State Kellogg who upped the ante by suggesting to French foreign minister Aristide Briand that the treaty be expanded into a general declaration outlawing war of any kind. This led to the Kellogg-Briand Pact in which sixty-two nations pledged in 1928 to abstain from "war as an instrument of national policy." Though there was a euphoric public reaction to what one newspaper called "The Magna Charta of Peace," more sober observers noted that the pact contained no time frame and no mechanism to enforce the pledge, and it did not address the race to rearm that was going on around the world. In Washington, the same Congress that ratified the treaty also appropriated new funds for the construction of fifteen cruisers and a new aircraft carrier for the U.S. Navy, just to be on the safe side.

On his return to New York from Geneva, Allen Dulles found himself something of a Progressive celebrity. He was eagerly recruited by Hamilton Fish Armstrong to join the Council on Foreign Relations and to take an active part in its various study groups on international issues. There quickly developed a close friendship between the ebullient, hyperactive Dulles and the quiet, deliberate Ham Armstrong that expanded beyond the meetings of the Council on Foreign Relations.

In the five years of its existence, the CFR, and its quarterly journal *Foreign Affairs,* had become a Progressive stronghold of internationalism, a kind of shadow State Department. At this distance, it is hard to appreciate just what a vacuum existed in how American foreign affairs were conducted during the 1920s. While the two secretaries—Charles Evans Hughes and Frank Kellogg—were men of ability, they still presided over a tiny, badly paid department, which by necessity was forced to react to events rather than formulate any forward-reaching strategic plan. Yet with the memory of the Great War's horror still fresh in the world's mind, there was a palpable hunger for some new way to be found to perpetuate peace.

While both Chatham House and the CFR had first been formed to help perfect the blemishes in the Versailles Treaty, both groups found themselves expanding into international forums where the major players came to reason over the issues of the moment. The list of speakers who came to New York to address CFR members—and thus a wider American audience through press coverage—encompassed nearly every player of consequence in international affairs: France's prime minister Georges Clemenceau, Britain's prime minister Ramsay MacDonald, Germany's chancellor Heinrich Bruening, and the Soviet Union's foreign minister Maxim Litvinov all appeared at CFR sessions. Many also wrote articles for *Foreign Affairs,* as did numerous Chatham House members including Philip Kerr (who had resigned from Lloyd George's service to resume editing *The Round Table*) and Eustace Percy (now a Member of Parliament).

While Allen's brother Foster had been one of the founding members of the CFR, he had remained preoccupied with Sullivan & Cromwell's aggressive deal making in Europe and was only an occasional participant in the Council's studies. But increasingly, whenever a study group was organized to consider the latest development in arms limitation or some European political dispute, Allen Dulles invariably ended up as the de facto chairman of the group. Together with Walter Lippmann, Allen and Ham became influential Progressive voices as a series of ill-fated conferences alternated between Geneva and London, even as the technology of war shifted the naval forces of the major powers from unwieldy battleships to more deadly aircraft carriers and submarines.

At this point in early 1928, most Progressives—especially the Dupont Circle set—made a curious set of political choices that had far-reaching consequences. With fellow House of Truth visitor Herbert Hoover a dead certainty to be the Republican presidential nominee and likely the next occupant in the White House, the Progressive movement instead rallied once again behind the controversial banner of Al Smith. While few of them disliked Hoover personally, his refusal to join the Democrats as their candidate in 1920 with FDR as a running mate was seen as an affront they could not forgive. Now, after eight years of Republican control, the Progressives were hungry, if not for jobs in government, at least for political influence.

Whether Smith really thought he could transcend the widespread distrust that many Midwestern Democrats had for his Catholic faith and anti-Prohibition stance is an open question. And as with Hoover's image of being the inevitable nominee for the Republicans, there was a general feeling among Democrats that "it's Al's turn." He had been a popular New York Governor who instituted numerous Progressive reforms; he led a powerful political network of big city machines, and he spoke for an emerging dominant bloc of Irish, Italian, and Jewish voters that was growing nationwide. And despite his Tammany ties, he was generally conceded to be an honest man.

But Smith was enough of a realist to fear that Hoover's popularity was so great that a Republican wave would not only defeat his own campaign but would also give GOP candidates a complete sweep of New York's state government as well. So at the Democratic nominating convention that June in Houston, Smith paid less attention to the party's choice for his vice-presidential running mate (an obscure Arkansas senator named Joseph Taylor Robinson) and more to courting a reluctant Franklin Roosevelt to come out of political retirement and run as his successor as New York's governor.

Roosevelt, who was now spending most of his time developing his Warm Springs treatment center and enduring painful exercises to strengthen his legs, had a number of reasons to decline an arduous statewide campaign just to ensure Smith would keep New York's electoral votes. FDR had invested a substantial amount of his personal fortune in the Warm Springs project. He not only believed in the greater good that the treatment center might bring to others, but he was also convinced in his own mind that his impressive progress in regaining mobility would require at least two years more of arduous therapy and would surely lead to his being able to walk again unaided. Moreover, he and Louis Howe agreed that Hoover's likely election probably meant their old acquaintance would remain in the White House for at least eight years. By 1936, they concluded, the time would be right for a revival of Democratic Party fortunes and his own re-entry onto the national stage.

Still, FDR's uncanny intuition about political trends clearly tempted him to venture back into the public eye if only to gauge whether he still had a following. There were clear signs that his friends among the Dupont Circle set and other Progressive allies were looking past Smith as their spokesman and searching for a future leader. He drew some quiet encouragement from the revived flow of letters he was receiving from old Dupont Circle friends such as Lippmann, Frankfurter, and others.

To test these waters in the weeks leading up to the convention, Roosevelt accepted an invitation from Ham Armstrong to write an essay for *Foreign Affairs* that criticized the Harding-Coolidge conduct of U.S. foreign policy in general and the naval disarmament issue in particular. Even though the magazine would not appear until weeks after the convention, FDR had advance copies printed and distributed to every delegate.[3] Among the consultants whose advice he sought were the omnipresent Colonel House, Lippmann, and his old protégé Sumner Welles.

Although FDR intended the article to form the basis for the party's foreign policy, Armstrong and other Progressives were frankly confused that much of what Roosevelt argued ran contrary to his previous positions throughout the 1920 campaign and during his time in the Wilson wartime administration. Where once he had been the most vocal advocate of the Big Navy interests, he now flatly saw "no real need for much more than a police force on the seas of the civilized world today." This was a misstep. Progressives may have been internationalists, but they were American internationalists, and a strong U.S. naval presence was considered prudent as long as other nations—the British and Japanese in particular—seemed bent on dominating the seas. FDR also tempered his advocacy of American membership in the League of Nations; now he said the United States could do well to be more cooperative as an outsider in League programs on health, education, and labor standards. Some of his demands for a less imperialistic policy toward Latin America bore the clear imprint of Welles. Other pronouncements were vague enough to be incomprehensible.

To Kenneth S. Davis and other Roosevelt biographers, FDR was habitually opaque on his personal beliefs throughout his life, so he could be free to jettison commitments on specific issues as the public mood or political opportunity shifted. What Roosevelt truly believed in, in short, was in Franklin Roosevelt and his destiny. As Davis describes it:

> If never openly contemptuous of pure thought—certainly he was never assertively so—he had nothing to do with it, personally. It was irrelevant to his vital concerns. It could even be hazardous to these—it might prevent his making the right career decision at a crucial moment—from small but important signs or cues presented him by and through his immediate environmental situation. For, to repeat, at the root and core of his

conception of self and world was the inward certainty that he was a "chosen one" of the Almighty, his career a role assigned him by the Author of the universe, and that the "part" he must "act" or "play" to the best of his ability, feeling himself into it, even identifying with it, up to a point, was of major historical importance.[4]

In what can only be considered a calculated preparation, Roosevelt agreed to act as Smith's floor manager at the convention and to reprise his 1924 nominating speech, this one carefully drafted by Smith's suspicious team of advisers. As he later confessed to Lippmann, FDR promptly rewrote the speech to accommodate his confident cadence, less for the convention delegates and more for the far wider audience of radio listeners who would hear the speech on an unusual nationwide broadcast. And ever aware of his stage presence, FDR recruited his teenage son Elliott for the hard physical task of walking with his father's iron grip on his elbow as a prop as he prepared to "walk" without crutches when he appeared on the platform to nominate Smith.

The gushing response to FDR's appearance on the stage in Houston and to his enthusiastic praise of the nominee may have surprised even Roosevelt, and it certainly gave Smith and his supporters pause. Newspapers, including those firmly in the Republican camp, praised both the speech and its dramatic impact. Floods of mail and telegrams congratulating him poured into his New York offices. Roosevelt, sensing the revived suspicion from the Smith camp, wisely retreated back to Warm Springs. And that might well have been the end of it had not Hoover's campaign begun to show signs of moving beyond victory and turning into a landslide that frightened the Democrats with virtual extinction.

Despite enormous popularity among the general population, Hoover recognized he was regarded with some hesitancy by the Old Guard of the Republican Party, some of whom still nurtured hopes of drafting Coolidge to run again. He had to face the fact that, while he had spurned his Dupont Circle friends among Progressives by becoming a Republican in 1920, he had not achieved a real claim on the affections of his own party except for his electability. He had not bothered to build the kind of intra-party base that Franklin Roosevelt had with his now huge collection of data cards of regional Democratic activists across the country. In truth, Hoover disdained rank and file politicians generally, and it showed. But he did go to some lengths the year before to remedy that deficiency, and the results frightened Democratic regulars.

The catastrophic Mississippi River floods of 1927 caused more than $400 million in destruction and killed hundreds of people and drove thousands more from their homes in a ten-state swath of high water that reached sixty miles wide. The Commerce Secretary became the national hero of the hour when he took over relief operations; in the process he gained enormous political support among white Southern politicians who historically had been loyal Democrats. At least part of this good will came at the expense of African American refugees who were treated shamefully. Where whites were rescued, black families were left in harm's way or relegated to barbaric camps where they were forced—sometimes at gunpoint—to labor to rebuild levees. Social historians generally cite this episode as a cause of the subsequent wave of migration that took thousands of African Americans out of the South and into the relative civility and jobs of Northern cities. Hoover stifled protests by black leaders by promising to address racial problems more aggressively when he became president, a promise he then broke, which touched off a second wave of migration in 1932 as blacks who could vote in major cities decamped to Franklin Roosevelt and the Democratic Party.

In the late summer of 1928, Hoover appeared invincible, and Smith renewed his efforts to coax FDR into running for the governorship. He shrewdly enlisted the support of the one person in FDR's inner circle who might be willing to lure him into the campaign. Eleanor Roosevelt had evolved into a highly respected political organizer in her own right and to a large extent had created her own existence and identity, one that was separate and distinct from her life with FDR.

There probably will always remain an element of speculation (some of it salacious) as to the exact nature of the friendship that sprang up between Eleanor, Nancy Cook, and Marion Dickerman. When Louis Howe had nudged Eleanor into a more active role in Democratic Party affairs in 1922, Cook and Dickerman were already prominent political figures and partners in a firmly committed personal relationship.[5] It is symptomatic of the cultural attitudes toward homosexuality of those days that same-sex relations between women drew merely raised eyebrows where the full weight of the law could be brought down on gay men. Cook was the executive secretary of the Women's Division of the party; Dickerman was a teacher at the exclusive Todhunter School for Girls in Manhattan, where the social activist curriculum reminded Eleanor of her own schooling in Britain. Over time, the three would become so close that they bought the school (Eleanor taught there part-time) and they established their own home at a cottage on the Hyde Park grounds that FDR had built for them and where Eleanor preferred to be during his lengthy absences.

That friendship clearly gave Eleanor the confidence to expand her horizons and reach out to other political women's groups, trade union officials, health advocates, and street-level political organizers. With Louis Howe's initial coaching, the three published a monthly political newsletter, and Eleanor began to earn respectable amounts of money on her own as an improved public speaker and an essayist in popular women's magazines.

Most importantly in 1928, Eleanor had earned a more cordial place in the Al Smith entourage than had her husband had. She had been a tireless campaigner for Smith in 1924 and had been an effective force in the 1926 election of Smith protégé Robert F. Wagner to the U.S. Senate. She was very active in Smith's 1928 bid as well, and it was to her the governor turned in October, just days before the New York Democrats were to have their own state convention, to reach Roosevelt. FDR did not have a telephone at the Warm Springs cottage, but it was Eleanor who lured him into a booth at a drugstore in a nearby village and then handed the telephone over to Smith who finally won his agreement to run for governor.

The irony is of course that Hoover's strategy prevailed. He not only carried five Southern states that had been resolutely Democratic since the Civil War, but he carried most of New England as well, including New York. Franklin Roosevelt, on the other hand, was narrowly elected governor by a twenty-five-thousand–vote margin and, preferences aside, found himself back on the national political stage both as the chief executive of a major state and as a potential heir to Smith's party leadership.

The presidency of Herbert Hoover demonstrates the shortcomings of political ideology when it comes in contact with an unexpected reality. He was fifty-five when he was sworn into office in March 1929 and was firm in his determination to pursue an enlightened foreign policy even as he pursued a domestic program that emphasized industry self-regulation and voluntary action by special interest groups; his faith in experts in specific industries to lead the way remained unchallenged.

The end result was that during the decade in which most of the Dupont Circle set and other Progressives had grown and expanded their system of beliefs to adjust to the revolutions going on in nearly all areas of life in the Jazz Age, Hoover remained locked into a set of responses to a world that no longer existed. Had the American economy remained on its upward trajectory, he might have had the time to adjust. As things stood, Hoover proceeded on from his election as if the wild bubble of speculation, inflated share prices, and paper prosperity would continue unabated.

Within days of his election in 1928, Hoover set out on an eight-week tour of Latin America that had partly been informed by a two-volume history of the Dominican Republic that Sumner Welles had just published and which had caused widespread favorable comment. *Naboth's Vineyard* was both a history of that troubled island nation and a scathing critique of U.S. policies in Latin America, which, Welles charged, "floundered too long between the sane and salutary, on one hand, and blustering intimidation on the other."[6] It was in the best interests of American security to foster economic growth and stability through cooperation with Latin American governments rather than impose it by military force.

Welles was not the only voice arguing for what would, under Franklin Roosevelt, become known as the Good Neighbor policy for the hemisphere. Hoover's choice for secretary of state was Felix Frankfurter's old mentor Henry Stimson, who just the year before had been sent to resolve conflicts with Nicaragua. At Stimson's urging, Hoover on his tour of South America won widespread applause for announcing that he would break with the hated policy set by Theodore Roosevelt back in 1904 that was known as the Roosevelt Corollary. This policy expanded the traditional U.S. policy called the Monroe Doctrine that banned European nations from interfering in Latin America. The new policy meant that the United States could do what it forbade European governments to do—to intervene with troops to collect government debts and even to interfere with governments—with impunity, especially when American commercial interests were threatened. From now on, Hoover pledged, U.S. Marines and soldiers would not be tools of American imperialism; there were promises that the restrictive trade barriers to imports from the region would be ended.

While, as one biographer noted, America under Hoover "began to act like a better, if not good, neighbor" in the region, U.S. troops remained guarding American property in hot spots like Nicaragua and Haiti but did not interfere in revived turmoil in Cuba (which had been commonplace before.)[7] However, Hoover's early hints at more liberal trade treatment and political outreach were never addressed. Part of this lack had to do with Hoover's somewhat distant relationship with the Republican majority leaders in the Congress, who were more interested in protecting the trade interests of their constituents. Then too, Hoover was deliberate by nature, and he thought, with reason, that he had plenty of time. In that he was cruelly mistaken.

Equally significant was the fact that whatever good will his Progressive past had brought with him to the White House was rapidly slipping away as his friends from the Dupont Circle days were growing more impatient, more assertive—indeed more radical—as their own careers matured. They came to agree that Hoover was not moving fast enough or going far enough on any number of issues to suit them. In the meantime, events were about to overtake Hoover's vision of the future and render it moot.

The irony of the 1929 stock market crash that sparked the Great Depression of the 1930s is that Herbert Hoover had been one of the few early voices who warned that a bubble was being created that would eventually burst. As early as 1926, the then commerce secretary had predicted that,

> Real estate and stock speculation and its possible extension into commodities with inevitable inflation, the overextension of installment buying, the continued instability of certain foreign countries, and the fever of speculation resting on overoptimism can only land us on the shores of overdepression.[8]

But like everyone else, Hoover saw the stock market turmoil through the early months of 1930 as an inevitable (and perhaps salutary) economic correction in American markets and not as the fundamental financial crisis that was gripping most of Europe. So, well-known financiers made flamboyant gestures of investing even more money into shares while government officials, including New York's governor-elect, assured the public that all would be well.

Hoover defenders like to point out that by 1932, many of the so-called New Deal programs credited to President Roosevelt were already in place: Emergency unemployment benefits, public works, farm aid, and government rules to stabilize prices all were authorized by Congress. But the hard truth was that Hoover drew back from making full use of these weapons because they conflicted with his free market faith.

Part of that faith was anchored in the widespread belief that American capital could still be used to stimulate the economies of Europe, and they, in turn, would stimulate their orders for American exports, thereby bringing stability and prosperity to both sides of the Atlantic. It did not occur to him—or to the heads of the Federal Reserve or their opposite numbers in the central banks of Europe—that the Fed's rapid expansion of credit and Wall Street's retailing of it abroad was the proximate cause and not the cure of the shaky financial foundations of the Western economies. As far as Hoover was concerned, he was taking steps to remedy the international situation, and the domestic crisis would, in time, correct itself without much Washington interference. In essence, Hoover was still trying to solve the problems left over from World War I without realizing he was just a few months away from the beginnings of a second global conflict.

In February 1929, one of his first acts, this one taken as President-elect, had been to urge the appointment of a special committee to re-negotiate the still-vexing question of German war reparations. Those debts had been officially reduced once already in the early 1920s. Now, Owen D. Young, head of General Electric, led a committee in Paris that cut the German obligations by 20 percent to roughly eight billion dollars. The meeting also led to the creation of the Bank for International Settlements, a formal mechanism that was to handle the actual transfer of debt payments—whether reparations or official loans—between nations.

As dramatic as the Young Plan appeared to be, it was too late. The German economy was trapped between its inability to buy needed raw materials from abroad and its inability to sell its exports abroad. France and Britain were in the midst of their own economic crisis as their own currencies were trapped between the limitations of the gold standard and the need to pump more liquidity into their economies to pay for social programs. Exacerbating the situation was a ramping up of naval and land-based weapons spending that was going on everywhere.

So when British prime minister Ramsay MacDonald came to the Council on Foreign Relations for a speech in the autumn of 1929 to suggest a new naval disarmament conference be held, Hoover jumped at the idea. Unlike the failed 1927 Geneva negotiations, Hoover handpicked the American negotiators—including Norman Davis and Allen Dulles—and put the power to reach agreement in the hands of the civilian delegates and not the admirals who accompanied them.

The London Naval Conference, which ran through the spring of 1930, proved to be the high-water mark of the disarmament movement. This time, all five major powers attended, and all five agreed to a five-year moratorium on battleship and large cruiser construction; there also were new limits placed on the use of submarines and aircraft carriers. Not all of the parties were completely happy with the pact. France and Italy were determined to checkmate each other in the Mediterranean, and Japan was already poised for the invasion of Manchuria, which it would launch in 1931. But Hoover could point with some pride that an agreement had been reached and that part of the arms buildup had at least been put on hold. Moreover, the conferees had agreed to a second round of further reductions in 1935, with planning to begin a year before.

Hoover might be excused for thinking he still had time to maneuver, but he was wrong. In June 1930, Hoover reluctantly signed into law the Smoot-Hawley Tariff bill that imposed prohibitive customs duties on most of the major goods sold in America by European trade partners. Although its Congressional sponsors had intended the new protectionist tariffs to shelter U.S. producers, it had the opposite effect, and the already high unemployment rate nearly doubled that summer. In the autumn elections, the Republican majority in the Senate was reduced, and the GOP leadership in the House hung on a single vote majority, which left the president's ability to push through any new remedies paralyzed.

If the Smoot-Hawley tariffs stifled American imports, they were a disaster that sent European finances into a downward spiral of frightening dimensions. Hoover tried one last effort. In the summer of 1931, he proposed a moratorium on all reparations and debt payments, but while all of Europe leapt to agree, the recalcitrant Congress balked at ratification until December, and even then refused him the authority to pursue another round of restructuring talks.

With the 1932 presidential elections looming, Hoover found himself politically neutered and completely repudiated by his former Progressive allies. Instead of waiting until 1936 to attempt their comeback, Progressives generally, and the Dupont Circle set in particular, began to consider who their leader would be that would bring them back to power.

Franklin Roosevelt, who had been lauded for his social reforms as governor (and handily re-elected to another two-year term in 1930) was just one of the possibilities.

Thirteen

THE MAKING OF A PRESIDENT

1932–1933

"He [Roosevelt] is a pleasant man who, without any important qualifications for the office, would very much like to be President."

—Walter Lippmann, *New York Herald Tribune,* January 1932

*B*Y EARLY IN 1932, THE DUPONT CIRCLE set and other Progressives sensed that their political fortunes had been revived by Herbert Hoover's perceived failures. But there was uncertainty about whom they should choose as their standard-bearer. Franklin D. Roosevelt was not an automatic heir apparent by any means. However, these old friends were sure of one thing: that they must take an active role in directing that choice in the months ahead.

Just as Sumner Welles had used his exile from government to establish his credentials as a leading expert on Latin America, others from the group also had achieved national reputations.

From his post at the Harvard Law School, Felix Frankfurter had become the nation's most visible and controversial legal advocate for labor and civil liberties cases. The 1920s had been highlighted by major court actions involving nearly every phase of American economic life and individual liberties. Nearly every facet of economic security we enjoy today—minimum wage standards, child labor laws, union contracts, etc.—all were hammered in court challenges that were headline news. As one of the early founders of the American Civil Liberties Union, Frankfurter worked tirelessly both in courtrooms and in arguments he wrote for *The New Republic* and elsewhere to spark the public conscience. But none of the causes he undertook was more emotionally charged than the seven-year controversy involving the murder conviction of two Italian anarchists named Nicola Sacco and Bartolomeo Vanzetti who, it now appears likely, were wrongly charged with a factory robbery in Massachusetts in 1920 where the paymaster and a guard were killed.

The visibly unfair series of court cases that followed the original conviction dragged on through the decade and became a touchstone of Progressive protests that spread worldwide and led to demonstrations in major foreign capitals and pleas for clemency from leading European statesmen. When in 1927 Harvard President A. Lawrence Lowell chaired a special citizens committee to review the case and concluded there was no reason to overturn the verdict, Frankfurter wrote a lengthy and impressive legal counterattack for *The Atlantic Monthly* urging a retrial.[1]

The article (which did not forestall the execution) made Frankfurter a national figure and underscored an ongoing battle he had been having with the Harvard administration. Lowell had systematically been trying to reduce the number of Jewish and African American students at the university by proposing various quota schemes.

The dispute led to an argument between Frankfurter and his old friend Walter Lippmann who, while opposing a strict quota on Jewish enrollees at Harvard, suggested that Jews might find it prudent to go to other universities to lessen their visibility at Harvard. But their friendship continued, bound in part by their loneliness; the marriages of both men had deteriorated to the point that their work and their political beliefs were more important. Lippmann was totally disenchanted with the more social and less politically interested Faye. Marion Frankfurter, who had always been highly strung, lapsed into a series of breakdowns that caused her to be institutionalized for long periods of time, leaving Felix bereft. The quarrel over the Harvard quotas and the rise of anti-Jewish senti-ment in the country underscored their outsider status.

Lippmann had always felt ambivalence about his Jewish identi-ty, and that feeling had been heightened by his emerging role as one of the most influential journalists and opinion makers of the day. He had resigned from *The New Republic* in 1921 and spent the rest of the year drafting what would become his most influential book of political thought, one that remains relevant and in circulation even today—*Public Opinion.* In far stronger terms and with more convincing examples, Lippmann expanded on his earlier theme in *Liberty and the News.*

Public Opinion argued that the pleasant image of the rational, well-informed citizen as the cornerstone of healthy democracy probably never existed in the past but certainly was not a reality in a modern mass society where, as he said, consent is "manufactured" by government institutions and commercial interests. "In the great blooming buzzing confusion of the outer world we pick out what our culture has already defined for us, and we tend to perceive that which we have pulled out in the form stereotyped for us by our cul-ture," he wrote.[2] What was needed, he repeated, was a reliance on experts to translate reality into palatable stereotypes so that public opinion could be marshaled in support of enlightened government.

The book was an immediate hit in Progressive circles and was another reason he agreed in 1922 to become an editorial writer on the *New York World.* The *World* had been the yellow journal-ism property of Joseph Pulitzer and a rival of William Randolph Hearst's sensationalist newspapers. But Pulitzer's heirs were deter-mined to transform the paper into a liberal intellectual showpiece. Under the editorship of the flamboyant Herbert Bayard Swope, the paper began to feature star writers such as Heywood Broun, George S. Kaufman, Edna Ferber, Ring Lardner, and Lippmann.

By 1924, Lippmann was chief of the editorial board, and dur-ing the seven years that the *World* remained in business he would write twelve hundred editorials, one third of them on foreign policy matters that became required reading not only in New York but in

Washington as well.[3] That same year he began to write for *Foreign Affairs* and soon formed a close friendship with Ham Armstrong that led him to take an active role in planning CFR studies on various international issues.

It was through Lippmann's prompting in 1928 that Armstrong had reached out to Franklin Roosevelt for the foreign policy essay that was supposed to be the Democratic Party's manifesto. By that time, Lippmann was bombarding Roosevelt with "Dear Frank" letters of advice on politics and social policy. Frankfurter was equally quick to revive his prewar friendship with Roosevelt, but unlike his old housemate Lippmann, he established a warm social relationship with the new governor and made himself an indispensable source of advice on political appointments as well as on policy issues. Roosevelt for his part was grateful for the flattery he received from Frankfurter, but he especially valued the law professor's ability to frame issues on complicated questions—struggles over electric power, highway construction, prison reform, and political appointments—so that the choices were easier to make.

In this Frankfurter differed sharply from Lippmann's faith in the preeminence of experts in political decisions. As he wrote to Roosevelt, he opposed "a new type of oligarchy, namely, government by experts . . . experts should be on tap but not on top."[4]

Roosevelt, however, became increasingly dependent on "experts" as he entered his second two-year term as governor and tried to see over the political horizon as the next presidential contest drew near. He began to seek advice—the "cues" Kenneth Davis called them—from a wide range of advisers, never committing to any one policy or attitude and often contradicting himself as the wind shifted. To Frankfurter's dismay, he found his recommendations on economic reforms having to compete with a group of Columbia University economists—Rexford Tugwell, Raymond Moley, and Adolph Berle—who advocated far more aggressive government intervention in economic affairs than he thought wise. The three would form the nucleus of FDR's famed Brain Trust during the early days of the New Deal, although Frankfurter would outlast them all in influence.

It was clear to Progressives that their first task was to find a candidate who could convince the voters that the Democratic Party could produce the remedies that would cure the economic crisis that was gripping America. Part of the problem was that there were too many choices. The 1924 nominee and CFR president John Davis had loyalists. Al Smith had made it clear he wanted another chance. And in their hearts, most Progressives still considered Newton Baker, the former secretary of war (now a judge of the International Court at The Hague), as the ideological ideal Democrat.

But a slow consensus was building that Franklin Roosevelt was the most electable prospect. His popularity as a visible big state governor, his skilled use of radio to reach nationwide audiences, and the tireless networking that the Cufflinks Gang kept up among party activists had to be weighed against the fear that he was a lightweight. As Frankfurter summed up his feelings in a letter to Lippmann, "I know his [FDR's] limitations. Most of them derive, I believe, from a lack of an incisive intellect and a kind of optimism that sometimes makes him timid, as well as an ambition that leads to compromises with which we were familiar in Theodore Roosevelt and Wilson."[5]

As much to hedge their bets as anything, many of the Dupont Circle set began to create a political identity for Franklin Roosevelt, which he was happy enough for them to do. Nowhere was the struggle more intense than on the issues of foreign policy, disarmament, and the search for peace.

Sumner Welles already was FDR's closest adviser on how to improve America's relations with its Latin American neighbors. From Paris, William Bullitt, through his letters to Colonel House, bombarded Roosevelt urging him to consider diplomatic recognition of the Soviet Union. In the summer of 1931, Roosevelt took the initiative of seeking out Colonel Edward M. House asking him for advice on campaign strategy with an emphasis on foreign policy matters just as he had for Woodrow Wilson fifteen years earlier.

House was now in his seventies and unwilling to take on more than a general advisory role. He turned to Ham Armstrong to help him fashion the international policies he wanted Roosevelt to follow if he were elected. Armstrong, in a memo to himself, recorded the conversation with House, one that reflected the general ambivalence among the Dupont Circle set:

> House said between you and me and the angels that he did not think Roosevelt a great man, and that he would not say he was the best man in sight for the presidency. Merely that he was an honest, able man and the most available candidate that stood the best chance of election if he were nominated. He pointed out that his present definite support is in just about the same states that Wilson had before his first nomination. . . . He said that he thought [Newton] Baker came nearer to being the Wilson type than any other man in the country today. I'd very much like to see Baker president, he said. But it would be much harder to elect him than to elect Roosevelt. . . . One of the things that makes House anxious to keep in close touch with Roosevelt is in order to influence his appointments in case he is elected. He said that his candidate for Secretary of State would be Baker.[6]

If Roosevelt was aware of the uncertain loyalties of many of his closest advisers, he never let on. When the Democrats gathered in Chicago on June 27, 1932 to begin the week-long nominating process, the team Roosevelt had on hand to help draft the foreign policy plank in the platform included Welles, Armstrong, and a young diplomatic journalist friend of Welles named Drew Pearson. Lippmann, for his part, remained aloof from FDR and worked behind the scenes at the convention to stir up delegate support for Newton Baker. Still, he was careful to avoid a break with his friends that would taint his access to Roosevelt.

The foreign policy pledge that the Democrats offered voters was hardly revolutionary; it pledged to lower tariffs on trade, to uphold the Monroe Doctrine, to oppose Hoover's call to renegotiate the remaining war debts and loans, and to try to foster the Kellogg-Briand pact that outlawed war. The voters, understandably, paid more attention to Roosevelt's pledge to repeal Prohibition, to reform Wall Street, to balance the budget, and to restore prosperity.

But even before the November election, Armstrong and House moved to nudge Roosevelt into a number of more progressive foreign policy initiatives. Their plan was to have House write an article for *Foreign Affairs* that would clearly state important objectives in that area without tying the president-elect to actions that he might later regret. On the Sunday after the election, Armstrong and his wife Helen took a draft of the House article to Hyde Park for FDR's approval. In a memo to himself, Armstrong described the event:

> Helen and I motored up to Hyde Park for lunch with the Roosevelts, and in particular so that I could go over with Governor Roosevelt the text of the article written by Col. House for the next issue of *Foreign Affairs*. We arrived at about twelve just as the family was getting back from church. Lord and Lady Astor were with them. Amelia Earhart and her husband were also staying at the house. . . . Lady Astor sat next to the governor and kept her end of the table in an uproar. She shook her finger under the governor's nose and said, "Franklin, don't get the idea that you want a second term. If you do, you will be a flop. If you can be a successful president for one term you will be much better remembered in history than if you were a bad president for two terms." The governor took it without a murmur, although I think he shrank a little from the attack.

After the lunch, Roosevelt met privately with Armstrong to go over the House article.

> On account of his paralysis he doesn't go upstairs if he can avoid it and they have turned the coat room into a sort of little study for him—very dark and crowded. There were piles of papers on all the chairs, piles of papers on the desk, piles all over the floor. He started by talking about the conference he is to have with Hoover on Tuesday about the war debt situation. He says it is a nasty situation, one which should not have risen in its present form. . . . He then looked at the House article and made editorial changes, reading it aloud with me going along on a carbon copy making the changes. "That's a good article. And I think it's a good plan to print it," at the end of the reading, he said. The

press had been waiting outside in the cold for quite a long time so the interview came to a close. He didn't give me the impression of hustling me out however, and all the way through was very friendly and cordial. He said quote, "That's a good-looking missus you have, and it's nice to see you both again. I want to have a longer talk with you when I get back from the South."[7]

The conversation between Armstrong and Roosevelt reveals several important points about the president-elect as he looked ahead. The most immediate one is that FDR was already behind the curve of events that were moving faster than he wanted to contemplate at that moment. Nevertheless, he was determined to keep control of his options while he made full use of the power he had just been given. He would not be bound by Hoover's promises on the debt question.

As carefully edited by FDR, the House article titled "Some Foreign Problems of the Next Administration," which appeared in the January 1933 issue of *Foreign Affairs,* was a vaguer version of the Democratic platform. It skimmed over the Japanese incursion into Manchuria, which had begun a year before. There was no concern voiced over the increasing bellicosity of Mussolini in the Mediterranean or the disturbing rise of Nazi power in Germany. Rather than fret over problems not immediately on the boil, the House-Roosevelt essay sent a clear signal that FDR intended to break with the foreign policy philosophy of the previous three presidents—and of many of his Progressive friends—who relied on multi-national conferences to reach broad consensus on issues of disarmament and economic disputes. Instead, there would be "a new deal in the spirit of our foreign policy," where the United States would negotiate bilateral understandings with one foreign partner at a time. In short, there would be no broad renegotiation of the huge sums owed by European borrowers of American dollars. He made it clear that President Hoover, in the interregnum between the November election and the inauguration in March, must not further commit to cancelling the foreign debts. Europe must settle its accounts with each other and with Wall Street. House also pledged that FDR would seek to lower tariff barriers to European and other exporters, but with the caveat that the objective was "to enable foreigners to earn enough dollars here to pay their debts and take our exports without the necessity of foreign loans"(italics included).[8]

Roosevelt also signaled that the Wilsonian dream of collective security was a dead issue. There was no revival of his spirited advocacy in 1920 of America joining the League of Nations. Here, Roosevelt was accurately reflecting a shift in the growing disenchantment with the League that many Progressives were feeling. While endorsing the Kellogg-Briand pact, FDR pointed toward the United States working for peace through direct negotiations with other nations on a bilateral basis. In part, Roosevelt was reflecting his personal suspicion of Britain's efforts to use its alliance with America to preserve its hold over its colonial territories in the Far East. He intended to keep America aloof from the contest for empires that was heating up among the European powers even as movements for self-government were springing up throughout the underdeveloped world.

Roosevelt made clear his determination to chart his own course when he and President Hoover met a few days later to discuss the transition of power, which would occur in March. FDR flatly rejected Hoover's suggestion that he signal his willingness to expand the temporary moratorium on all international debt schedules as a way to reverse the worsening global depression. Instead, Roosevelt emphasized his first objective would be to attend to America's immediate economic crisis regardless of the consequences abroad. In the weeks that followed, he reaffirmed his decision by naming as his secretary of state a man whose only foreign affairs qualification was that he was an ardent low-tariff advocate.

Cordell Hull was a tall, silver-haired, and pleasant man who had spent most of his life either as a congressman or senator from Tennessee. He had been a long-time friend of Roosevelt's, dating from the 1920 campaign when he had been chairman of the Democratic Party. Hull also had welcomed Eleanor Roosevelt's first forays into political activity and had appointed her to a number of party posts. At the 1924 convention, FDR had repaid the friendship by trying to get Hull nominated as vice president. Other than sharing the faith of most Southern politicians that high tariffs only served the interests of wealthy Northern manufacturers, Hull was singularly unacquainted with diplomatic matters, and that was what recommended him to Roosevelt, who intended to be his own foreign policy architect. Naming Hull gave Roosevelt a man who would not set himself up as a rival on foreign policy matters. Hull could also be counted upon to be a loyal lobbyist for the president among the Southern Democrats who controlled so many of the key Senate committees.

What Roosevelt did not know, and what Hull went to lengths to conceal, was the fact that the sixty-three-year-old Cabinet officer had just been diagnosed with diabetes and with tuberculosis lesions on his lungs. Although he would remain in office until 1944 and outlive Roosevelt by ten years, Hull was often sidelined with health issues that left his deputies in charge. And even when he was in remission from his illnesses, Hull often would—weather permitting—take his immediate staff off in the afternoon for an energetic croquet match at his estate that bordered on Rock Creek Park. From FDR's point of view, however, Hull could be counted upon to stay firmly loyal to the president despite being marginalized and often bypassed completely when important decisions had to be made.

However, other friends of FDR were determined to have an influence on the molding of his foreign policies even though it was clear the president's most pressing concerns were to revive the domestic catastrophe that gripped America. For one thing, the— Department of State was caught in its own budgetary crisis that virtually paralyzed it as an effective force even if the secretary had intended otherwise. In 1933, the department's staff numbered 708 in Washington with another 633 abroad in the Foreign Service posts around the world; this was actually fewer than there had been in 1920. Worse, Congress had so slashed the department's budgets that salaries were cut by 15 percent, and key allowances were cancelled. The exodus of talented careerists who could find work in the private sector continued to drain the department until well after 1936.[9]

The Council on Foreign Relations moved quickly to fill the vacuum in Roosevelt's policy planning process. Although *Foreign Affairs* never achieved a circulation beyond fifteen thousand during this time, it was considered mandatory reading among opinion-makers across the country. Moreover, branches of the Council were established in twenty-one major cities as forums where business leaders who shared the internationalist viewpoint held regular study sessions and conferences on regional questions.

So not only did the CFR carry a certain amount of weight with public opinion that FDR depended upon, there was also a growing sense of urgency among the old Dupont Circle habitués that the old concerns of the 1920s had been overtaken by events. While all of America and most of the rest of the world watched Franklin Roosevelt's dramatic efforts to stem the economic collapse during his first hundred days in office, Adolf Hitler and his Nazis were sweeping aside all opposition and beginning the systematic destruction of Germany's democracy as a prelude to his planned conquest of the rest of Europe.

Unlike Mussolini, whom some of the Progressives admired (despite his bombast and posturing) for uniting fractious Italy, it was hard to take Hitler seriously at first. Indeed, when Allen Dulles and Norman Davis made an early pilgrimage to Berlin to meet the new Reich Chancellor, they reported to President Roosevelt that Hitler would likely be toppled by the Nazis themselves and replaced with someone more substantial like Hermann Goering.[10]

Ham Armstrong, however, came away from his meeting with Hitler a few weeks later with a far darker understanding of what Hitler represented. In the July issue of *Foreign Affairs,* he declared,

> A people has disappeared. . . . So completely has the Repub-
> lic been wiped out that the Nazis find it difficult to believe that
> it ever existed, at any rate as more than a bad dream from which
> they were awakened by the sound of their own shouts of com-
> mand, their own marching feet.[11]

The essay was prescient to the extreme, considering it was written in the weeks after Hitler's accession to power. Yet it was clear to Armstrong or anyone who listened that Hitler's goals were as predetermined as they were frightening: a massive program of rearmament followed by (and here Armstrong listed specifically) the—annexation of Austria, the return of Danzig and Silesia from Poland, territories from Denmark, Lithuania, Belgium, as well as the Saar and Alsace from France. "National Socialism will last in Germany," he concluded.

What that meant is that even though the diplomats of the great powers would continue to meet in Geneva and London at various conferences on achieving further disarmament, it was a dead issue already. It would take Mussolini's invasion of Ethiopia in 1935 and the exodus of Germany and Japan out of the League for the death of the disarmament movement to be official. But the issue that now faced Roosevelt and the other Progressives of Dupont Circle could be summed up by another word that came into increasing use: neutrality.

If Europe was bent on another war and if Japan's increasing aggression in the Far East went unchecked, could America remain aloof? Just before Christmas 1933, Allen Dulles received a letter in Paris from Walter Mallory, the CFR's executive director, summoning him back to New York to act as secretary for a top-level conference on the neutrality issue to be held in early January 1934. The panel would be chaired by no less a figure than Henry Stimson, Hoover's secretary of state. The other invited conferees were the top rank of the American internationalist advocates and former Cabinet officers like Elihu Root, Newton Baker, Norman Davis, and John Davis, as well as senior executives from major corporations and Wall Street investment houses. The question to be posed at the January conference was to the point: Do the experiences of the war period, of postwar agreements and developments, or both, lead to the conclusion that there is room for modification in our traditional neutrality policy; if so, along what lines should such modification be made?[12]

Allen Dulles, Clover, and their three children had been commuting between houses on Long Island and Paris where Allen had divided his time since 1930. He had become his brother Foster's point man for the major financing deals Sullivan & Cromwell arranged with European industrialists and governments and at the same time was called upon as the unofficial U.S. legal representative at the almost-constant series of preliminary meetings and major conferences that sought to defuse the explosive slide toward war. In both cases he operated out of Sullivan & Cromwell's large offices on the Rue Cambon. He usually worked in tandem with Norman Davis, an official of the Morgan Bank interests, and his old friend Hugh Gibson, who continued in the Foreign Service. No one saw any conflict of interest in this relationship, and with the State Department on such short budgetary rations, Davis and Dulles were praised for their selfless service.

By then both men had come to agree with Armstrong's warnings about the new threats to U.S. security. As alarming as Hitler and Mussolini were becoming, there was an equally troubling shift in attitude within the United States itself. During most of the previous decade, America had been largely apathetic to foreign matters and preoccupied with the excitements of prosperity and jazz at home. But now, amidst the fears of economic collapse, a virulent form of isolationism had taken root. Various members of Congress began to charge that the big manufacturing firms—the "merchants of death"—who had prospered during the Great War were trying to push the country back into another foreign war so as to enhance their profits. This was given credence by recently disclosed evidence of how lobbyists for the various steel producers had wrecked the 1927 naval treaty meetings. There was a real battle brewing over America's role in world affairs, and that fight would be back in the United States, not in Paris. It was time to go home.

Other friends from the Dupont Circle days already had arrived back in Washington to seek places in the administration. William Bullitt had returned to America in 1932 and, through Colonel House, ingratiated himself with Roosevelt with a one-thousand-dollar campaign contribution and a detailed report on the European financial crisis that the candidate put to good use. In the months before the inauguration, FDR dispatched him back to Europe to conduct further private conversations with European leaders. And even though Bullitt leaked news of the task to the press and caused some embarrassment, he felt sure enough of his standing with the president-elect that he leased a large mansion in the exclusive Kalorama neighborhood that was just north of Dupont Circle and the old House of Truth.

Sumner and Mathilde Welles also had moved to even grander quarters than her mother's ornate mansion on Massachusetts Avenue. In part because he wanted to position himself in elective politics, he and Mathilde had bought a 250-acre estate about a half hour's drive from downtown Washington overlooking the Potomac River at Oxon Hill in Maryland. The Oxon Hill mansion and complex of barns and stables was a baronial estate that was created by the leading designers and architects of the day at a cost in current terms of more than two million dollars.

From Oxon Hill, Sumner began to take an active role in Maryland's turbulent political scene while at the same time working enthusiastically to advance Roosevelt's prospects. Both Franklin and Eleanor were delighted to accept Sumner's invitation to use Mathilde's Massachusetts Avenue mansion as their temporary quarters in the weeks before the inauguration; they ended up staying at the Mayflower Hotel because campaign advisers warned it looked unseemly to be staying in such posh surroundings in the midst of an economic crisis. Not that it mattered; Sumner and Mathilde were as much a part of the official party at the inauguration festivities as any of the Roosevelt children.

It was clear that Roosevelt was determined to surround himself with people whose personal loyalty to him was unquestionable. So his old boss, Navy Secretary Josephus Daniels, now in his seventies, was made ambassador to Mexico; another friend, Breckinridge Long, was named ambassador to Italy. FDR did not keep his protégé Welles in suspense for long; he would be made assistant secretary of state for Latin American Affairs.

Roosevelt also brought another important figure back into his life, although it was to remain a closely guarded secret at the time. Lucy Mercer Rutherfurd was sent tickets to the inaugural ceremonies, and FDR provided her with a car and driver so she could

witness him being sworn in. They had been carefully correspond-
ing in guarded letters for more than five years, and while there is
speculation that they might have had clandestine meetings when
she lived with her husband in Aiken, South Carolina, and he was
nearby in Warm Springs, Georgia, it is clear she was now back in
his life to stay.

Franklin Roosevelt now had the cadre of faithful supporters
around him that he had carefully selected more than a decade earlier. Louis Howe and Missy LeHand would actually be installed
in rooms in the already-crowded White House so as to be at hand
twenty-four hours a day. Steve Early and Marvin McIntire were
made special assistants as well. So with the Cufflinks Gang by his
side and the Council on Foreign Relations group in support, Roosevelt could confidently tell himself, as he would tell the nation in
his first inaugural address, "We have nothing to fear but fear itself."

Fourteen

Messy Foreign Affairs

1933–1936

"If the President contemplates sending to the Senate for confirmation an appointment of Sumner Welles to a position in the State Department, or in the Foreign Service, please withhold such action until I be given an opportunity to submit to him, or to someone representing him, certain serious facts on matters bearing directly upon his fitness for such a position. I prefer these matters to be presented to the President, rather than to make formal charges to the Senate Committee."

—Horace G. Knowles in a letter to Louis Howe,
January 1, 1933[1]

*F*RANKLIN ROOSEVELT'S LANDSLIDE victory in the 1932 presidential election ended the exile from political power for most of the Progressives from the Dupont Circle set. Herbert Hoover had fled Washington, his once great reputation shattered by his inability to restore public confidence during the economic crisis. He would linger in the background of Republican politics nurturing fading hopes of a comeback in both 1936 and 1940, but the party's hierarchy preferred to choose standard-bearers that were more amenable to their anti-New Deal, isolationist mood. As for Roosevelt, he continued to nurture an angry resentment against Hoover—he had, after all, spurned FDR's invitation in 1920 to head the Democratic presidential ticket—and others took their cue from the president. Thus Hoover became a non-person in American politics for nearly twenty years.

From the start of his administration, FDR ran true to form and quickly began to recruit many of his loyal old friends without paying too much attention to what they had been doing for the previous dozen years or what qualifications they might bring. So Grenville Emmitt, his old law partner, was made minister to the Netherlands. Breckinridge Long became U.S. ambassador to Italy; Josephus Daniels, FDR's old Navy Department boss now in his seventies, was sent to the embassy in Mexico. The Cufflinks Gang—Marvin McIntyre, Steve Early, Louis Howe and, of course, Missy LeHand—all got White House jobs, with the latter two moving into the family quarters there. But no one tried harder to land a position in the government than Felix Frankfurter, who began to commute between his Harvard Law School post and Washington to be on the scene while he peppered Roosevelt with "Dear Frank" letters of advice, flattery, and veiled offers to help create the White House post of chief of staff which had never existed before. Playing to FDR's ego in one letter just before the inauguration, Frankfurter was especially effusive about Roosevelt's top cabinet appointments but could not resist observing, "A Cabinet is like a symphony orchestra—qualities that come out of the individual members in no small extent depend on the qualities which the leader draws out of them. The New York Philharmonic is a very different thing when Toscanini leads, rather than someone else."[2]

To his chagrin, FDR merely offered to make him Solicitor General in the Justice Department, a post Felix rejected as uninteresting and, instead, he accepted an offer to return to Oxford for the 1933–1934 academic year as a visiting law professor. Undaunted even from that distance, Frankfurter continued to provide Roosevelt with policy advice and to urge a chief of staff job be created, if not for himself, then for his protégé Thomas "Tommy the Cork" Corcoran, whom he had recruited as a law clerk for Justice Holmes. Here he was more successful. Roosevelt appeared more than willing to take into government any number of what became known as "Felix's Happy Hot Dogs." These were former Supreme Court clerks that Frankfurter had talent-spotted at Harvard and then placed with Justices Brandeis and Holmes—men like Ben Cohen, Dean Acheson, and Donald and Alger Hiss. The ebullient and brilliant Corcoran, who had been Frankfurter's favorite pupil at Harvard, quickly installed himself in the president's office as a combination court jester, speechwriter, and political fixer. As with Missy LeHand and Louis Howe, FDR soon became so dependent on "Tommy the Cork" he assigned him a bedroom in the already-overcrowded White House living quarters so he was always at hand. This meant that Frankfurter would continue to be kept at arm's length as an adviser by Roosevelt (until his Supreme Court appointment five years later), but nonetheless Frankfurter had Corcoran in his debt and by the president's side for the time being.

Two other Dupont Circle job seekers were something of a problem for the new president. Understandably, Roosevelt's overriding concern when he took office was to fashion a dramatic response to the dire economic crisis that had gripped America for more than three years. His now-fabled "First Hundred Days" burst of New Deal reforms were certainly dramatic, and many of those remedies first tried back then have been tried again in the current crisis. The nation's banks were first closed and then reopened to a round of forced mergers of weaker banks into stronger ones as well as infusions of new capital into the sound banks. Government salaries and jobs were slashed in an effort to balance the federal budget. An attempt to control wages and prices was made under the ill-fated National Recovery Act, and the first plans were drafted for what would in two years become the Social Security pension system.

But while he wanted badly to concentrate on the Depression at home, the president was distracted by foreign policy questions that were equally pressing, since the Depression at home was merely part of a global economic contraction that threatened to unhinge the fragile peace that had existed since the end of the Great War. For help on these foreign vexations, FDR turned to two men who would prove bitter rivals for his affection—Sumner Welles and William Bullitt.

If Franklin Roosevelt can be said to have had a close personal friend—that is, an equal and not a devoted aide—it was Sumner Welles. From 1928, when Welles provided policy advice on Latin American affairs for FDR to pass on to Al Smith, Welles had emerged not only as a personal confidant of both Franklin and Eleanor but also as the candidate's chief source of foreign policy advice who trumped even the efforts of Colonel House and the Council on Foreign Relations to influence him. A year before the 1932 campaign had begun, Roosevelt had wanted to attack the Hoover administration's policy of recognizing Latin American dictatorships as long as they did not threaten U.S. commercial interests. He knew that as New York's governor he lacked the standing, so he persuaded the disarmament negotiator Norman Davis to permit Welles to ghostwrite a lengthy article to appear under Davis's name in *Foreign Affairs* that outlined what would become FDR's Good Neighbor policy for the hemisphere. Despite the fact that editor Hamilton Armstrong was not pleased by the subterfuge, the article was widely praised internationally, and it soon became generally known both that Welles was the author and that Roosevelt had been the moving force behind it.[3] Fully expecting Roosevelt to name him secretary of state, Davis was so pleased by the notoriety that he told Welles he would certainly ask him to be his undersecretary.

Roosevelt depended on Welles to an even greater degree during the 1932 campaign. Welles was asked to set up an impromptu think tank, a kind of mini-Inquiry, in Washington to provide FDR with the latest intelligence and foreign policy advice. With the help of his close friend journalist Drew Pearson, Welles also began to build a network of social contacts among influential members of Congress who might be made more sympathetic to the new administration. Pearson was rapidly becoming something of a political celebrity. With a partner, Robert S. Allen, Pearson had used his entrée as a diplomatic correspondent for various newspapers to gather inside gossip about the private lives of many key Hoover Administration officials and their wives into a best-selling book, *Washington Merry-Go-Round.* The pair had then written a sequel and launched a nationally syndicated newspaper column that featured high-level political gossip that soon became required reading in Washington. Since he was sympathetic to both Welles and Roosevelt, Pearson readily allowed the column to be used by FDR to launch trial balloons about controversial policy changes. Not surprisingly, there were many early and flattering references to Welles and his likely role in the expected batch of new State Department appointments.[4]

But the president-elect had domestic political pressures that overrode his personal friendships when it came to the top posts at State. FDR scored important points within the Congress by appointing the popular Senator Cordell Hull as secretary and an old Harvard chum and career Foreign Service officer, William Philips, as undersecretary. Another factor, never stated but understood, was that Welles was still a controversial figure in official Washington. The scandal over his marriage to Mathilde Townsend and his firing by President Coolidge may have faded but was not forgotten. Then too, there was the gossip about his other indiscretions which Roosevelt certainly was aware might have become an open scandal. Not only had former Ambassador Horace Knowles brought accusations to FDR about Welles's sexual escapades in the Dominican Republic, there were also rumors of a confidential State Department dossier about his conduct on other occasions that had been compiled during the Coolidge administration. Louis Howe had been concerned enough about it to demand a search of State Department files before the inauguration, but when Welles confronted him about it, Howe had replied that the records he had examined had not contained anything that would bar him from an appointment. Then after months of frustrating indecision for Welles, events suddenly accelerated beyond his control.

In April 1933, FDR finally named Welles Assistant Secretary of State for Latin American Affairs, a post that was the bare minimum in prestige that he would accept. But by May, that was abruptly changed, and Welles was hurried off to Havana as ambassador. Cuba was still a quasi-protectorate of the United States from the Spanish-American War, and Roosevelt was determined to end that client relationship as part of his Good Neighbor initiative. But the corrupt government of Gerardo Machado was brutally repressing protestors to the point that civil war might erupt at any moment and threaten the more than two billion dollars of U.S. investments in the Cuban economy. Welles was sent to coax Machado into holding free elections that would allow him to be replaced peacefully by a more stable regime.

Welles succeeded too well at his task. While he adhered to his orders to avoid bringing U.S. military intervention to bear, the Welles mission succeeded in driving Machado into exile too quickly to permit a stable transition. By the time Welles returned to his desk at State in December, Cuba had been convulsed by a series of increasingly violent coups that ended with the country coming under the grip of an even more repressive strongman, an ex-Army sergeant named Fulgencio Batista who would stay in power until he too was ousted thirty years later by Fidel Castro.

⚜

DESPITE SOME CRITICISM IN the press, Welles found his reputation much enhanced when he returned as assistant secretary. The next three years would be probably the happiest of Sumner's adult life. Bolstered by the president's personal commitment to improve hemispheric relations, Welles and Hull won praise at the end of 1933 for negotiating a treaty in Montevideo, Uruguay, with nineteen other governments of the hemisphere that was the basis for the Roosevelt version of the Good Neighbor policy of nonintervention, freer trade, and economic alliance. Welles also found himself thrust into a series of foreign policy challenges that ranged from instability in Panama to the civil upheavals in Mexico and a direct role in ending a particularly bloody border war between Bolivia and Paraguay. It all culminated in the weeks after the 1936 re-election when Welles was the advance man for Roosevelt's historic journey to Buenos Aires, where treaties were signed that pledged the nations of the hemisphere to a policy of collective security in the case of an international crisis—the pact would prove crucial during the early days of World War II.

In his triumph, Welles inadvertently made a grudging enemy out of his immediate superior Cordell Hull. The secretary had felt upstaged by Welles at both the Montevideo and Buenos Aires conferences where the younger man's popularity with Latin American delegates, his flawless Spanish, and his tireless energy overshadowed the older statesman. Worse, Roosevelt visibly preferred getting terse, to-the-point briefings from Welles instead of Hull's often long-winded discursions on policy matters. Early in the administration, the president and his friend began to bypass the secretary of state on important decisions. The final straw came in 1936 when Roosevelt somewhat cruelly allowed Hull to think he might be chosen as FDR's vice-presidential running mate. Instead, at the Philadelphia convention the choice went to the incumbent, John Nance Garner of Texas, while Welles (with Pearson's help) drew praise for swinging Maryland's rebellious delegation firmly into the Roosevelt camp. Hull, who worked hard to maintain an impassive dignity that masked a fiercely proud temperament, had become an implacable enemy of Welles.

Franklin Roosevelt's other vexation in the foreign policy arena had been what to do about William Bullitt. Both Colonel House and old Harvard friend Louis Wehle had strongly advised FDR to find a place for the now forty-one-year-old Bullitt. Always confident in his own importance, Bullitt had begun campaigning for a place in FDR's foreign policy circle as early as January 1932 and had caused a minor flap that summer when he went on a tour of European capitals—including Moscow—where he strongly hinted to diplomats and journalists alike that he was fact-gathering at Roosevelt's orders, which he was not. Still, Roosevelt could not help but be impressed with Bullitt's contacts among foreign leaders, and the breezy, gossip-filled letters that flowed from Europe to Hyde Park were very much to the candidate's taste.

Upon his return to New York in July, Bullitt was relegated to speech writing duties in the campaign offices of Louis Howe and did not actually get to renew his personal contacts with Roosevelt until close to the election in November. After twenty years as a political pariah for having denounced President Wilson and the Versailles

Treaty, the renegade Bullitt was finally readmitted to FDR's personal circle. Bullitt was sent back to Europe on two separate trips to report to the president-elect on just where the various European debtor nations stood in their ability to pay back the billions of dollars still owed to Wall Street or the U.S. Treasury. While FDR voiced increasing confidence in Bullitt's judgment, he balked at giving him the post he wanted most—U.S. ambassador to France—and instead named another, a major campaign donor.

Frustrated, Bullitt moved to Washington to campaign for a job after the inauguration in the spring of 1933. He leased a large mansion at 2414 Tracy Place a few blocks north of Dupont Circle in the tony Kalorama neighborhood. He continued to pay flattering social calls on Roosevelt and to court Cordell Hull at State where he was temporarily ensconced as a special assistant while a better job was being weighed for him. Ever alert to the opportunities to advance his career, Bullitt also began to make a play for FDR's "other" wife, Marguerite "Missy" LeHand.

Now thirty-five, Missy had spent a dozen years in the hermetically sealed world of Franklin Roosevelt and his inexhaustible need for affirmation. Where he had gone, she had been the one—not Eleanor— who most often accompanied him, whether it was in the cramped quarters of a houseboat in Florida or the rustic isolation of Warm Springs. During this time, she had never had an apartment of her own. Her bedrooms in the Albany governor's mansion and at Hyde Park adjoined Roosevelt's. Ensconced in the White House, she was even more confined to the cramped family quarters or the Oval Office.

Although Bullitt was seven years older than she and was prematurely balding, he was still an attractive and vigorous man who could be extraordinarily attentive and charming. He began to squire Missy to many of the official social events staged by Washington society to welcome the new administration. Early on, the couple began to enjoy intimate dinners at the Tracy Place mansion; in one early note from Bullitt he returned some pearls to Missy "that must have gotten lost in the car."

Their affair was interrupted briefly in June when Roosevelt sent Bullitt with the official U.S. delegation to a London economic conference that President Hoover had previously endorsed to broker a readjustment in the international debt burden. Unlike Hoover, however, Roosevelt was determined not to agree to any reduction in the sums owed to American lenders by the Europeans. Despite his orders, some members of Secretary Hull's team raised the hopes of foreign leaders that the president might soon take the U.S. dollar back to an exchange rate fixed to the gold standard and reduce some of the demands on Europe's debts owed to America. When an angry Roosevelt repudiated the efforts at a press conference, the London negotiations broke up without any agreement, and Hull returned home in embarrassment.

Bullitt escaped any censure because, again on his own, he had absented himself from the conference sessions and had concentrated on confidential talks with Maxim Litvinov, the Soviet foreign minister who had come to London. Stalin's regime was keen to win U.S. recognition of their government. The Russians feared an impending Japanese invasion and calculated that a closer tie with the United States might cool Tokyo's ambitions in Asia for a while; it was a strategic move that appealed to Roosevelt as well. So there was a willingness to believe Litvinov when he promised Bullitt that the Kremlin favored a wide range of trade and economic partnerships as well as a repayment of some if not all of the Czarist era bond debts that had been repudiated during the 1917 revolution.

Bullitt's star rose even higher that autumn as Hull, trying to recover some prestige from the London debacle, strongly endorsed his argument to establish official relations with Russia. He also got a boost in influence when Hull secured an assistant secretary appointment for an old Congressional friend, R. Walton Moore, a Representative from Virginia who just happened to have been the law school roommate of Bullitt's father.

With the benefit of hindsight, it is easy to fault the naive credulity that made Bullitt—and through him, FDR and other administration officials—so eager to seek close ties with Stalin's Soviet regime. But like many other foreign visitors to Russia, Bullitt had been impressed with how Russia had leapfrogged its way from a medieval backwater to an industrial power in the decade and a half since the 1917 Bolshevik revolution. As would also be the case with Mussolini's Italy and the reawakening of Germany under Hitler, it was possible to overlook the violent despotism and sheer terror that gripped Russia, especially since much of the repression that Stalin's apparatus imposed remained hidden in the inaccessible vastness of its far provinces. Even doctrinaire capitalists such as Henry Ford were willing to build factories inside Russia in the belief that Marxist tyranny could be organically cured by exposure to Western industrial democracy.

So the Russia that Bullitt saw on the prosperous modern streets of Moscow merely confirmed the dream that he and John Reed had nurtured from the beginning. He was not alone by any means. Frightened by the uncertainties at home, many Americans were fascinated by the resolute image of the Soviet experiment as it was portrayed to them. In his chilling book *The Forsaken,* author Tim Tzouliadis reports that when the Soviet trade offices in New York advertised job openings for six thousand skilled American workers, it received more than a hundred thousand applications. And uncounted thousands of them actually picked up and made the long journey to what they hoped was a more open society. In what he calls "the least heralded migration in American history," Tzouliadis describes "A cross section of America, they came from all walks of life: professors, engineers, factory workers, teachers, artists, doctors, even farmers, all mixed together on the passenger ships. They left to join the Five-Year Plan of Soviet Russia, lured by the prospect of work at the height of the Great Depression."[5] With the laudatory reportage about the Soviet experiment in such major publications as The *New York Times* and *Time* magazine, along with the effusive praise of celebrity visitors like George Bernard Shaw, most Americans can be excused for having an unrealistic opinion of events in Russia.[6]

By mid-October, Bullitt's back channel communications had progressed to the point that Foreign Minister Litvinov, accompanied by the *New York Times'* Moscow correspondent Walter

Duranty[7] journeyed to Washington, where he quickly agreed to most of Roosevelt's conditions which specified payment of the Czarist debts, civil liberties for the Americans who traveled to Russia, and a cessation of Soviet propaganda efforts through the Communist Party of the U.S. to overthrow the government. On November 17, the agreement that established diplomatic ties between the two giant nations was formally signed at the White House. FDR promptly followed the announcement of recognition with the appointment of William C. Bullitt as ambassador to the U.S.S.R.

Bullitt wasted no time in heading off for his exciting new assignment, but he was careful to solidify his relationship with Missy LeHand as the two indulged themselves in farewell romantic interludes at his mansion. He sailed for Europe on November 29 with his nine-year-old daughter Anne and steamer trunks of finely tailored suits and formal dress with which he intended to dazzle his deliberately dowdy Russian counterparts. To his delight, the Soviet government gave him a near royal welcome when he arrived in Moscow on December 11, and in the days that followed, he was cheered as a friend of Russia whenever he appeared in public. After presenting his credentials and having an introductory meeting with Stalin, Bullitt returned to Washington for the Christmas holidays and to arrange to have State Department staff and office supplies shipped to the new embassy's temporary accommodations in Moscow to begin the New Year. He was in understandably high spirits.

Missy, on the other hand, was bereft. The emotionally immature woman clearly adored Franklin Roosevelt and would continue to do so. But Bill Bullitt made her believe that she was loved, and that led to what can only be described as a girlish crush. From her desk at the White House, she began a flow of love letters to Bullitt that were sent via the diplomatic pouch and which alternated between coy flirtation and desperate pleas for affection. The letters, which are preserved in Bullitt's collection at the Yale University library, began the week after he started on the return journey to Russia in January 1934.

In the first, Missy reported,

> I'm just back from lunching with the Jimmy Dunns [a State Department official] . . . and it being Saturday afternoon, I am longing to take a taxi to 2414. For some curious reason, life seems to go on in Washington—Marguerite suddenly has become athletic in the extreme and has ridden (desperately hard) twice and swum each day since Tuesday. Unfortunately however the day ends—enough of that! I hope you find an Embassy ready for you which will have at least the essentials of comfort. I hope too that this note will be there to say I'm thinking of you and that a week filled with happiness is still fresh and clear in my memory. I had intended not writing until I heard from you, but a lonely Saturday afternoon overcame me. I shall not indulge myself this way often, however. My love to you—much more of it than I like to confess. M.[8]

Although only a few of Bullitt's responses to her are preserved in the collection, it becomes clear that he used their relationship to enhance his personal contacts with Roosevelt. When he sent examples of European and Russian postage for the president's prized stamp collection, they went to Missy to hand personally to FDR. Despite the considerable technical difficulties, Bullitt also kept up an almost-constant stream of telephone calls to Roosevelt, always routed through Missy. But just as often, when the ambassador came back to Washington for consultations, she would be neglected and would become depressed again. "Bill, dear," one note complained, "I was so disappointed to hear that you are not going to be here for the holidays that I very nearly burst into tears! It was very childish and I am sorry. Silly isn't it, that I mind being without you for a few days when there have been so many, but I do mind! M."[9]

The Bullitt mission to Moscow turned out to be a flamboyant failure in part because of his own emotional makeup as well as a misreading of Stalin's intentions. As historian Beatrice Farnsworth observed, "In fact, Bullitt was not ideal for the Russian post. . . . The nature of his personality (combined with his emotional attachment to Soviet Russia) was to make him particularly susceptible to disappointment, for Bullitt needed to be liked." Farnsworth also presciently notes that Bullitt had clearly shifted the intense emotional commitment he had once invested in Woodrow Wilson onto the shoulders of Franklin Roosevelt; such transference could and did prove dangerous for all concerned.[10]

Through 1934 at least, Bullitt made quite a splash as the most visible American in the Soviet Union, although one has to wonder what Stalin and the other Kremlin leaders made of it. He announced plans to build a mammoth new U.S. embassy that would resemble Monticello and gave a lavish banquet and ball that featured wildly expensive wines and gourmet delicacies that had to be brought in from abroad. When American workers who had emigrated to jobs in various Russian cities formed a baseball league, Bullitt ordered up shipments of bats, balls, and uniforms to be distributed. In a bid to establish contacts within the Red Army officer corps, he introduced polo matches on the embassy grounds. In the meantime, he sent Soviet security forces scurrying after him when he uncrated a Douglass two-seater airplane and—with some ancient railroad maps for navigation—began flying to distant parts of Russia to see the famine conditions firsthand. All of this was given international headlines by a press corps starved of much hard news that was not dictated by the Soviet propaganda machine.

Almost at once, the lavish welcome the ambassador had received when he arrived began to vanish. Promises of adequate embassy facilities were ignored, and substantive talks on trade deals died. The thorny negotiations over how much and in what ways the Russians would honor the estimated six hundred million dollars in bonds and loans owed by the Czarist and Kerensky governments to U.S. creditors were abruptly stalled. The reason was clear enough, but Bullitt refused to face the change and instead spent much of that year blaming the Foreign Minister Litvinov for sabotaging his friendship with Stalin. The real answer was simple: the one thing Stalin had wanted all along from ties with the United States was a "nonaggression pact"—a mutual defense agreement that if another nation (certainly Japan, but also perhaps Germany) attacked Russia, America would come to its aid. But Franklin Roosevelt had never intended such a commitment, and Bullitt could not even consider such a proposal. With Japan's army now committed to extensive campaigning in Manchuria, the threat of an invasion of Russia had also diminished. Stalin, ever the strategist, turned his diplomatic sights back to Western Europe, where clandestine talks with both France and Germany were resumed; the Soviet Union even joined the League of Nations to help facilitate its maneuvering.[11]

The final straw for Bullitt came in the summer of 1935 when there were reports that the Comintern, the Communist International organization of sixty-five national Communist parties, was to have a long-scheduled meeting in Amsterdam. Bullitt became alarmed by rumors that the meeting venue was being transferred to Moscow and that American Communists would be participating. He protested that this would violate the "gentleman's agreement" that FDR had reached with Litvinov during the recognition negotiations but was blithely assured by Russian officials that the rumors were false. But the Comintern Congress did convene in Moscow a few weeks later, and top officials of the CPUSA were prominently applauded for their efforts to destabilize the capitalistic American government. The ambassador's sense of outrage was turned to fury when Soviet officials stonily dismissed his new protests with the pretense that Russia had no direct influence on the international communist movement. Bullitt had to face the fact that he had been deliberately played upon by the Russians, and the idea was an intolerable affront. He began to startle and then alarm the Moscow press corps with increasingly inflammatory criticism of the Soviet system and of specific Kremlin officials, just short of insulting Stalin himself.

In the meantime, Roosevelt too had become less interested in advancing American interests with Russia. The same month the Comintern was gathering in Moscow, FDR was busy signing a host of important New Deal domestic economic reforms into law including the Social Security Act and banking law reforms. And reflecting a new concern with the revived militarism in both Italy and Germany, he also reluctantly put his signature to the Neutrality Act of 1935, which imposed a blanket embargo on shipping any arms or war materiel to all parties in a war regardless of whether they were an ally or enemy of U.S. interests. While he resented the restraints imposed by the act, many of its Congressional sponsors were Democrats from the states of the Deep South, and he needed their support badly in the coming year's presidential elections, which would be a referendum on the still-moribund domestic economy and his administration.

Bullitt too had looked ahead to the coming election campaign and saw an opportunity to give up the frustrations of the Moscow posting and get closer to Roosevelt. He brought Anne back to the United States for the Christmas holidays and entered her in the exclusive Foxcroft School for girls in the Virginia countryside near Washington. He paid a visit to the White House in January 1936 to put in a bid for a position in the re-election campaign, but FDR cheered him immeasurably by hinting that a more important job was in the offing. When Bullitt finally returned to Washington for good in June, he was briefly given the position he had said he wanted: writing speeches for Roosevelt's early campaigning. All that took an abrupt turn when the American ambassador to Paris suddenly resigned for health reasons, and by August, Bullitt was back on a ship headed to a post he had dreamed of for nearly twenty years—U.S. ambassador to France.

The world had turned upside down in the less than three years since William Bullitt had engineered the U.S. diplomatic relationship with the Soviet Union. By the summer of 1936, Italian troops had been fighting for more than a year in Ethiopia, and the Japanese army had taken over huge portions of Manchuria while the League of Nations dithered. The start to the bloody Spanish Civil War was just weeks away. And in Nazi Germany, a program of rearmament and military buildup was underway as Hitler began to reclaim territories given up by the Versailles Treaty.

For Franklin Roosevelt and his friends from the Dupont Circle era, there was no question of America getting involved in any of these disturbing threats to world peace. The impact of the president's dramatic reforms of the American economy had not yet taken effect. It was imperative that he be given another four years in office to guarantee that his critics not be given the chance to undo those changes. The various crises in foreign affairs must not be allowed to interfere. Yet how could that be prevented? No one knew for sure.

Fifteen
War Clouds on the Horizon

1934–1938

"It is obviously useless for the United States to fight in Europe every twenty-five years, let us say in 1914, 1939, 1964, and thereafter if, during the intervening years we follow the policy of nonintervention in European affairs to which both our traditions and our sentiments have committed us."

—Allen W. Dulles, *Foreign Affairs,* 1934[1]

ℱOR MOST OF HIS CAREER, Walter Lippmann had aspired to the role of the compass that would always point to a Progressive true north for others to follow. But where he sought certainty he more often found doubt, and when he erected philosophical signposts, the landscape around him would abruptly change. By the end of the 1930s, Lippmann's political opinions resembled a weather vane that swung wildly with the prevailing wind.

Instead of discrediting him as a political observer, this tendency made Lippmann more widely respected as an opinion leader. This was largely due to his uncanny ability to echo the ever-shifting mood of the American people as they moved from the careless euphoria of the Jazz Age to the shock and dismay of the early Depression years. If Lippmann's newspaper columns and steady stream of books seemed to contradict themselves from one year to the next, it was because Lippmann could spot how shifting public opinion could change the reality of political responses to the seemingly unending stream of threat and crisis that gripped America and the rest of the world. What the world may have been like in 1919 was no longer relevant fifteen years later as the slide into a new world war got underway.

Through much of the 1930s, Lippmann was so celebrated that his name had become a popular punch line in cartoons and Hollywood movies.[2] When the Pulitzer family halted operations at The *World* in 1931, his services were eagerly sought by rival newspaper publishers. The *New York Times* wanted him to run their Washington bureau while the Hearst chain dangled a syndicated column. Instead, Lippmann accepted a lucrative offer to write three signed columns a week under his old "Today and Tomorrow" logo for the Ogden family's *New York Herald Tribune*. The paper was the flagship and national syndicate for the bluestocking, internationalist Republican business and high society where Walter and Faye now had most of their social friendships. Many of the old Dupont Circle set were appalled.

As Frankfurter wrote to another friend:

> There is no incongruity in Walter's association with the *Tribune*. For he has steadily moved to the right. . . . Of course I know that you believe that Walter will tincture the *Tribune* and its readers with liberalism rather than strengthen the conservative forces. I think I know the argument and understand it, but am wholly unpersuaded by it. This doesn't mean that Walter won't from time to time and perhaps even frequently write articles which I shall read both with stimulus and with gratitude. But it does mean that the acquisition of Walter by the *Tribune* is not an occasion for jubilation by me.[3]

But Lippmann's old friends were not quite accurate in their fears that he was turning into an advocate of conservative political thought. To be sure, he had joined the social milieu most associated with Wall Street and old privilege. He became one of the token Jewish members of a number of WASP clubs and took up golf and tennis. In place of his old bohemian friends from Greenwich Village and the House of Truth, he now courted the likes of Norman Davis and Thomas Lamont, the wealthy partner of financier J. P. Morgan. He and Faye took their vacations at Florida resorts that only the privileged few could afford. His yearning to belong to the establishment was palpable and provided reasonable doubt for some about his motives.

But a closer look at the man and the times confirms that Lippmann also was continuing to seek that certain mix of philosophy and political action that would match his ideals. The best example of what was going on in Lippmann's mind had come earlier in 1931 when Thomas Lamont organized a testimonial dinner for Lippmann under the auspices of the American Academy of Political Science to honor him for his contributions to journalism. More than five hundred blue-ribbon guests from the top ranks of Wall Street and government service gave him a standing ovation and lauded him as a "prophet of Liberalism."

In his speech to the group, Lippmann cast off allegiance to the old Progressive faith that had carried him from his days in the House of Truth. In its place, he urged, what was needed was this new concept called Liberalism, a still-vague and uncertain term but one that aimed more closely at the new realities of the world of the 1930s than the old Progressive radicalism of Theodore Roosevelt or the idealism of Woodrow Wilson. The old class struggle between giant corporations and the working class was out of date, he argued.

> The fighting faith of the reformer of twenty years ago no longer arouses the generation to which we belong. Who but a political hack can believe today, as our forefathers once sincerely believed, that the fate of the nation hangs on the victory of either political party? . . . Who can believe that the cure for the corruption of popular government is to multiply the number of elections? Who can believe that an orderly, secure and just economic order can be attained by the simple process of arousing the people against the corporations? . . . The progressives of the last generation were attempting to police what seemed to them

an alien intruder upon their normal existence. For us the problem is to civilize and rationalize these corporate organizations.[4]

The first practical test of Lippmann's new faith would come a year later when he acknowledged that (after a White House luncheon interview) Herbert Hoover was a spent force and could not pull the nation out of the Depression. But despite the fact that Frankfurter and other friends appeared to be coalescing around the candidacy of Franklin Roosevelt, Lippmann held back. He liked FDR personally and had campaigned for his election as governor of New York in 1928 and again in 1930. But when it came to who would be most capable of assuming the Presidency in the midst of crisis, Lippmann was put off by Roosevelt's easy charm and was unable to divine the steely determination that lay at FDR's core. He wrote to the man he supported for the Democratic nomination, his old boss Newton Baker, "that [Roosevelt] just doesn't happen to have a very good mind, that he never really comes to grips with a problem which has any large dimensions, and that above all the controlling element in almost every case is political advantage." FDR, he concluded, was "an amiable boy scout."[5]

These, and a number of slighting references to Roosevelt in his columns, would be used against him by his critics, first when he grudgingly endorsed FDR's election and a year later when he became an unabashed cheerleader for both the New Deal and its chief executive. Indeed, Lippmann became so partisan in urging the president to exercise even more power during his first hundred days in office that Roosevelt called on Frankfurter to convince Walter to tone down the rhetoric because it was causing a backlash among the Democratic leaders in Congress who were wary of the new pace of change.

But then, just as abruptly, Lippmann changed his mind again about Roosevelt. By 1935, the columnist concluded that FDR was overreaching himself with programs that were intended more to gather new power to the Presidency and less to cure the still-persisting depressed economic condition of the country. This was the period when the U.S. Supreme Court had begun striking down key parts of the New Deal, including National Recovery Act price and wage rules, which were proving unwieldy and confusing. Instead of listening to

Lippmann's counsel that it was perhaps time to pause in the pace of New Deal reforms, Roosevelt plunged ahead with new government initiatives. Annoyed, Lippmann endorsed and voted for the Republican nominee in the 1936 elections. Kansas governor Alf Landon had been an old ally of Theodore Roosevelt's campaign of 1912 when he broke away from the Republicans and ran as a Progressive. But Landon proved a lackluster campaigner, and FDR not only carried forty-six states handily but also increased the Democratic majorities in the Congress.

Undaunted, Lippmann continued to volunteer personal advice to the victorious president. Roosevelt, to his credit, continued to welcome Lippmann's suggestions with his usual evasive cordiality, never giving in to pique when Lippmann attacked, as he would do increasingly during 1937 when the president's attempts to pack the Supreme Court with a friendly majority provoked a political backlash of firestorm proportions.

Nor did Lippmann confine his criticism of the Roosevelt Administration to its domestic programs. In the area of American foreign policy, Lippmann charged the president with standing aloof from the alarming rise of military aggression that was going on around the world. Here again, Lippmann's views were in flux. When isolationists in the Congress forced through the first Neutrality Act in 1935 over FDR's objections, Lippmann decried the self-absorbed spirit behind the act but also allowed it might stiffen the resolve of Britain and France to actively oppose Italy and Germany's aggressiveness if they realized America might not come to their rescue in another European conflict.

It becomes clear at this point that both Lippmann and Roosevelt—and most Progressives—had given up any dream that the League of Nations was a workable guarantee of collective security. In response to a letter from his close friend Ham Armstrong, Lippmann wrote from his Florida vacation home in the spring of 1935:

> My net conclusion is that a system of collective security, having no real legislative powers cannot in any expansive sense hope

to alter the status quo. It must in its very essence freeze the status quo in all its essentials. And it must, therefore, expect every so often to be faced with what amounts to a revolution by the dissatisfied backers. Some of these revolutions will be suppressed; some of them will be successful; when they are successful a new system of collective security will be imposed for a time. The only hope in preventing these revolutions lies in the formula which Wilson aimed at but couldn't carry through, namely the reduction of national frontiers to a level where they mark cultural rather than economic boundaries . . . To say all this is to be obviously pessimistic and frankly I am. I have ceased hoping for permanent peace and now have reduced my hopes to the idea of long periods of tranquility such as the world knew in the Victorian Age. It is possible that we might have such an era once the Central European issue is decided by war or by revolution. Isn't this horrible?[6]

Interestingly, Lippmann had been prompted by a previous letter from Armstrong that included "a rather indiscreet memorandum" of an off-the-record conversation between an official of the Federal Council of Churches (FCC) and President Roosevelt. In the memo, FDR reportedly told the church group leader of his reluctance to reform much less join the League of Nations at this late date because of what he called "a monumental obstacle to any comprehensive system of international security based on collective action." Like Lippmann, Roosevelt looked back to Wilson's efforts to combine both the Versailles peace treaty with the formation of the League and judged it to have been "the best that idealistic men could conceive of and make realistic to men less idealistic." But if that approach had failed, then what other way would be better? Until that question could be answered, Roosevelt judged that "discussing the reformation of the League or the form of some new League is to risk inflicting fresh disappointment on a world already dangerously disillusioned about the inventive genius of statesmen and political scientists."[7]

Two points of significance about the memo are worth mentioning. The Federal Council of Churches had become the largest and most active in the United States of the religion-based peace movements that were springing up in Europe and North America. With a membership of three-dozen Protestant denominations claiming more than twenty-five million adherents, the FCC had been actively urging Roosevelt for some time to become more vocal in his warnings to the dictators. The other point is that the official who had briefed Armstrong about his talk with FDR was almost certainly the FCC's most important lay leader—John Foster Dulles, one of the founders of the Council on Foreign Relations.

As with others of the Dupont Circle set, Foster Dulles had undergone a fundamental change in his beliefs from the days when he had negotiated the reparations clauses in the Versailles Treaty in 1919. Then he had been fully committed to the Wilsonian faith in the treaty and in the League as an effective mechanism to enforce peace. A key to that faith was his belief that American membership in both the League and the Reparations Commission the treaty set up to oversee Germany's repayments of its obligations would guarantee a flexibility that would ensure Germany's continued economic growth and guarantee its transition back into the community of nations. But even after it was clear that America would belong neither to the League nor the Reparations panel, Dulles continued to argue that a revived German economy was essential to restoring Europe to a stable peace.

The key to understanding the evolution in John Foster Dulles lies in the two major strains in his personality. As the oldest son of a Presbyterian minister, Foster inherited a deeply religious core that nearly led him to follow his father into the ministry. But the logical certainty of the law appealed more to his precise intellect, and the older partners at Sullivan & Cromwell cheerfully made him the firm's point man for rounding up foreign borrowers and matching them with Wall Street lenders in increasingly profitable bond issues. In a speech he gave in 1928 to answer critics of the huge sums of American capital being invested in Europe (and not in the U.S.), Dulles made headlines with what appeared to be irrefutable logic. He noted that in the seven years since 1921, $11 billion in financing had flowed from Wall Street to Germany and other Eastern European borrowers. In that time Europeans had purchased $47 billion in U.S. exports and had earned $39 billion from the sale of their exports to us. That left them with an indebtedness of $11 billion—the amount of Wall Street's loans outstanding. The conclusion, Dulles argued, was that the loans clearly were critical to America's own prosperity.[8]

While the math was sound, the economics were still risky. Dulles—that is, Sullivan & Cromwell—had been the guiding force behind most of those loans and had focused the capital investments where Dulles felt a greater kinship with the borrowers. And the hard truth is that Dulles had come to dislike the French intensely from his Paris experiences and had come to admire the Germans for their apparent efficiency and crisp, businesslike attitudes. Dulles also traveled widely in Eastern Europe and found much to attract him about the newly formed governments of Czechoslovakia and Hungary; by the same token he avoided London because he hated the food and the British air of superiority over Americans. The end result was his conviction that Germany held the key to European stability. That meant that he and his Wall Street colleagues found themselves so heavily invested in German industries when the Depression sent the world into a tailspin that their response was to keep lending and hope for the best.

It also was because Dulles traveled so widely throughout Europe in the 1920s and early 1930s that he saw, sooner than many Americans did, how powerless so many of his friends in foreign governments were to stop the erosion of stability and the rise of militarism that grew as the global marketplace degenerated. The religious current in his makeup had never been far below the surface, and he increasingly turned to it to help explain to himself and others what was going wrong and where the remedies might lie. He had been something of a celebrity when in 1923, at his father's urging, he was defense counsel for a famous clergyman named Harry Emerson Fosdick in a heresy trial before the Presbyterian Church. Reverend Fosdick, brother of Rockefeller Foundation secretary Raymond Fosdick, had been preaching modernist theories that challenged church rules on divorce and the literal truth of the Bible. Although the minister chose to resign from his pulpit, it was

Dulles's defense that prevented official censure, and the case was a milestone in the liberalization of religious doctrine. Fosdick was immediately hired by John D. Rockefeller Jr. to be the minister at the new Riverside Baptist Church that the family had financed, and Dulles was rewarded with appointments to various advisory positions with the Rockefeller family. That same year, Foster had been the general counsel that incorporated the Federal Council of Churches, and he became increasingly involved in pro bono work for the group over the years. So when he traveled through Europe on law firm business, Dulles actively participated in conferences of Protestant church leaders and laymen in other countries.

The high point in Foster Dulles's search for a religious context for building peace came in July 1937 when he attended a World Conference on Church, Community, and State at Oxford, where he engaged with the likes of theologians Reinhold Niebuhr and Paul Tillich and intellectuals including T. S. Eliot. It was Foster who was asked to draft the group's concluding statement, which called for a new world consensus for peace that would transcend national boundaries. At this point, Foster Dulles was further along in his thinking than either Roosevelt or Lippmann in their rejection of the League approach to collective security.

As early as 1935, Dulles had been arguing that while the Versailles Treaty and the League had been well intended, any effective proposal for international peace "must recognize the need for change and provide peaceful mechanisms to obtain it." Both the Treaty and the League, in effect, sought to preserve the status quo, and the emerging aggressiveness of nations like Italy, Japan, and now Germany merely reflected their rebellion against that rigid system. Unless some way could be found to recognize the needs of the newly emerging powers, the threat of violence could only increase. Nor were a new round of treaties or peace declarations (like the Kellogg-Briand declaration) of any use, for they were "not designed to provide a status of reasonable flux between the static and dynamic forces of the world."

What was needed, Dulles concluded, was what he called "a central authority which owes and feels a duty to the group as a whole and to all of its constituent parts," and which "must create a condition of flexibility, which will give qualified and balanced satisfaction to both dynamic and static" nations. He called it "a new world order," and it was the germ of the idea that would lead after much tortuous debate to the consensus to scrap the League organization and start a new world peace mechanism—what would become the United Nations.[9]

Foster's brother Allen also was being forced to reconsider his long-held beliefs. By 1934, he had become America's internationally recognized expert on disarmament technicalities. At the series of disarmament parlays that had continued almost nonstop since the 1922 Washington Naval Conference, he had mastered an astonishing background on specific weapons systems held by the various powers. Along with his British counterpart Anthony Eden, Dulles and Norman Davis had come very close at a Geneva meeting in the summer of 1933 to achieving the first agreement among the major League members to cut back on specific land-based weapons including tanks and airplanes, only to have the conference dissolve when Hitler abruptly pulled Germany out of League membership.

A year later, President Roosevelt asked him to try again. The treaty limits on battleships and other heavy naval craft that had been set in 1922 would expire in 1935, and the last thing FDR wanted was to have to find the money for a new round of warship construction. Reluctantly, Dulles agreed to head for Geneva despite his doubts that anything could be accomplished. He had already voiced those doubts earlier in the year in a *Foreign Affairs* article on Germany's abandonment of the League. "If the problems which confront the European countries are to be worked out by agreement it is not merely a Disarmament Conference which Europe needs, but a second Peace Conference in which the disarmament question would be only one of the major problems to be solved."[10]

Before Dulles and Norman Davis could leave on their new assignment, isolationists who wanted to further hamper President Roosevelt's cautious forays into foreign affairs targeted both of FDR's emissaries for attack. Davis was for the time being too prominent, but Dulles was vulnerable on a number of fronts. On

October 4, Davis telephoned Dulles from Washington with a warning that journalist Drew Pearson was about to attack Dulles for the work he did for Sullivan & Cromwell while he was representing the government in Geneva and London. Although Pearson was still an ardent New Deal supporter, he pretended to impartiality in his columns by occasionally jabbing at the administration. Dulles had been targeted in the column before with charges that he had helped rig the Colombian elections of 1932 to secure oil concessions for the law firm's clients.

When Pearson's "Washington Merry-Go-Round" column appeared on October 10, it merely reported that officials of the Navy Department had protested to the State Department about Dulles being sent to another disarmament conference because he was judged to be anti-Navy.[11] But Pearson had perfected the style of starting with a fairly innocuous charge against a target and then following up in later columns with ever-more damaging evidence to give the appearance of a breaking scandal. What Davis and others feared were accusations that could lead to a Congressional hearing where both men would be challenged by the president's enemies. For his part, Dulles also feared Pearson might be about to report Allen's episodic philandering with women he had met during his travels—including a much talked-of affair with British writer Rebecca West when the two were guests at the Astor estate at Cliveden. So before Pearson's first column could appear in newspapers across the nation, Dulles telegraphed Secretary Cordell Hull to resign, and Hull promptly accepted it with a public statement of regret. FDR quickly followed with an official letter that praised Dulles for his long service to various presidents. Whatever serious scandal Pearson was prepared to reveal about Allen Dulles remained unpublished.

While Allen Dulles cannot have been happy about such an abrupt end to his government service, he realized other claims on his time were more pressing. He and Clover had come close to divorce, and his three children were having problems with his extended absences. In a bid to shore up his family life, he moved them out of Manhattan to Long Island to a community that included Foster's family and other friends and a more sedate social life.

Foster also needed Allen closer to hand at Sullivan & Cromwell. Foster had been made a partner of the huge law firm in 1922 on his return to work from the Paris conference. The firm's directors were so pleased with his ability to broker the huge bond offerings with European clients that they made him the managing partner four years later at the young age of thirty-eight. But now, ten years later, many of the lucrative deals that S&C had put together were coming unstuck as European banks collapsed and European manufacturing froze for lack of markets for their products.

A lot of pernicious comment has been written about Sullivan & Cromwell's dealings in Germany after the rise of Adolf Hitler trying to make the case that Foster Dulles was personally sympathetic to the Nazi regime. His authoritative biographer, Ronald W. Pruessen, handily refutes these allegations in one succinct paragraph.[12] Indeed, both Foster and Allen had worked against long odds to raise a five-hundred-million-dollar loan in 1932 to bolster the tottering government of Germany's democratic chancellor Heinrich Bruning specifically to forestall the Nazi takeover of a year later.

Despite the almost-universal conclusion that Hitler would not last in power for more than a year, by the spring of 1935, Allen Dulles on a return visit to Berlin realized that Ham Armstrong had been correct. Hitler and the Nazis were in power to stay. As he later noted, long-standing clients now begged him to find ways to smuggle their assets out of Germany and evade the increasingly restrictive laws being imposed. "You couldn't practice law there. People came to you asking how to evade the law, not how to respect the law. When that happens you can't be much of a lawyer."[13] After a stormy meeting, Foster reluctantly gave into his brother's demands, and Sullivan & Cromwell's Berlin office was shut down.

While Foster became more involved in his search for a religious path to peace, Allen now spent more time at the offices of the Council on Foreign Relations. He had developed a close bond of friendship with Ham Armstrong. The energetic lawyer and the restrained journalist-scholar seemed to compliment each other's strengths as analysts. They shared the same birthday and took to celebrating it together. Armstrong and Dulles also began a writing partnership that articulated a growing alarm among the various CFR study groups that the political popularity of neutrality legislation being churned out by the Congress was a danger to long-term U.S. security interests. As early as 1934 Dulles had concluded:

> We should now realize that we cannot find safety solely in avoiding entangling alliances and through traditional neutrality. . . . No nation can reach the position of a World Power as we have done without becoming entangled in almost every quarter of the globe in one way or another. We are inextricably and inevitably tied to world affairs. We should not delude ourselves that like Perseus of mythology we can put on neutrality as a helmet and render ourselves invisible and immune to a world in conflict around us.[14]

For the last half of the 1930s, Armstrong and Dulles became the leading voices for the cause that became known as "preparedness." Each made an increasing number of speeches to public affairs groups (often on the new medium of radio), and they churned out a series of jointly signed articles, all rejecting the popular notion that America could—by geography and superiority—remain aloof from the world's descent into war. In two best-selling books based on CFR study group findings, the two argued, "It seems impossible to believe that the elaboration of a complicated system of safeguards to protect American neutrality can be the sole or even the principal aim of American foreign policy. The Government, both in its executive and legislative branches, must take constant account of the fact that the United States has a continuing responsibility which is broader than the aim to escape from some particular difficulty or danger."[15]

Armstrong's friendship with Allen Dulles began to fill an enlarging vacuum in his life as his earlier devotion to Walter Lippmann eroded. In truth, Lippmann was becoming estranged from many of his old Dupont Circle friendships. He had quarreled violently with Felix Frankfurter, who had rebuked him for a slighting reference he had made to Jews in one of his columns about virulence of Hitler's persecutions.[16] Lippmann's marriage to Faye had deteriorated into a mere habit for him and a bore for her. She shared none of his interest in world affairs, and he considered her yearning for an active social life to be an irritation.

Despite the rush of recognition, the hefty income, and the access to the world's most important leaders, Lippmann was frankly bored and had half a mind to abandon journalism. But to do what? He had plenty of university faculty posts offered, but he recoiled from the notion. One response was to travel more, and during the early 1930s, he had gone on a number of lengthy trips—part holiday, part fact-finding—with his devoted friend Ham Armstrong. And where Lippmann and Armstrong went, Faye and Helen Armstrong went with them, for long motor excursions into the Balkans and Italy and even longer tours to Egypt and North Africa. When they were apart, the correspondence between Walter and Ham portrays Armstrong as the kind of uncritical, always-praising friend that Lippmann needed voraciously.

Lippmann had also grown fond of Helen Armstrong. She was unlike the blonde effervescent Faye in every way. A dark and slender brunette with high cheekbones and violet eyes, Helen Armstrong had the assurance of a wealthy background and an inquisitive mind that was as absorbed in the great issues as either of the men's minds were. Earlier in their marriage, she had also written about international affairs and contributed essays to *Foreign Affairs* in its early days, so she could hold her own whenever Ham and Walter discussed weighty matters.

Early in 1937, Walter had decided he must end his marriage to Faye but hesitated because he could not decide what he wanted after he took such a painful step. Faye, after all, was not really at fault, and he hesitated to hurt her. Fate took a hand when Ham told him he would be tied up in a meeting and asked if he would take his wife out to dinner just to keep her company.

In the art deco splendor of the Rainbow Room atop Rockefeller Center, Walter unburdened himself to Helen about his unhappy marriage, his doubts about his career, and his general unhappiness. Surprised, but also intrigued, Helen agreed to meet him for other private dinners in out-of-the-way restaurants. Within weeks, they were involved in a hurried, fevered romance, and Helen rather briskly arranged to rent a small, furnished apartment where the two could meet in secret.

The secret could not last for long. Helen, Ham, and their daughter had been committed to a lengthy trip through the Balkans that summer, but Ham was to return to New York in August, and mother and daughter would spend that month in the south of France with friends. The lovers arranged that Walter would come to France, and the two would meet at a rendezvous south of Paris for some time together. The meeting was all the more urgent because each wanted some firm commitment from the other—Helen wanted to know if Walter was really going to divorce Faye, Walter, to know if Helen would really leave his friend Ham. Daily letters between the two crossed the Atlantic that summer.

Finally, it was the volume of letters that brought matters to a head. Four of the more fervent letters from Walter to Helen missed her at her hotel in southern France and were forwarded to Ham at the Council on Foreign Relations offices in New York. Armstrong's secretary, recognizing Walter's tiny, cramped handwriting addressed to Helen, grew suspicious. She opened them and handed them to Ham.

The disclosure was an emotional catastrophe for all four. The only advantage was that delaying decisions was no longer an option. Helen moved at once to the Armstrong's country place in Long Island, Walter went into a hotel, and they continued to meet in their little apartment. Faye, at first stunned by the news, moved quickly enough to turn to Morgan banker Thomas Lamont to negotiate a settlement from Walter, who gave her not only an established income but also the Lippmann family silver. Very shortly afterwards, Faye married a neighbor best known for his polo playing prowess, and she continued to live in Wading River, Long Island. Helen, as was the custom, went to Reno, Nevada, where a six-week stay at a resort would qualify for an easy divorce decree. Ham Armstrong turned the painful negotiations involved in dividing property and child custody decisions over to his new friend, Allen Dulles, who handled the sad affair with dispatch and without a fee.

The breakup was of course a shock to the establishment of both New York and Washington, where affairs were commonplace but divorce was still something unsavory and not done. But more thoughtful observers worried about greater fallout. It was not just that the two close couples would never see each other again. Ham Armstrong, not surprisingly, made it known that Walter Lippmann was now blackballed from both the Council on Foreign Relations and the pages of *Foreign Affairs* that he edited. Would this breakup interfere with the internationalist confrontation of the totalitarian menace? At the least, the unhappy event robbed Walter Lippmann of a venue where his views carried weight with others who were trying to chart America's future course. And it left Armstrong, both Dulles brothers, and the rest of the CFR elite without Lippmann's often-contrary opinions at a time when the newly formed Axis alliance moved steadily toward conquest as their response to their national frustrations.

During this time, the isolationist mood in America grew with each threat from abroad. From 1935 onward, successive Neutrality Act legislation sought to restrain the Presidency from any act that might involve the United States in what many felt were the moral failures of foreign leaders. This was a time when university students piously pronounced they would refuse to fight in a future foreign war, whatever the provocation. Congressional isolationists hinted darkly that all wars were merely due to the cunning manipulations of "merchants of death."

Franklin Roosevelt, like Woodrow Wilson before him, knew better than to waste his political influence trying to reverse such a tidal wave of opinion, dangerous though it might be. He also knew that tides ebb and recede and was patient enough to wait. But in the meantime, who would speak for America's international obligations? Equally important to devising a preparedness strategy for the likelihood of America's involvement in yet another global war was the question of what would happen after that war. It was increasingly clear to establishment Progressives—at CFR, at the State Department, and even inside the White House—that the time to plan America's strategy for after a new Great War was before that war started in earnest.

But who would do the planning? And what would the plan look like?

Sixteen

LOOKING OVER THE HORIZON

1939–1941

"What I expect you to do is to have prepared for me the necessary number of baskets and the necessary number of alternative solutions for each problem in the baskets, so that when the time comes all I have to do is to reach into a basket and fish out a number of solutions that I am sure are sound and from which I can make my own choice."

—Franklin Roosevelt's orders to Undersecretary of State Sumner Welles on plans for a postwar United Nations[1]

*J*UST WHEN FRANKLIN ROOSEVELT needed him most, the darker side of Sumner Welles's life threatened to bring them both to ruin. It all began with a piece of routine political theater—a funeral.

In the early spring of 1940, William Brockman Bankhead, the Speaker of the U.S. House of Representatives, began to campaign to win the Democratic Party's presidential nomination to succeed Franklin D. Roosevelt in the autumn elections. It was widely assumed that FDR would keep to the tradition of two-term presidencies and not try for a third election.

For his part, the president kept silent that spring. He appeared to observers to be increasingly isolated in the White House, and many of the Brain Trust and other early advisers who had started out by his side in 1932 were now gone from Washington. The hard truth for many Roosevelt backers was that while they were still committed to the New Deal reforms, the Depression still persisted, and many blamed the president's capricious style of governing. Worse, war had begun in Europe in September 1939 and now hung like a threatening cloud on America's horizon. There also were whispers that Roosevelt's health had deteriorated badly.

By contrast, the sixty-six-year-old Bankhead was eight years older than the president, but, as a former University of Alabama football player, he was in fighting trim. Tall, darkly handsome, and a brilliant orator, friends teased him that he had greater dramatic talent than his famous daughter, actress Tallulah Bankhead. Better still, he had impeccable New Dealer credentials. As Majority Leader and then House Speaker, Bankhead had shepherded much of the Roosevelt legislative agenda through Congress since 1933. He had gone against the isolationist sympathies of many in his own party to dismantle some of the most recent Neutrality Act restraints on Roosevelt's efforts to send weapons and aid to France and Britain. Like Roosevelt, Bankhead had no wish to see the United States dragged into the war itself, and helping Britain and France stand against Germany and Italy would help prevent that.

There is considerable disagreement about whether Franklin Roosevelt intended all along to seek an unprecedented third term in office. But FDR knew better than to try to get ahead of public opinion, and at all cost, he would not risk having to fight for his party's nomination. In the early weeks of 1940, not only was Bankhead but also were John Nance Garner of Texas, FDR's vice president, and his Postmaster General James Farley of New York poised to run. If he could not appear to be an inevitable victor, Roosevelt would not try. So he coolly kept everyone guessing while he waited for a sign.

Two external factors also had to be weighed by Roosevelt. After the German conquest of Poland in the autumn of 1939, there had been a pause in the conflict through the winter months while the Wehrmacht regrouped. The period was dubbed the "phony war" by U.S. isolationists, who argued that since some peace settlement appeared likely, the European conflict posed no threat to America. Neutrality, they concluded, was working.

The second factor FDR had to consider was the Republican Party's ultimate choice for their candidate. East Coast establishment Republicans—the Dulles brothers included—toyed for a while with the name of Thomas Dewey, New York's crime-busting district attorney, but he was too young. In the spring, the leading GOP contender was Ohio senator Robert Taft, who charged Roosevelt with trying to force the U.S. into the European war as a way to expand his socialist agenda. While Taft attracted the support of some Midwestern and Southern conservatives, he dismayed the Eastern internationalists. Instead, the nomination went to Wendell Willkie, a Wall Street industrialist who promised to make existing New Deal programs more effective and to provide military supplies to the French and British. If there did not seem to be much different from the Roosevelt position, it's because there was not. Willkie held himself out as being untainted by party politics and a more efficient administrator if elected and hoped that would be enough to defeat any possible successor to the president, if not to FDR himself.

The abrupt reversal of American isolationism began on May 10, 1940 when German troops invaded France and marched into Paris a month after that. The collapse of France and impending invasion of Britain destroyed whatever faith there had been in neutrality as a foreign policy. Voters began to look for a president who would ensure the country was prepared to defend itself. When Willkie's campaign began to gain some traction, Democrat leaders from across the country put aside their doubts and began to bombard Roosevelt with pleas to run again.

Speaker Bankhead loyally withdrew his candidacy in support of the president at the 1940 Chicago convention. He hoped the sacrifice would earn him the vice-presidential nomination, but Roosevelt refused, instead choosing his secretary of agriculture, the eccentric Henry Wallace. Despite his disappointment, Bankhead agreed to give the key speech in Baltimore in September that launched the Roosevelt re-election campaign. However, before Bankhead could speak, he collapsed with an abdominal hemorrhage and, after being rushed back to the Bethesda Naval Hospital, died within a few days.

Roosevelt, ever alert to political symbolism and drama, chartered two special trains and on September 16 took most of his Cabinet, sixty-three members of the House, thirty senators, and much of the White House press corps to attend Bankhead's funeral in the tiny town of Jasper, Alabama. The newsreel cameras recorded an estimated throng of sixty thousand Alabamans gathered in the sweltering ninety-degree heat outside the rural church where the president and his delegation sweated through an interminable funeral service conducted by half a dozen local clergymen. Once over, the exhausted party fled back to the trains, which set out at once for the long overnight return to Washington. FDR went immediately to his sleeping compartment in his specially fitted car and did not appear again during the trip.

In the enforced idleness of the presidential train, many of FDR's entourage repaired to the dining car and began to drink heavily. While most retired early to their berths, several settled in for a long session of highballs and political shoptalk. Among them, Sumner Welles was one who stayed longest and became steadily more inebriated.

Not that this was remarkable in the Washington culture of the times when alcohol was a recognized social vehicle for relaxation. And if anyone on the president's train had stopped to think about it, Sumner Welles certainly deserved a chance to blow off steam and relax. Everyone recognized he had been under tremendous strain over the last few years doing his job and the job of, many said, Secretary of State Cordell Hull's as well. But what happened next would touch off a crisis within the administration that would have far-reaching consequences.

Although there are some small variances in the different reports, the events on the president's train on its overnight journey back to Washington are well documented.[2] By 2:00 AM on the morning of the eighteenth, Welles was left drinking in the dining car with vice-presidential nominee Henry Wallace and John M. Carmody, head of the Federal Works Administration. Welles had been rambling about his much-publicized "peace mission" interviews with the heads of the warring European powers—including lengthy talks with Hitler and Mussolini—when Wallace and Carmody retired as the train neared Bristol, Tennessee.

John Stone, a senior Pullman car waiter, responded to a call for coffee from Welles's compartment at about 5:30 AM as the train headed for Roanoke, Virginia. Welles suddenly offered Stone twenty dollars to disrobe and perform oral sex while he remained clothed. Politely but firmly, Stone refused and returned to the dining car. Four more times, the visibly drunk Welles rang to demand coffee, and each time a porter or waiter arrived, he repeated his demand for sex. One waiter was briefly trapped in the compartment when Welles suddenly barred the door. By now, the alarmed staff had alerted dining car manager W. F. Kush and a conductor, W. A. Brooks. They in turn roused a Pullman company inspector and Luther Thomas, the Southern Railways special assistant for security, to listen to the outraged porters. Dale Whiteside, head of FDR's Secret Service detail on the trip, was called, and he and Thomas ordered another porter to take coffee to Welles and leave the compartment door open so they could hear whether the offers would be repeated. But Welles spotted Whiteside lurking in the hallway and slammed his door shut, coming out only when the train reached Washington's Union Station later that day.

Given the pervasive public horror of homosexual acts at that time, Whiteside's report of the incident to Colonel Edmund W. Starling, overall head of the Secret Service back in Washington, should have led to Welles's immediate dismissal from government with some spurious story about his health given out to the press. This was, after all, just a few weeks before the election, and Willkie had been hammering the Administration for bad judgments. But nothing happened. Nor was any action taken a few weeks later when reports reached the White House that on October 11, Welles had gotten drunk again on a trip to Cleveland to make a speech and had importuned a Pennsylvania Railroad waiter and a porter to perform the same acts. FBI Director J. Edgar Hoover was ordered to conduct interviews of all the Southern Railroad personnel involved in the first incident. At the end of January 1941, Hoover delivered the only copies of that report to a noncommittal FDR, who had them locked away in the files of his military aide General Edwin "Pa" Watson. And there matters stood with Welles apparently untouched by the affair but with the time bomb of the scandal ticking away.

There had always been two opinions about Sumner Welles. Friends were devoted to the brilliant, idealistic, generous man whose shy reserve hid a gentle sense of humor. Others were put off by that same reserve, which they saw as punctilious snobbery, and while they conceded his brilliant intellect, they also charged Welles with using it ruthlessly. Both views were accurate, but the brittle outer shell of humorless dignity that Welles had built around his public persona had grown thicker in the years leading up to World War II. This was partly due to the strain caused by his ever-increasing workload, but it did seem that the harder he worked, the more enemies he accumulated.

In a town where strong personalities and high politics fueled passionate arguments at the best of times, Welles seemed to defy his detractors with his tailored suits from London, his ever-present walking stick, and his coldly solemn manner, which contrasted with the backslapping good fellowship of most power brokers. Many New Deal appointees despised Welles, but they also knew that Eleanor Roosevelt steadfastly considered him part of her family. More importantly, the president, by the start of his second term in office, had made Welles the only man he listened to in a State Department he had always distrusted.

In May 1937, when Roosevelt's second term got underway, he moved to make the State Department more responsive to presidential desires. He filled the post of undersecretary, which had lain vacant for a year. Welles's rival had been Assistant Secretary R. Walton Moore, the isolationist ex-congressional friend of Secretary Hull and mentor of Bill Bullitt, FDR's ambassador to France. The president forestalled any protest but pleased no one by naming Welles undersecretary and reviving the moribund post of counselor for Moore, both having equal rank and the same $10,000 salary. The president made it clear, however, that Welles was second in command to Hull. Bullitt was especially miffed, for he had journeyed to Warm Springs to plead Moore's case with Roosevelt and felt personally insulted. Still, Bullitt and Welles exchanged coolly friendly letters of cooperation, and he began to send Welles rare flower seedlings from France for the lavish gardens at Sumner's Oxon Hill estate, where he knew Roosevelt often went to relax.

One point that Bullitt recognized and initially welcomed was what Hull and Moore feared: The elevation of Welles signaled a shift in American foreign policy attitudes. The State Department at that time still had a total of roughly seven hundred Foreign Service officers spread around the world and a budget ($16 million) that was smaller than what it had been in 1932. American diplomacy had been a backwater of government service that could only react to crises after they occurred; there was no capacity to anticipate or plan strategy, let alone move it forward.

Welles moved quickly to change that culture. While he would in the future appear to advance policies that were more aggressive than the president's at the time, it is more accurate to say that Sumner Welles and Franklin Roosevelt shared the same vision of America's future role in world affairs. Both men recalled how, in 1918, Woodrow Wilson had hoped a League of Nations would become the functioning mechanism to prevent war among other nations so the United States could return to its mission of building a just society at home. Two decades later, FDR and Welles had developed a different vision.

Christopher D. O'Sullivan, a historian of the founding of the United Nations, notes:

> Welles was a self-professed internationalist, and his vision of a postwar world aimed to promote largely national objectives of security through international means. His promotion of idealistic principles such as liberal democracy and self-determination perhaps owed more to calculations of America's national interests than to high ideals or selfless altruism. While an idealist in

his public pronouncements, he endeavored to promote the more specific needs of America's expanding economy and strategic interests. Welles would perhaps have felt quite at home with a definition of internationalism that placed it in the service of the pursuit of national interests. He believed the two concepts were perfectly compatible.[3]

That description fits Franklin Roosevelt equally well. It underscores how the Wilsonian dream to keep the turmoil between other nations from intruding on the quest for domestic perfection had evolved into the recognition by FDR and other Progressives that there was no escaping America's responsibility to be the leading force for good in the world. There was another key difference between Roosevelt and Wilson as each viewed their options on the eve of a great war. FDR repeatedly told intimates that Wilson had erred by waiting until the United States had actually entered the First World War to plan his postwar strategy. He would not make that mistake. Roosevelt saw early on that another war in Europe was likely. Contrary to conspiracy theorists' beliefs, he did not want the United States to fight in that war, but he did recognize that such a conflict would thrust a new set of responsibilities on the nation, whatever the postwar environment might be. This explains his orders to Welles for "a basket" of options that he could choose from when the time was right. Like Wilson, he wanted his own Inquiry to tell him what the facts were, and, like Wilson, his faith in his own instincts for the right was unshakable.

Welles understood and agreed. He moved quickly to reshape the State Department with a speed that stunned Hull, who was frequently away during those months when the lesions on his lungs left him breathless and bedridden. Welles consolidated the Latin American and Mexican divisions into a single American Republics staff. He did the same with the Eastern and Western European divisions. Both moves allowed him to oust officers who had long opposed his Good Neighbor policy for Latin America and the new friendly relationship the president wanted with Soviet Russia. At the same time, he brought in powerful new allies including Norman Davis, the distinguished arms negotiator, and Adolf Berle, an original Brain Trust adviser on economics and finance.

Against all protocol, Welles also established daily direct contact with Roosevelt, sending him a stream of personal memos and getting called to the White House for advice on matters that were often referred to Hull only after decisions had been made. Hurt and increasingly bitter, Hull nevertheless felt he could not resign since he represented a political constituency in the Congress and a deeply held attitude of prudence and caution that he was certain Roosevelt lacked and needed. To quit would be dishonorable. So he suffered and fumed and blamed Welles more than Roosevelt for creating such dissension.[4] Welles compounded the secretary's anger by becoming a skillful selective leaker of information and trial balloons of FDR's ideas to Drew Pearson and other leading Washington correspondents—leaks that often underscored Hull's isolation from affairs.

A lively academic debate continues over just how both Roosevelt and Welles interpreted the threat posed by the dictators who were roiling Europe in those final years before the war. It is true that within the ranks of the Foreign Service (and among many citizens), opinion continued for some time to be mixed between grudging admiration for the superficial appearance of progress and order achieved by Hitler and Mussolini along with distaste for the flamboyant militarism and absurd saluting of the tyrants' henchmen. Europe, for many Americans, was still "over there" and only of passing concern when weighed against the problems closer to home. Public sympathy and calls for protests over worsening Nazi persecution of Germany's Jewish citizens grew and were often brought by Eleanor in personal entreaties to her husband. Roosevelt deliberately remained aloof, in part no doubt to deny further ammunition to his enemies who hinted that FDR himself was Jewish, and that his "Jew Deal" programs were part of a Zionist plot. As unseemly as the negative tone in today's political arena surely is, none of it can compare with the sheer vitriol and slander that was aimed at FDR and Eleanor by the demagogues of the day.

Instead, taking a leaf from Abraham Lincoln's instinctive finessing of the slavery issue in his early call to save the Union, Roosevelt cast the rising Nazi menace in Europe as a threat to U.S. safety by pointing to Latin America's increasing trade with and financial ties to German and Italian firms. German economic penetration in key Latin American investments in commodities, banking, new airlines, and communications were of particular concern. Roosevelt began to worry in public that if Hitler did succeed in dominating the European continent, his next target would be South America, which would put him within striking distance of the United States. Through most of 1938, Welles and Treasury Secretary Henry Morgenthau Jr. arranged a series of export credits and other aid to Latin American governments to help insulate them against foreign market penetration. Secretary Hull was kept busy attending a series of hemispheric conferences in the winters of both 1937 and 1938 that gradually stiffened the resolve of South American governments to oppose non-American intrusion in the region. Lurid press reports of German agents plotting on the Mexican border and alarm over "fifth columnists" stoked public alarm.

If Roosevelt and Welles were too disengaged from Europe, part of the blame lay with the Europeans themselves. Until it was too late, most French and British leaders refused to believe that Hitler would ever risk a military adventure in Western Europe. This was a time when British prime minister Neville Chamberlain and his French counterparts were widely applauded for surrendering Czechoslovakian independence in the Munich Pact as a hostage for Hitler's pledge of "peace in our time." Just as Hitler had confounded early predictions of his downfall, his ability to gull foreign negotiators with his protestations of peace is incredible in hindsight. Nancy Astor and her Cliveden Set of influential aristocrats reflected the opinion of many Europeans who conceded that the Versailles Treaty had treated Germany unjustly. Many dreaded the threat of Bolshevism and another European war far more than they were outraged by Hitler's aggression.

To complicate matters, the president received vastly conflicting intelligence from his principal embassies in London, Paris, and Rome. Joseph Kennedy, the ambassador to the Court of St. James, remained pessimistic to the end about Britain's willingness to go to war with Hitler over any issue. William Bullitt, whose popularity and access to top French officials was extraordinarily intimate, predicted the ultimate victory of the French army until the last moments before its surrender. William Philips, FDR's old friend in Rome, firmly believed in Mussolini's abilities to control Hitler's intentions.

No one had his attitudes more knocked about by events during this time than Philip Kerr, the House of Truth regular visitor from Britain and long-time friend of the Dupont Circle set. After resigning as David Lloyd George's private secretary on foreign affairs in 1922, Kerr returned to journalism and held a series of government appointments. In 1925, he became the director of the Rhodes Trust that administered the prestigious Rhodes Scholarships, which brought elite scholars from North America, the Dominions, and Germany to study at Oxford. Like its founder, the imperial industrialist Cecil Rhodes, Kerr advocated transforming the British Empire into a commonwealth of democracies, and he dreamed of some day including the United States in a powerful force for world peace unified by common language, law, and culture. Germany, with its Anglo-Saxon heritage, would be a more preferable ally to such a common cause than the undependable French.

In 1930 Kerr inherited his family's ancient Scottish title, and as the eleventh Marquess of Lothian, he took a seat in the House of Lords, which provided him with expanded opportunities to advocate his ideas. He continued to visit his old Dupont Circle friends, especially Frankfurter and Lippmann, and through his leadership in Chatham House studies, he was a regular contributor to the CFR's *Foreign Affairs* quarterly and to the increasing exchange of data between the two institutions that went on through the final years of the decade. Starting in 1935, the CFR and Chatham House entered into a series of joint confidential studies on the key issues of debts, trade, and currency instability that threatened world peace.

Supported by his old friend Eustace Percy, who was in the House of Commons and held a number of important government posts, Lord Lothian also stepped up his visits to Germany on Rhodes Trust matters but came to see himself as an unofficial peace negotiator with the Hitler government. The Germans, well aware of his Cliveden Set friendship with Nancy Astor and other high officials, played him skillfully. While the Nazis were busy rooting out suspect church groups and intellectuals, they carefully restrained any overt oppression of either the German Rhodes Scholars or the Christian Scientists until the very end. It was a clear effort to placate the concerns of what the Germans hoped would be an important constituency inside British society—Kerr, the Astors, and a host of other influential officials who came later to be branded as "The Cliveden Set Appeasers." To the intense irritation of the British Foreign Office, Lothian was granted a number of private interviews with Hitler and other top Nazi leaders between 1935 and 1937 that convinced him, "I think Hitler genuinely means peace on its merits."[5]

Lothian quickly realized his mistake in October 1938 after the ominous truth of the Munich Pact had sunk in. In the attempt to appease Hitler, Italy, France, and the UK had allowed Nazi Germany to annex Czechoslovakia without resistance. In speeches in the House of Lords and a flood of articles, he began to advocate a "union" of democracies to oppose the dictators. In a series of memos sent through Chatham House to Armstrong at CFR, and from him to Welles, Lothian went further and envisioned a grand alliance of the British Commonwealth and the Pan American Union, an enlarged Good Neighbor organization that explicitly would be directed by London and Washington as a bulwark against totalitarianism. However impractical the idea might have appeared at first reading, it nevertheless appealed to Welles and Roosevelt. Both privately signaled their willingness to at least consider closer ties with Britain and that, to the consternation of the British Foreign Office, prompted Prime Minister Chamberlain—now desperately trying to prepare his nation to defend itself—to ask Lothian to go to Washington as ambassador to the United States. He sailed for America in December 1938 to get a firsthand assessment of American attitudes.

Lothian got a shock in his first conversation with President Roosevelt on January 2, 1939. As the president later wrote to a friend:

> I wish the British would stop this "We who are about to die, salute thee" attitude. Lord Lothian was here the other day,

started the conversation by saying he had completely abandoned his former belief that Hitler could be dealt with . . . and went on to say that the British had been for a thousand years guardians of Anglo-Saxon civilization—that the scepter or the sword or something like that had dropped from their palsied fingers—that the U.S.A. must snatch it up—that F.D.R. alone could save the world, etc., etc. I got mad clear through and told him that just so long as he or Britishers like him took that attitude of complete despair, the British would not be worth saving anyway. What the British need today is a good stiff grog, inducing not only the desire to save civilization but the continued belief that they can do it. In such an event they will get a lot more support from their American cousins.[6]

Lothian recognized that Roosevelt knew the American mood far better than he did, and so he quickly changed his message. Throughout 1939 and 1940, the new ambassador tirelessly traveled about the country speaking enthusiastically about Britain's will to fight but also warning that if Hitler did conquer Britain, its Royal Navy would cease to be the shield of the U.S. Atlantic coastline. With the U.S. Navy most heavily committed in the Pacific, America would truly be vulnerable. A united front of the British Commonwealth and the American democracies was the world's only hope for a restoration of peace.

In truth, Roosevelt, Welles, and the participants in the CFR study groups were already thinking along similar lines. They dreaded the prospect of the nation having to go into a war caused by others. But a resolve was forming—even as most of the nation still clung to hopes of neutrality—that America's role in international affairs after the imminent war had to be the dominant force. Both Ham Armstrong and Allen Dulles were now writing regular essays in *Foreign Affairs* and giving radio addresses urging a more thoughtful foreign strategy than reliance on neutrality legislation to keep America safe. In a draft of an essay Dulles prepared for the quarterly, he asked,

> Have not the events of the past few years in Europe and the Far East had a sufficiently sobering effect on public opinion to justify

our State Department in instituting further studies to see whether
legislation might not be proposed which would make the United
States a more positive influence for peace? . . . There is no gainsay-
ing the fact that we are viewed with a certain cynicism abroad. The
dictators are convinced that the United States would do no more
than give lip service to the cause of peace unless the United States
were directly and immediately attacked. They count on a passivity
quite alien to the American temper. If we are to have an influence
for peace or war—a decision in which every living American has a
direct stake—we will need more effective weapons in our hands.
There may not now be much time left in which to forge them.[7]

What Dulles advocated was a program of systematic research
and policy planning about the myriad issues—political and economic—that the United States would face after the allied democracies had triumphed over the fascist dictatorships. Interestingly,
there appears to have been no serious contemplation by Dulles or
anyone else of any compromise settlement with totalitarianism.

Contrary to other accounts, neither Welles nor the CFR waited
until the war began in earnest in September 1939 to begin looking
past the conflict to how America would be transformed. In November 1938, a full three years before the U.S. would be drawn into
the war, the first meeting of a European policy study group took
place at the CFR offices led by Allen Dulles and George S. Messersmith, an assistant secretary of state and ally of Welles. A series
of other meetings followed into the spring of 1939 as the Council's
experts set agendas and the parameters for policy recommendations
on U.S. foreign strategy for Asia and Latin America as well as Europe. The meetings between the Dulles-Messersmith committee
were kept secret from Hull.[8] Also kept secret was a formal pact with
the Chatham House experts to coordinate postwar policy research,
which would be offered to both governments.

Messersmith remained the contact point between Welles and
the CFR in September 1939 when Germany invaded Poland.
Hamilton Armstrong and CFR's director Walter Mallory came to
the State Department a few days after the invasion with a formal
offer to undertake the research to provide the government "concrete

proposals designed to safeguard American interests in the settlement which will be undertaken when hostilities cease."[9]

A series of secret meetings then took place through the autumn, often at Messersmith's home in Washington to avoid Secretary Hull's discovering the formation of such a planning group. Hull would have feared that public disclosure that FDR was even considering postwar planning would create a backlash fear that America was deliberately being led into the war. Hull also clung to his fundamental belief that all that was needed to stabilize the world situation was a general free trade treaty and further disarmament talks. Also, the very notion that the plans had been instituted by Welles would have angered him further.

Surprisingly, the secret held for a while. On December 8, 1939 at Messersmith's home, CFR and the State Department agreed to the details of a War and Peace Studies program that would be conducted by Council committees and funded by a special grant from the Rockefeller Foundation. The program initially would be a stand-alone project, but it was foreseen that it would be folded into a formal State Department staff once official funding was obtained. The steering committee included Norman Davis, Hamilton Armstrong, Walter Mallory, and veterans of the Paris Peace Conference such as Allen Dulles, Isaiah Bowman, and Whitney Shepardson. There were to be four main areas of study: arms control, economic and financial problems, territorial claims, and "political problems."[10]

While the agreement studiously avoided spelling it out, both CFR and State organizers of the War and Peace Studies were already agreed that one of the matters that the experts on "political problems" would concentrate on was the creation of an international forum after the war to peacefully resolve disputes among nations. There was no notion of reforming the League of Nations in Geneva. A new organization would be created. It would be based in the United States and, at least initially, directed by the United States much the same way the alliance of the Pan American bloc was influenced through a combination of aggressive diplomacy and economic aid.

The participants could not know it, but they were exactly two years away from America being pulled into a conflict even more horrible than the Great War they had vowed would never happen again. Many questions were left to be resolved about this new organization—its name, its specific areas of activity, what nations would belong, and what role America's allies would play in its formation. But significantly, the seed that would become the United Nations had been planted in the minds of the planners. They would move with surprising speed to make the idea a reality. Speed was essential because events were crowding in on America in these days as its isolation was ending.

Seventeen

SUCCESS THREATENED BY SCANDAL

1940–1943

"Mr. Bullitt, why don't you shoot that man (Sumner Welles) for me?
You men are terrible. You protect each other even when you commit
crimes. I don't see why you or Cordell hasn't had this man put in
jail or shot."

—Frances Whitney (Mrs. Cordell) Hull, April 25, 1943[1]

IT WAS ALWAYS IMPOSSIBLE TO KEEP a secret in Washington—
D.C. gossip is currency in the political marketplace—and in
the autumn of 1940, the capital was awash with such uncertainty
that rumors crowded in on one another in confusion.

Franklin Roosevelt had a lot on his mind during the final days
of 1940. That may be the best explanation for why he ignored the
reports of Sumner Welles's bizarre behavior on trains. Whenever
FDR was faced with a hard choice, he often stalled for time until
he saw a way clear. He had an election to win, and Wendell Willkie
appeared to be doing far better than Alf Landon had in 1936.[2] In
Europe, the war appeared to be going from bad to worse. France
and Norway had fallen to the Nazis. Britain was being pounded by
the nonstop bombing of Hitler's Luftwaffe. Winston Churchill had
become prime minister in May, but Roosevelt was determined not

to commit America to propping up the British Empire, and he worried whether the two leaders could agree on an overarching strategy to defeat the dictators.

Although the joint War and Peace Studies project was just being organized, FDR pushed Welles to expedite the research, and there were a series of confidential White House meetings where Ham Armstrong was brought in to hear the president brainstorm about his postwar vision.

At this point, Roosevelt had no specific structure in mind for the international peace organization he wanted. He was understandably preoccupied with the more immediate task of getting the United States armed against the dangers rising in both Europe and Asia. So when he described the "basket" of options he wanted prepared, he spoke in deliberately vague terms. Even so, it was clear to both Welles and Armstrong that Roosevelt wanted something that would unite other democracies—particularly those of the Western Hemisphere—under American leadership. These united nations (still in lower-case letters) would first defeat the forces of Nazism and Fascism and then be the nucleus of a movement toward the higher ground of permanent world peace and economic stability.

To further complicate matters, the increasingly bitter power struggle at the State Department between Secretary Hull and Welles was now heightened by the arrival on the scene of William Bullitt, who had come home for good in late July of 1940 from the abandoned embassy in Nazi-held Paris. Bullitt and Welles had maintained a superficially cordial relationship until a few months earlier. In previous years, Sumner and Mathilde had invited Anne Bullitt to Oxon Hill while she was at Foxcroft School in Virginia; Bullitt had helped guide one of Sumner's sons when he had visited France. But Bullitt had convinced himself that Franklin Roosevelt had deputized him to be his main source of intelligence and advice on European matters, and it was a turf he was determined to protect from interlopers. Bullitt had ambitions for higher office but had always aspired to the role of the president's top adviser on foreign affairs. Welles was clearly a rival who must be marginalized.

But earlier in February 1940, however, FDR had succumbed to hints from Berlin that Hitler's regime might welcome the president attempting to do what Wilson had tried in 1916: to broker a peace with France and Britain that would leave Germany with the lands in Eastern Europe already under Nazi control. Instead of Bullitt, the president sent Welles to make the initial contacts. Despite warnings from Lord Lothian that London would oppose any American interference at that point, Welles set out with a large entourage—including Mathilde and servants—in what the press at once hailed as "a peace mission."

For six arduous weeks he crisscrossed Europe meeting with all the major leaders and for a time was convinced that Hitler meant to work out a deal, that Mussolini would restrain Hitler from further depredations, and that the British and French would come to terms eventually. It was, as he later ruefully admitted, "a forlorn hope." The reality was quite different. Hitler and Mussolini told Welles what he wanted to hear in the midst of their own secret negotiations that would send Italy's troops into the Balkans when the Germans struck west into France. The French were in confusion, but the British had at last roused themselves into a stubborn refusal to consider anything but defeating Germany once again. Welles was made to look foolish, and FDR was embarrassed once they realized the truth.

Worse, now Bullitt was beside himself with rage. He had returned to Washington for a brief holiday just as Welles was setting out without anyone having thought to ask his opinion. Bullitt refused to meet with Welles and sulked off to Florida during the mission. Upon his return to France just before its surrender, Bullitt became increasingly strident in his demands that Roosevelt send warplanes and arms to the French military, and the president feared the ambassador might go public with his complaints in the midst of the election campaign. Instead, Bullitt struck a heroic pose as the German troops neared Paris and the French government retreated to its eventual new base in the spa town of Vichy in the south. Refusing Hull's orders to stay with the evacuating French government, Bullitt stayed in Paris and became its self-appointed mayor, saying he would lead any resistance if the Wehrmacht began to destroy the city. The Germans had no such intentions, and Bullitt found himself no longer wanted as the U.S. representative to the Petain regime. Even though the U.S. was still nominally a neutral nation, Bullitt's strident anti-Nazi stance had made him persona non grata among the collaborators who were in control in Vichy.

Bullitt returned to Washington for good in late July and kept a low profile because the president had hinted that he might make him the next secretary of the Navy. But once FDR privately decided to run for a third term, he moved quickly to appoint two leading Republicans to his cabinet—the veteran Henry Stimson as secretary of war and Frank Knox as Navy secretary. To compound Bullitt's disappointment, the move also put a stop to the president's private assurances that he would prefer Cordell Hull as his successor in the White House, hints that had kept the secretary loyally quiet despite his frustration with being kept out of key policy decisions. The fissures that had developed between Welles and Hull began to crack the State Department hierarchy into two warring camps. Matters that had been secret now became weapons in the struggle.

Hull had learned about the confidential War and Peace Studies program early in 1940 but had held his fire through the election campaign. Early in 1941, however, he moved to establish his own research planning staff for postwar strategy. Leo Pasvolsky, an economist and expert on trade policy on the State staff, was appointed director.[3] He soon became the secretary's most trusted foreign policy adviser, in effect serving the same function that Welles provided the president. Hull then demanded and got Roosevelt's approval to fold the CFR program research effort into this new department. Most of the CFR members—Ham Armstrong, Isaiah Bowman, Norman Davis—kept their membership in the new joint project, but Hull assumed the chairmanship with Pasvolsky in charge of the actual operations.

Since Welles and Pasvolsky had sharply different views of what postwar strategy should be—especially on the question of an international peace organization—the stage was set for confrontation. Pasvolsky saw any new United Nations forum as an improved version of the League of Nations where all nations would have an equal vote in resolving international problems—something along the lines of the way today's UN General Assembly operates. Welles (reflecting FDR's determination) was not opposed so much to the idea of a general forum, but he insisted that the United States, backed by its strongest wartime allies—Britain, Russia, and China—have an overriding power (akin to the way the UN Security Council operates) to take direct action in a crisis. One of the more contentious debates that went on between the two camps was whether this new United Nations should be provided with its own army and navy forces that would be separate from control by member nations.

Welles may have lost some prestige for the moment, but he remained Roosevelt's main conduit for foreign policy, including a new mandate to provide urgent military aid to the Soviet Union once the Germans had invaded Russia. But the campaign to oust him from the State Department had begun in earnest, with William Bullitt serving as the point man for his enemies.

There is some difference of opinion as to who first learned of Welles's sexual misadventures on the train, Bullitt or his old mentor, State Department Counselor R. Walton Moore. One version has Southern Railway officials at the head office in Philadelphia taking their investigation directly to Bullitt a few days after the episode in September 1940.[4] In Bullitt's own papers and in statements he made at the time, the Southern Railway's security chief, Luther Thomas, took his interviews with the train staff to his Virginia friend Walton Moore.[5] But Moore apparently neither acted on the information nor informed Secretary Hull until well afterward. That winter, Moore contracted pneumonia and, in failing health, resigned from the State Department, handing over the incriminating documents to Bullitt. He died in February 1941. With his usual taste for drama, Bullitt claimed he had made a deathbed promise to Moore to bring the information to the president's attention as an urgent matter since the scandal made Welles a dangerous security risk from blackmail and a political risk to FDR personally.

Bullitt was impetuous but not foolhardy. He was on thin ice with Roosevelt already. FDR was annoyed with his indiscrete press comments and was resentful over the cavalier way Bullitt was treating Missy LeHand. There had been no job of any kind waiting for him when he got back from France, and he had gamely resigned from State. Yet at FDR's request, he had given a series of rousing speeches in the ensuing months urging support for the president's preparedness program even though he disapproved of parts of it—most notably, FDR's efforts to rush aid to the Russians. His hopes of forcing FDR to find him a Cabinet post only produced offers of ambassadorships to lesser countries that were beneath him.

Through his off-again, on-again romance with Missy LeHand, Bullitt also knew that the president's emotional life was in considerable private turmoil. To attack Welles, the one man upon whom Roosevelt placed such explicit trust, was a dangerous move at the best of times. Hull, unwilling to risk his own neck, kept urging Bullitt to press the case more aggressively. Welles must go.

While he waited for an opportune moment to confront Roosevelt about Welles, Bullitt could not resist telling others what he knew. Among those he confided in was his old lover Cissy Patterson, who was the owner-editor of *The Washington Times-Herald* and an implacable foe of the New Deal and FDR personally. Though Patterson refused to print anything in her newspaper, she and others spread the gossip throughout the city, and important members of Congress who were opposed to Roosevelt's war policies began to take notice and plot. Owen Brewster, a Republican senator from Maine and leading isolationist, began to demand to see the FBI report from J. Edgar Hoover and to threaten a public hearing. For the moment, Brewster could be stalled since the chairman of the committee that would conduct such a probe was a staunch FDR loyalist, Senator Harry S. Truman.

Other journalists caught the scent. Columnist Drew Pearson refused to believe the rumors of his old chum from his bachelor days; *New York Times* correspondent Arthur Krock and a young bureau reporter, James Reston, both saw copies of the railroad interviews but wrote nothing. Homosexuality was still not a topic that any mainstream newspaper could portray with any comfort, and even when stories were printed, they invariably used euphemistic phrases like "vice" and "indecent behavior." With the added complication of African American Pullman car staff being the targets, the Welles story was just too hot not to be spiked. As for Welles, when a reporter did confront him with the rumors, his response made it clear that he had completely suppressed the memory of the affair; he had been so drunk he had no recollection of either incident.

Bullitt's gossip about Welles had a particularly vicious tone that was at considerable odds with an important part of his personal life. In 1934 when he was setting up the U.S. Embassy in Moscow, he recruited an expert shorthand stenographer and speed typist named Carmel Offie from the State Department's clerical staff. The twenty-five-year-old Offie made up for his lack of formal education with a fierce dedication to his job and a willingness to work the punishing hours that Bullitt demanded. Offie soon became an indispensible aide and companion. When Bullitt took over the embassy in Paris, Offie went with him as the chargé d'affaires and doubled as a courier of sensitive letters and gifts that the ambassador sent across the Atlantic to Missy and the president, both of whom thought him "a nice young man."[6]

But Offie also was openly and promiscuously homosexual and had a series of fraught encounters with male prostitutes in Paris and London that sometimes required Bullitt's intervention. The Ambassador could hardly take a censorious pose with Offie because his own serial romances with various married women had forced him to set up a separate apartment away from the Paris Embassy and his estate near Chantilly to avoid his own scandals. It is clear that Bullitt was very fond of Offie and relied on his loyalty through the years.

But that friendship makes the particularly virulent campaign against Welles that Bullitt waged between 1941 and 1943 puzzling. All the stranger is the attitude of Cordell Hull, who reserved his most brutal Tennessee epithets for Welles's conduct. Even as he and Bullitt were fulminating against the undersecretary, an undercover Washington policeman arrested Offie for soliciting in the public toilets on Lafayette Park across from the White House. Hull personally intervened with a letter saying Offie was on a top-secret mission for the State Department to meet an informant there.[7]

One factor that may have driven Bullitt was his sense that he had lost what he had always assumed was a special place in Franklin Roosevelt's affections. Throughout the early years of the Administration, Bullitt had fantasized that his combination of unctuous flattery and cheeky but insightful advice had won FDR over completely. For his part, Roosevelt had always been skeptical about Bullitt ("He talks too much") even when he, in turn, treated him with hearty familiarity. The president also was aware of how quickly Bullitt could turn against a patron if he was disappointed—his savaging of Woodrow Wilson was still remembered—and he considered it better to keep the man inside the tent but on a short leash.

Roosevelt had been gradually growing more irritated with Bullitt ever since his dramatic departure from France. Bullitt was talking too much to newspapermen about sensitive policy matters, and the spreading gossip about Welles was getting back to the White House as well. Another factor was that FDR resented how unhappy Missy LeHand was becoming about her love affair with Bullitt. There had been an informal engagement for a while, but now it was off.[8] Both Bullitt and Missy reportedly were drinking more heavily than they had in earlier years when they did see each other. Missy's health (she had rheumatic heart problems) became a matter of concern to the president, who depended on her so completely.

The president's own chaotic private life could not have helped Missy's stress levels at that moment. The marriage between Franklin and Eleanor Roosevelt had by then evolved into a sterile symbiotic relationship. While they went through the superficial gestures of affection with each other, Eleanor now saw herself as a kind of moral alter ego for the president, who could be evasive and contradictory when faced with hard choices. This probably suited Roosevelt, for it left the detail work of attending to vexing questions about social justice and reform to Eleanor while he focused on the broad horizon. So with humorless determination, the First Lady would risk the president's occasional wrath and force him to do things he would have otherwise let slide.

Her own emotional life was nurtured by her continuing close ties to her friends from the Todhunter School days—Nancy Cook and

Marion Dickerman—and a new and intense relationship with Lorena Hickock, an Associated Press reporter who became a confidant and companion. FDR might deride "those she males," but he recognized they provided Eleanor with emotional sustenance she could not get elsewhere. The argument against Eleanor's having any sexual relations with any of these women is supported by the openly intense affection she lavished on Earl Miller, her bodyguard in the Albany governor's mansion. Like her husband, Eleanor Roosevelt greatly needed unquestioning affection, and she got it where she could.

Increasingly, however, the complicated burdens of preparing an unwilling nation for the prospect of war put damaging stress on Roosevelt's own health. He needed increasing periods of rest and relaxation, and that, in turn, increased the distance between husband and wife. The famed "children's hour" cocktail break before White House dinners for years had been an enjoyable ritual for FDR and his secretaries and intimates.

The president prided himself (somewhat questionably) on his skill as a mixer of the latest drink fad—martinis, Manhattans, and Old Fashioneds—and imposed an ironclad rule against discussing any business while they all wound down. But Eleanor too often would intrude on the interlude with a batch of urgent papers for his attention and would provoke a burst of anger from him that would dampen the affair. Increasingly, Roosevelt began to avoid Eleanor when he needed a respite. He took to waiting until she had left the White House for some evening function, and would then summon younger staff members to the family quarters and demand a flow of diverting gossip and chatter while he poured fairly lethal drinks for them.[9]

He also turned increasingly to the company of "Mrs. Paul Johnson," the code name given by the Secret Service to Lucy Mercer Rutherfurd. Lucy had never gone completely out of Roosevelt's life. They had corresponded during the 1920s, and he had invited her to attend both the 1933 and 1937 inauguration celebrations. White House telephone operators had "Mrs. Johnson" on their list of privileged callers who were to be put through at once to the Oval Office. Biographer Joseph Persico lists half a dozen such calls in just the first hundred days—calls that were discreetly placed by Lucy from a telephone in Augusta, Georgia, which was fifteen miles from the Rutherfurd estate in Aiken, South Carolina.[10] The president also managed a number of clandestine visits with Lucy whenever he was on a train trip that took him near Aiken or the other Rutherfurd estate in New Jersey.

In the spring of 1941, FDR and Lucy got together more often and more openly. Lucy's husband Winthrop Rutherfurd, seventy-nine and in failing health, suffered a stroke, and Lucy prevailed on the president to get him admitted for treatment at the Walter Reed Army Hospital. FDR began to meet Lucy at roadside encounters in the Virginia countryside, and they soon began to have more intimate get-togethers at the home of a mutual friend in nearby Leesburg. With the connivance of FDR's daughter Anna and Missy, "Mrs. Johnson" sometimes came for tea whenever Eleanor was safely out of town on some official business.

While Missy appears to have been willing to bring Lucy and Franklin together, she was not prepared to face the emergence of a third rival for his affections in the statuesque form of Princess Martha of Norway. Martha and her husband, Prince Olav, and the rest of the Norwegian royal family had fled the Nazi conquest of their country in 1940 and set up a government-in-exile in London. But she had been ordered to take her three children to the safer environs of America, and both Eleanor and Franklin had welcomed the royal refugees into quarters at the White House where Martha soon began an open flirtation with the obviously enchanted president.

Missy could hardly be jealous of the fiftyish Lucy, who had become a gracious and affectionate friend to both the secretary and to Anna Roosevelt, the vulnerable daughter. But Martha was a Nordic beauty in her early thirties who reacted with girlish adoration when FDR began to play the role of the naughty uncle, teasing her with risqué stories and jovial embraces. When a suitable house was found for Martha in suburban Maryland, Roosevelt regularly spent long afternoons there, and the princess took over the seat at White House dinners next to FDR that once had been Missy's place of honor.[11] Missy, who was smoking three packs of cigarettes a day by now and drinking more than was good for her, began to fray at the seams.

It was in this environment that Bullitt made his first foray to get Roosevelt to fire Sumner Welles. In April 1941, Bullitt records that he went to the White House to turn down an offer of a post in a civil defense organization the president wanted to set up. Taking a breath, he informed the president of the deathbed promise exacted by Walton Moore and handed him a copy of the Luther Thomas affidavits on the Welles incident.

The president read the first page of this document and looked over the other pages and finally said,

> I know about this already. I have had a full report on it. There is truth in the allegations . . . . I then said that Judge Moore had felt the maintenance of Welles in public office was a menace to the country since he was subject to blackmail by foreign powers and that foreign powers had used cases of this kind to get men in their power and that the Judge also was convinced that this matter was of utmost danger to the President personally since it was the most scandalous behavior of any public official within his memory. A terrible scandal might arise at any time which would undermine the confidence of the country in him, the President . . . I asked the President if he knew that Welles had behaved in the same way on the Pennsylvania Railroad in the first half of October. The President said he knew that Welles had behaved in the same way . . . on that trip but added that he thought that Welles would never behave that way again since he was having Welles watched by a guardian day and night to see to it that Welles did not repeat such a performance. I said that the question was not one of future acts but of past crimes committed. I said the Secretary of State had said to me after discussing this matter that he considered Welles worse than a murderer.[12]

When the president argued that he needed Welles at State, Bullitt pulled out the emotional stops and reminded FDR that, "He was thinking of asking Americans to die in a crusade for all that was decent in human life. He could not have among the leaders of that crusade a criminal like Welles." That was enough for Roosevelt, who abruptly ended the meeting.

What the president could not tell Bullitt was that Welles was needed more than ever to help prepare for the next step in Roosevelt's strategy. If America was to be drawn into the European conflict, Roosevelt knew it was imperative to first reach an agreement with Winston Churchill on what the relationship would be between Britain and America in that war and what would be the ultimate objectives of that partnership. Hammering out the details of such a pact had been complicated by the sudden death in December 1940 of Lord Lothian, whose Christian Science faith had prevented him from seeking medical treatment for a worsening heart condition. Lothian was replaced in January by Lord Halifax as ambassador, but by then, Roosevelt and Churchill had begun to communicate directly with each other as each sought to forge close ties between the two governments without either surrendering any influence to the other.

The end result of these secret negotiations came four months later on August 9 when the Royal Navy battleship *HMS Prince of Wales* with Churchill aboard sailed through a cordon of American warships into Placentia Bay in Newfoundland and anchored near the U.S. Navy cruiser Augusta, where Roosevelt was waiting. Both leaders had slipped in secret away from their capitals to meet in this remote harbor to agree on a common strategy that could be embraced by other free nations.

Neither Churchill nor Roosevelt got what he wanted. FDR refused the British leader's pleas for a formal pledge to enter the war in Europe or to increase pressure on the Japanese in China. Roosevelt tried without success to win Churchill's commitment to guarantee independence for the colonies of the Empire.

Yet what came to be known as The Atlantic Charter would become a cornerstone of the world system we have today. It was a deliberately vaguely worded document that pledged lower trade barriers, freedom of the seas, a world "free of want and fear," undefined rights of self-determination, and no territorial gains for either country. The immediate impact of the statement of common goals brought the enthusiastic endorsement of all the nations at that moment either conquered or threatened by Germany—most significantly, the Soviet

Union. By January 1942, the charter had become the founding document for more than two-dozen nations in the Declaration of United Nations, the wartime alliance of democracies that would be committed to total defeat of the Axis Powers.

While all the issues confronted by Welles and the British staff negotiators were contentious, the most politically sensitive from Roosevelt's standpoint was the agreement of how the world would be governed through a postwar mechanism—a League-type international peace organization—and who would be the dominant powers in that organization. Without actually pledging such an international body, two of the eight clauses of the Atlantic Charter make it clear that such a forum would be set up. The sixth clause promises "an established peace which will afford to all nations the means of dwelling in safety within their own boundaries," while the eighth foreshadowed "the establishment of a wider and permanent system of general security."

Welles had gone to the conference hoping for a more explicit pledge for a postwar global peace organization but found to his chagrin that it was Roosevelt, not Churchill, who temporized because he sensed (probably correctly) that American public opinion would have recoiled from the idea of another League of Nations being imposed on them. He could take comfort in the more immediately important agreement with Churchill that after the war, the Roosevelt-Welles vision would prevail. What Roosevelt wanted was what came to be known as "the Big Four" powers—the U.S., Britain, the U.S.S.R., and China—to have the final say in any world body set up after the war. Churchill grudgingly did not press the traditional Anglo-American commonwealth ideal since FDR was so adamant about colonial independence. But both men agreed that France had forfeited any claim to international influence through its collaboration with its German conquerors.

Hull, who had been deliberately excluded from the meeting in Placentia Bay, was alarmed that even the vague wording of the Atlantic Charter was too much of a commitment to war, a view shared by many of the still-vocal isolationists in the Congress. Welles began to be referred to by some columnists as "President Roosevelt's

Colonel House." But Hull was absent from his desk for health reasons during much of this time and so could not lodge a protest with the president. For his part, Roosevelt now turned his full attention to war mobilization and strategy planning with his military advisers and left the details of filling the postwar policy "baskets" to Welles for the rest of the autumn.

That interim period of comparative leisure came to an abrupt end on December 7. Looking back, the ability of the United States to mobilize its military might from a standing start on the eve of the Pearl Harbor attack to the landing of American troops in North Africa ten months later is even more impressive than the arrival of the AEF (American Expeditionary Forces) in France in 1917. More important, in the midst of the herculean military response, the commitment and work of the postwar planning effort at State accelerated at an equal pace on a parallel track.

It seemed as if everyone wanted to be involved in postwar planning. Treasury Secretary Henry Morgenthau began to advance a plan to eviscerate Germany's industrial capacity after the war to thereby render it powerless. His undersecretary, a brilliant monetary economist named Harry Dexter White, began to devise a plan for postwar currency stabilization that would compete with an alternative version being advanced by the British economist John Maynard Keynes. Vice President Henry Wallace asked to form a Bureau of Economic Warfare (BEW) under his office, and Roosevelt, always willing to spur competition among his subordinates, agreed. Wallace turned out to be an inept administrator, however, and the BEW soon was folded into the State-CFR program. One of the things Pasvolsky and Welles did agree on was the need for an immediate expansion of subcommittees to begin planning on specific issues and on the need for far more staff.

Most of the Dupont Circle set had been intimately involved in the debate over a new international structure for world stability for years. Now many of them began to take direct roles in the formal planning for peace.

Among the first to get directly involved were the three Dulles siblings. John Foster Dulles became even more involved in the expanded

CFR study groups, providing his legal expertise to studying how to make the peace treaties that would have to be reached with the defeated Axis powers both more just and more ironclad.

Well before the Pearl Harbor attack, Allen Dulles had left Sullivan & Cromwell to become a deputy of William Donovan's new clandestine intelligence and covert action service, the Office of Strategic Services (OSS), that was to report directly to FDR.[13] (It is the predecessor of today's Central Intelligence Agency.) In October 1942, Dulles would move to his old hunting perch in Berne, Switzerland, where he would operate a fabulously successful spy operation into the heart of Nazi Germany.

Eleanor Dulles had continued to mix her career as an economist through the 1930s with research and publications on social welfare and monetary exchange rate theory. She and David Blondheim had married in 1930. But in 1934, soon after the birth of their son, Blondheim committed suicide.[14] The next year, Eleanor (who had conducted a special study of Britain's social welfare system for President Hoover) accepted a post at the newly formed Social Security Administration. Once the war started, she moved first to Wallace's dysfunctional BEW but was soon drafted by Pasvolsky to State, where she spent the next two years in a battle of memos with Treasury's Harry Dexter White over the details and functions of what would become the International Monetary Fund.

Felix Frankfurter, who in 1939 was appointed to the U.S. Supreme Court, continued without pause to offer Roosevelt a flood of confidential political advice and to serve as a talent scout. A supporter of the general idea of an international peace organization, Frankfurter was most concerned that any postwar realignment honor the promise of a Jewish homeland in Palestine, which had been made twenty-five years earlier. FDR, true to form, refused to commit, even resisting pressure from his wife Eleanor and Jewish friends like Morgenthau. Even before the war, Frankfurter had inserted a number of talented protégés inside State as a way to keep his finger on the pulse of what was going on. Two that he managed to shift from other government posts were the talented Hiss brothers, Alger and Donald. Alger Hiss would rise quickly in the ranks and become a liaison between the staff and John Foster Dulles's work on treaty structure. Despite allegations as early as 1942 that Hiss was providing classified intelligence to the Russians, he became so important in the final construction of the United Nations that he came close to being the first secretary-general of the organization after the war.[15]

Walter Lippmann continued throughout the war years in his often-contradictory role of gadfly and weather vane. He maintained a basic skepticism of the faith that both Ham Armstrong and Sumner Welles had in their ability to create a new iteration of the League of Nations that would succeed. In articles and correspondence with Roosevelt and others, Lippmann argued that the United States should not plan to be an occupying power in either Europe or Asia once the war had ended. Lippmann blamed Woodrow Wilson's abrupt demobilization in 1918 for provoking the economic unrest that led to the rejection of the Versailles Treaty. As he wrote to Henry Wallace in January 1943:

> It follows, I believe, that an international post-war program should be preceded[16] by a program for domestic demobilization, thus establishing the government's first concern for its own people. To this end I believe that within the next few months, Congress should be asked to enact a series of authorizations dealing generously with soldiers, workers, farmers, businessmen. They should be on the statute book before authorizations are asked for any kind of post-war international relief and rehabilitation.[17]

The legislation authorizing what became the landmark G.I. Bill of Rights was introduced in Congress with bipartisan support a year later.

The advent of the war in no way dissuaded either William Bullitt or Cordell Hull in their determination to get rid of Sumner Welles. At the end of 1941, FDR sent Bullitt on a fact-finding tour of the Middle East—from the French colonies of Africa to Iran. On his return early in 1942, he continued to press the president both for an important post and to get Welles out of the State Department. Roosevelt by this point had an added grudge festering against

Bullitt. Missy LeHand had collapsed one evening in June 1941 and suffered a massive stroke soon afterwards. She continued to linger disabled in the care of her sister in Massachusetts until she died in July 1944, comforted only by the rare letter of concern from Bullitt. Roosevelt perhaps unfairly blamed Bullitt's cavalier treatment of her for her collapse. When Bullitt—anxious to find a job and needing money—returned to Philadelphia to run for mayor, FDR managed to sabotage the campaign in retribution.

Finally in the summer of 1943, Bullitt convinced Hull to work in concert with him and to force the president to act. The secretary demanded to see the FBI report locked in General Watson's files. Until then, he had cautiously confined his complaints to the president to charges that Welles improperly bypassed the official chain of command at State. Now genuinely outraged, Hull feared that when the rumors became so common that his wife got complaints from the wives of members of Congress, the administration could be ruined if the scandal touched off a formal inquiry.

On July 27, Bullitt made the first move. He met with the president to discuss some of his advice from the Middle East trip; he arrived at the Oval Office walking on a cane and with a foot bandaged from an injury he had suffered. When he raised the Welles question, Roosevelt flushed and angrily accused him of showing the Luther Thomas affidavits to "that bitch Cissy Patterson." Bullitt swore he had not done so. But FDR was not mollified. In a memo after the event, Bullitt quoted Roosevelt's tirade: "You have ruined Welles's reputation and his life. . . . What if he does behave that way when he is drinking? It is cruel and un-Christian for anyone to talk about him."

When Bullitt reminded him that Walton Moore had compelled him to pursue the matter, the president replied, "I never would have taken those papers from Judge Moore."

To which Bullitt said he replied, "Balls." Later, Roosevelt would tell friends he had consigned Bullitt to hell, but the memo quotes a more Rooseveltian dismissal: "Well, Bill, I hope your foot is well soon." It was the last time they would speak.[18]

Hull followed up on August 15 and threatened to resign if Welles did not. At that point, Roosevelt had to make a hard decision. The

1944 elections loomed ahead, and Republican criticism of the war effort was building. The president could not risk losing Hull, who retained an immense general popularity and a great influence within the Democratic Party as well. Then too, the heavy lifting of the postwar planning effort was pretty well set.

Welles was now expendable, at least as undersecretary of State. FDR offered him the alternative of a roving ambassadorship to Latin America or a special mission to the Soviet Union. Welles, distraught and angry, resigned abruptly and fled to his vacation home in Maine. His friend Drew Pearson provoked a firestorm of controversy by writing that Hull had forced Welles out because he was judged too sympathetic to the Soviet Union, now America's ally in the war. FDR and Hull reacted angrily to the charge, with the president publicly calling the journalist a "polecat," but his friend Welles remained deliberately silent. The president's official announcement of Welles's resignation finally came on September 26, 1943. While Washington insiders knew the truth of the ouster, the press treated the story as the result of a political struggle between diplomats, and it soon faded from sight.

In the final analysis, it was a Pyrrhic victory for both Hull and Bullitt. Welles was out, but neither would reap much in return. Hull's health continued to deteriorate until he was forced to resign in 1944. He would win the 1945 Nobel Prize for Peace and be called "the Father of the United Nations" by the president, but he and Roosevelt knew otherwise. Bullitt never held another post in government, and his campaign against Welles was interpreted by Washington insiders as yet another example of his habitual treachery.

Ironically, even though he was out of government, Welles continued to be Franklin Roosevelt's most valued friend and adviser on foreign affairs until the president's death in April 1945. Once things had calmed down, he returned from Maine to Oxon Hill and resumed regular visits to the Oval Office and consultations with Roosevelt.[19]

While the formal construction of the United Nations organization and its ancillary arms—the World Bank and International Monetary Fund—would take two more years of tedious and contentious negotiation, the foundations were set by then. Franklin Roosevelt could take some comfort that he had prevailed in his postwar objective. He would be absorbed in the daily struggle of winning the war and then would be forced, at Yalta and after, to address the stresses in the Allied partnership with Russia that would deteriorate into the Cold War. But for the moment, he and Welles, and the rest of the Dupont Circle set, could take momentary satisfaction in redeeming the promises they had all made together when they were very young and arguing passionately around the dinner table at the House of Truth.

They had remade the world. The world we inhabit today.

Conclusions

THE LEGACY OF THE DUPONT CIRCLE SET

THERE ARE NO HISTORICAL MARKERS around Dupont Circle to identify the scenes where our young Progressives came together nearly a hundred years ago. The Little White House on N Street where Franklin and Eleanor Roosevelt first lived is gone. So is the mansion of General Foster and the Dulles siblings on Seventeenth Street. Both have been replaced by anonymous apartment houses. The House of Truth survives quietly at 1727 Nineteenth Street, a private residence, its current inhabitants unaware of the history that unfolded there.

Yet the neighborhood still can evoke the ghosts of those young men and women if one knows where to look. Connecticut Avenue and the circle itself look much the same. There are enough of the grand old beaux arts mansions along Massachusetts Avenue, though most have been taken over by embassies, law offices, and foundation headquarters. Just as one can hear the echoes of history by standing in the Rotunda of the U.S. Capitol or touring the East Room of the White House, the aura of great happenings remains palpable even now on the tree-shaded side streets of Dupont Circle.

What can we say about our young Progressives who started out in the House of Truth and elsewhere around Dupont Circle so many years ago? That they made history is obvious. But more, they made the world we inhabit even now.

One only has to listen to a president—any president—affirming the objectives of America's place in the world to hear our youthful Wilsonians as they argued around the dinner table at the House of Truth. Their assumptions of our exceptionalism, of our duty to foster our kind of democracy for diverse people, of our commitment to intrude commercially, militarily, culturally, drive us ever onward. The empire they dreamed of, an empire not of wealth but of civic values—American values—has spread to every corner of the world. If their triumph has not brought the peace for which they strived, most Americans still have faith in the objective. At least, so far.

The Dupont Circle set were the heirs of a long tradition of perfecting American society, just as we are their inheritors today. They were elitist, but their sense of superiority and entitlement came from their own struggle for education and advancement and not from any aristocratic noblesse oblige.

They got some things wrong. While all were idealistic, they had blind spots that stand out by today's standards. They were often too ambivalent about discrimination against minorities. Many held bizarre beliefs in genetic improvement. They lacked understanding of economic forces and could be startlingly naive about their own ability to influence despots. Their private lives could be chaotic and destructive to themselves and others. While they kept their eyes on the horizon, they often were unwilling to look far enough beyond to predict the results of their actions.

The generation of young men and women typified by the Dupont Circle strivers may have been frustrated in Paris in 1919, but one has to admire their determination to try again in 1939. And more historically important than the residences where they began their careers together are the landmark institutions they helped create that still are important decades later.

One has to admire the sheer stamina of the Dupont Circle set. The second chance that ended in the creation of the United Nations was by no means the end of the crusade for many of our characters of so long ago. There were important third acts in the lives of nearly all of them.

—Franklin Roosevelt died of a cerebral hemorrhage on April 12, 1945 in Warm Springs, Georgia, with Lucy Mercer by his side. His remarkable career ended only months into an unprecedented fourth term as president and mere weeks before Germany would surrender. An editorial by The *New York Times* declared, "Men will thank God on their knees a hundred years from now that Franklin D. Roosevelt was in the White House." His legacy dominates our lives today and is the standard measure for other presidents. He may have been as humanly flawed as any president before or since. His mistakes will occupy historians for generations. But he knew one thing—how to gauge the ever-shifting mood of the fractious American people—better than any one of his time, and he had the cool wit to act when that mood shifted in his direction. He never doubted either himself or his nation.

—Eleanor Roosevelt would go on to be called the First Lady of the World. She was a U.S. Representative to the United Nations General Assembly from 1945 to 1952 and would end her public service on President Kennedy's Commission on the Status of Women, which contributed to the feminist movement. She died in 1962.

—Walter Lippmann continued to be America's most influential intellectual commentator on public affairs until his death in 1974. He was openly critical of America's Cold War strategy against the Soviet Union but continued to argue for a strong American foreign policy. He received the Medal of Freedom from President Lyndon Johnson for his contributions but characteristically angered LBJ by opposing continued American involvement in the Vietnam War. He and Helen lived quietly in Washington, D.C., most of their lives.

—Sumner Welles had considerable success after leaving the State Department as a public speaker, syndicated columnist, and author of major books on foreign policy. But in 1949, Mathilde suddenly died, and Welles fell under the influence of a servant who pandered to his alcoholism and homosexual appetites. He began to drink heavily and suffer serious heart problems that led to periods of depression. In 1956, *Confidential,* a scandal magazine, published an exposé of Welles's sexual escapades, including some of the more recent solicitations. The article is believed have been submitted to the publisher by Carmel Offie at the behest of William Bullitt. Dissuaded from suing for libel, Welles spent the next five years in retirement and in failing health. He remarried and died in 1961.

—John Foster Dulles was the principal architect of the surrender agreement and postwar treaty with Japan. At the same time, he was the primary U.S. legal consultant at the UN conference in San Francisco in 1945. After the war, he served briefly in the U.S. Senate but lost his bid to be elected to a full term. Dwight Eisenhower named him secretary of state in 1953, a position he used to wage an unrelenting challenge to the imperialism of the Soviet Union. In a partnership with his brother Allen and President Eisenhower, Foster Dulles negotiated a turbulent time of post-colonial struggles, a threatening Cold War, and the revival of a democratic Europe from the rubble of the previous war. He resigned as secretary in 1959 and died shortly afterwards from cancer.

—Allen Dulles returned from his OSS triumphs in World War II to become president of the Council on Foreign Relations. He recruited Eisenhower, then president of Columbia University, for a special CFR study of postwar European security that led to the general assuming command of NATO forces in 1951. From that position two years later, Eisenhower would be elevated to the Presidency and bring into his administration many of his CFR mentors. In the meantime, President Truman asked Dulles and two other intelligence experts to design the architecture of a new intelligence service. The recommendations became part of the National Security Act of 1947 that, among other innovations, created the Central Intelligence Agency. Dulles became the deputy director of the CIA and then the director in 1953, a post he held until he was asked to resign by President Kennedy in 1961 after the failed Bay of Pigs attempt to topple the Castro regime. He continued to serve in a variety of advisory posts, including as a member of the Warren Commission. He died in 1969.

—Eleanor Dulles served on the U.S. delegation to the Bretton Woods conference in 1944 that created the World Bank and IMF. In 1945, she directed the Allied economic reconstruction of the Austria economy and later the revitalization of Allied zones of the city of Berlin. During the 1950s, she directed the State Department's study of economic programs in undeveloped countries in Latin America, Africa, and South Asia. She was ousted from State in 1962 by the Kennedy administration. She returned to teaching and writing until her death in 1996 at the age of 101.

—William Bullitt left Washington shortly after the Welles affair and accepted an officer's commission to fight in the Free French Army led by General Charles De Gaulle for the rest of the war. He was awarded both the Croix de Guerre and the Legion of Honor. He returned to writing after the war and was bitterly critical of Franklin Roosevelt's policies. He supported Thomas Dewey for president in 1948 and became an early backer of then Senator Richard Nixon. In 1966, Bullitt finally published his scathing profile of Woodrow Wilson, which he allegedly had written in the 1930s with Sigmund Freud. The book was widely panned by reviewers; the most damaging challenge came in a lengthy article in *Look* magazine written by Allen Dulles. The Freud family later disavowed the book. Bullitt died near Paris in 1967.

—Hamilton Fish Armstrong went on a number of important overseas missions for FDR during the war. He remained the editor of *Foreign Affairs* and an active force in the Council on Foreign Relations until his retirement in 1972. He continued to write articles and publish books on a wide range of foreign policy issues. He married twice more and died in 1973.

—Lord Eustace Percy served in a wide number of important posts in a succession of British governments, most notably as head of the national agencies for education and health. He was dubbed by the press the "Minister for Thought" and led postwar reforms in both departments. He remained an active Chatham House study group participant and was a key adviser in the creation of the United Nations Education, Scientific, and Cultural Organization (UNESCO). He died in 1958.

—Felix Frankfurter remained an Associate Justice of the U.S. Supreme Court until he suffered a stroke and retired in 1962. He received the Medal of Freedom in 1963. While Frankfurter remained a behind-the-scenes advocate of Progressive policies during the Roosevelt administration, he evolved into a conservative jurist on the High Court. He advocated judicial restraint in Supreme Court decisions on whether to overturn lower court rulings or Congressional mandates. In *Brown v. Board of Education*, Frankfurter is credited with insisting that the court order forcing desegregation of public schools include the phrase "with all deliberate speed," which many Southern states used for years to justify delays in complying. He died in 1965.

—Herbert Hoover was immediately brought back into government service after Franklin Roosevelt's death. President Harry Truman sent Hoover to Germany in 1946 to report on food shortages, and on his initiative, a program of school meals for 3.5 million children was begun in the U.S. and British zones of occupation. Both Presidents Truman and Eisenhower put Hoover as head of important study commissions on government reorganization. He died in 1964.

Chatham House and the Council on Foreign Relations still dominate the transatlantic dialogue on global issues by bringing a diversity of viewpoints to bear on issues as complex as threats to the environment, migration, and human rights, while still studying the traditional vexations of trade, finance, and politics. The United Nations they constructed may have been unable to prevent armed conflicts around the world over the last sixty years, but it fairly can be credited with preventing a third world war. The ancillary agencies of the UN—the World Bank, the International Monetary Fund, the World Health Organization, the World Trade Organization, to name a few—first revived the war-shattered nations of Europe and Asia and then were crucial to lifting even the poorest nations of Africa and Latin America into the global marketplace.

Today our world is a dangerous and unhappy place. It may seem in our darker moments that mankind may be unable to exist on this planet for much longer unless we can reverse our heedless depredations of the very land, water, and air that sustain human life. Some nations have achieved standards of well-being for ordinary citizens that were once beyond the powers of princes to command. Elsewhere, however, whole populations are sliding back into a new Dark Age of poverty and tyranny where a fanatical explosion of violence appears to be the only option available.

Except for the fact that the global arena is now more compressed and crowded and that time is exponentially accelerated, the threats we face are not much different than those faced by our youthful strivers when they first arrived on Dupont Circle. Poverty, injustice, and tyranny still threaten human existence. But it also is true that the world is far better off than it might have been without the efforts of the Dupont Circle set and the far larger group of young men and women for whom they are a metaphor. Not everyone of that generation of Progressives became an internationally recognized figure; some, like my schoolteacher friend from Mississippi who had wanted to work for the League of Nations, had modest lives but did inestimable good.

What is important about the Dupont Circle set in the final analysis is that they made a commitment to a set of broad ideals with firm, if at first unrealistic, convictions about the way the world worked and how to make it better.

They made a promise to themselves and to the rest of the world—call it the American promise. They gave their word. That is their legacy to us, the successor generations, and many of us have kept that word in the small acts of community involvement, Peace Corps tours, and even greater sacrifices of life and limb in far-off places.

Do we have the same faith in ourselves today to go on building on the legacy of the Dupont Circle set? This is a question beyond just of being worthy of that inheritance, of living up to that word. As the poet W. H. Auden observed, "Civilization can endure a good many ills, but unless people will fulfill their word, there can be no civilization."[1] We do not seem to have a choice but to keep trying to do better.

Notes

Preface

1. Daniel Okrent. *Last Call: The Rise and Fall of Prohibition.* (New York: Scribners, 2010).

Chapter One

1. Walter Lippmann Papers, hereafter WLP. HM 257, Part I, Selected Correspondence 1906–1930, Unit 1, Series I, Reel 257, Sterling Library, Yale University.

2. John M. Jordan, *Machine-Age Ideology, Social Engineering & American Liberalism, 1911–1939* (Chapel Hill, NC: University of North Carolina Press, 1993), 21.

3. Valentine was Commissioner of Indian Affairs from 1909–1912; he died suddenly in 1916, but the House of Truth remained a popular residence for young Progressives until the 1920s. Jeffrey O'Connell and Nancy Dart, *Catholic University Law Review* 79 (1985–1986): 79–81.

4. Mark N. Ozer, *Massachusetts Avenue in the Gilded Age* (Charleston, SC: The History Press, 2010).

5. Lord Eustace Percy, *Some Memories* (London: Eyre & Spotswood, 1958), 40.

6. WLP. A Letter to Theodore Roosevelt Jr. dated February 18, 1915 updates previous advice Lippmann provided TR on a new labor-management strategy. Lippmann's admiration survived a row with TR at the end of 1914 when *The New Republic* had chided the former president for attacking Woodrow Wilson for timidity in dealing with Mexico. Roosevelt had been enraged at what he saw as disloyalty and denounced *The New Republic* editors as "three uncircumcised Jews and three anemic Christians." Ronald Steel, *Walter Lippmann and the American Century* (New York: Atlantic, Little-Brown, 1980), 76.

7. Lippmann, in what later would prove an embarrassment, went so far as to write that these new arrivals were largely to blame for the rise in anti-Semitism that older Jewish immigrants had avoided. In a 1922 essay in a Jewish magazine, he argued, "the fundamental fact in the situation is that the Jews are fairly distinct in their physical appearance and in the spelling of their names from the run of the American people. They are, therefore, inevitably conspicuous." Heinz Eulau, "From Public Opinion to Public Philosophy: Walter Lippmann's Classic Revisited." *American Journal of Economics and Sociology* 15, no. 4 (July 1956): 443–445.

8. Edward Mandel House (1858–1938) was heir to a Texas cotton and sugar fortune who had earned the honorary title of Colonel for helping to elect a series of governors of that state. He met Woodrow Wilson in 1911 when the governor gave a Bible history lecture in Dallas and then helped Wilson's 1912 election bid by persuading rival William Jennings Bryan to endorse his candidacy. House later moved to New York but for a time also had quarters in the White House as Wilson became more dependent on his advice. He became Wilson's personal envoy to try to broker peace among the warring European powers when the war broke out in 1914.

CHAPTER TWO

1. Resa Willis, *FDR and Lucy: Lovers and Friends* (New York: Routledge, 2004), 30.

2. There is a whole shelf of books devoted to the details of Franklin Roosevelt's relations with women, including his often-simultaneous romances. There are, in addition, other volumes devoted to Eleanor Roosevelt's friendships and emotional ties to other men and women. Among the former: Joseph E. Persico, *Franklin & Lucy: President Roosevelt, Mrs. Rutherfurd and the Other Remarkable Women in His Life* (New York: Random House, 2008); Resa Willis, *FDR and Lucy*. And among the latter: Blanche Wiesen Cook, *Eleanor Roosevelt, Volume One, 1884–1933* (New York: Penguin Group, 1992); Joseph P. Lash, *Eleanor and Franklin* (New York: W.W. Norton & Co., 2004).

3. The Papers of Breckinridge Long, 1916–1945, are housed in the Manuscript Room of the U.S. Library of Congress, Washington, D.C. See also the memoir by Louis B. Wehle, *Hidden Threads of History: Wilson through Roosevelt* (New York: The MacMillan Company, 1953).

4. Benjamin Welles, *Sumner Welles: FDR's Global Strategist* (New York: St. Martin's Press, 1997), 16–21.

5. Samuel Slater is credited with creating the American textile industry when, in 1790, he memorized the closely guarded technology of British spinning mills and then moved to Rhode Island with that knowledge.

6. Welles, *Sumner Welles,* 26–36.

7. *Ibid.,* 37.

8. George Bernard Shaw, *The Fabian Society: Its Early History* (London: The Fabian Society, 1906). Fabian philosophy, in contrast to Progressivism, was at the same time more gradualist and favoring a strong national government (indeed a strong British Empire) in its reform program than American Progressives, who distrusted big government and concentrated their

early efforts on reforming government at the local level. In addition to Shaw, early Fabian advocates included H. G. Wells, Leonard and Virginia Woolf, Bertrand Russell, Sidney and Beatrice Webb, Suffragist leader Emmeline Pankhurst, and future prime minister Ramsay MacDonald.

9. Oliver Wendell Holmes, Junior, (1841–1935) was appointed to the U.S. Supreme Court in 1902 by President Theodore Roosevelt. As a Harvard law professor (briefly), and a Massachusetts state court judge, Holmes developed a Progressive philosophy that the law was not a rigid, unchangeable set of precepts; rather, it was a plastic and malleable set of goals that must be altered to fit changing circumstances as society itself changed. During his thirty-year tenure on the Supreme Court (he retired in 1932), he became best known for his advocacy of freedom of speech and his decisions supporting economic reforms.

10. The 1981 film *Reds,* starring Warren Beatty as Reed and Diane Keaton as his wife, the writer Louise Bryant, is a fanciful version of their life together.

11. James Weinstein, *The Decline of Socialism in America, 1912–1925* (New York: Vintage Books, 1969). The author estimates that in 1911, seventy-four U.S. municipalities had Socialist mayors.

12. Walter Lippmann, *A Preface to Politics* (Charleston, NC: Bibliobazaar, 2010).

13. Philip Henry Kerr (1882–1940) became the eleventh Marquess of Lothian in 1930. The Lothian Papers are housed at the National Archives of Scotland (Series GD40/17). See also J.R.M. Butler, *Lord Lothian* (New York: St. Martin's Press, 1960).

Chapter Three

1. Edward M. House, *Philip Dru: Administrator* (New York: B.W. Huebesch, 1912). There are a number of online versions of this novel available.

2. Walter Lippmann. Both *A Preface to Politics* (1913) and *Drift and Mastery* (1914) were originally published by Mitchell Kinnerly (New York). *The Stakes of Diplomacy* (1915) was originally published by Henry Holt (New York), but other editions are now available. See Steel, *Walter Lippmann,* 90–92. Also see John Morton Blum, ed., *Public Philosopher: Selected Letters of Walter Lippmann* (New York: Ticknor and Fields, 1985).

3. Charles Evans Hughes, an associate Justice of the U.S. Supreme Court (1862–1948), was the Republican nominee.

4. Blum, *Public Philosopher,* 49–59. Letter dated May 29, 1916.

5. WLP. Folder 128: John Silas Reed, 1913–1916. Letter dated February 21, 1916.

6. Reed's book was *Ten Days that Shook the World* (Digireads.com, 2007). Bryant's was *Six Red Months in Russia* (Ann Arbor, MI: University of Michigan, 2009). Reed died there in 1920 during a typhus epidemic.

7. Michael E. Parrish, *Felix Frankfurter and His Times* (New York: The Free Press, 1982), 76–78.

8. Felix Frankfurter, Letter to Katherine Ludington, April 10, 1917. Box 79, The Papers of Felix Frankfurter, Library of Congress. Hereafter FFLOC. Also, Parish, Felix Frankfurter, 80.

9. The Cantonment Commission headed by FDR and Lippmann ultimately built thirty-two Army and Navy training camps, each capable of processing forty thousand troops.

10. Harlan B. Phillips, ed., *Felix Frankfurter Reminisces* (New York: Reynal and Co., 1960), 146–149.

11. Lawrence E. Gelfand, *The Inquiry: American Preparations for Peace,* 1917–1919 (New Haven, CT: Yale University Press, 1963), 122–124. Note: Many of the papers of The Inquiry staff are housed in the Sterling Library at Yale.

12. Frankfurter to Baker, August 7, 1917. Box 189, FFLOC. See Parrish, *Felix Frankfurter,* 51–52, 86.

13. Sidney Edward Mezes, who was married to House's sister, was president of the City College of New York from 1914 to 1927.

14. Gelfand, *The Inquiry,* 116–119, 256.

15. James Srodes, *Allen Dulles: Master of Spies* (Washington, D.C.: Regnery, 2000), 50–65.

CHAPTER FOUR

1. Percy, *Some Memories,* 59.

2. Including the author's grandmother, who was traveling in Europe with her three young children. They were finally able to reach the United States in April 1915 on the penultimate voyage of the Lusitania. The ship was torpedoed by a German submarine on the return voyage on May 7 with a loss of 1,189 of the 1,959 passengers.

3. Joan Hoff Wilson, *Herbert Hoover: Forgotten Progressive* (New York: HarperCollins, 1975), 45–48. George H. Nash, *The Life of Herbert Hoover* (New York: W.W. Norton, 1988), 15–20.

4. Yardley would be the post-war head of the famous "Black Chamber" code-breaking office for the U.S. government.

5. James Rives Childs, *Let the Credit Go* (Hollywood, FL: Frederick Fell Publishers, 1983), 40–45.

6. In a speech to Congress in January 1918, Wilson outlined America's objectives for the war. Known as The Fourteen Points (and drafted in part by Walter Lippmann), they stated:

Any secret treaties should come to an end.
All nations should have freedom of the seas.
There should be free trade between nations.
There should be significant reductions in armaments.
Colonial claims for independence must be adjudicated fairly and impartially.
Foreign troops must leave Russia, and it must be allowed to develop its own form of government.

Belgium must be restored as a nation.

Alsace-Lorraine must be returned to France.

Italy's borders must be realigned "along clearly recognizable lines of nationality."

The various nationalities of Austria-Hungary should be free to set up their own governments.

The Balkan nations should be restored.

A Turkish government should govern Turks; there should be self-government for non-Turk groups within the old Ottoman Empire.

An independent Polish nation must be established.

The League of Nations should be founded to provide "mutual guarantees of political independence and territorial integrity to great and small nations alike."

CHAPTER FIVE

1. From July 1917 onward, the War Industries Board standardized military purchase orders, pressed for mass production, rationed raw materials, and granted wage increases to unions in exchange for accelerated work schedules. In addition to its chairman, Bernard Baruch, the board also contained two other notables: St. Louis businessman Robert S. Brookings, who later founded the Brookings Institution for economic study, and New York financier Eugene Meyer, later the owner of *The Washington Post.*

2. Eleanor Lansing Dulles, conversation with author. Notes filed with the author's Allen W. Dulles Papers Collection, George C. Marshall Library, Lexington, VA.

3. Lenin actually left Bern on the famous sealed train through Germany to Russia on April 9, a Monday.

4. Steel, *Walter Lippmann,* 134.

5. *Ibid.,* 144. Also Gelfand, *The Inquiry,* 121.

6. Wilson to House, September 3, 1918. Edwin M. House Papers, Sterling Library, Yale University.

7. One of the fables of the Conference has Lloyd George using a gold sovereign coin to impress the wax seal on his signature to the Treaty of Versailles. Clemenceau admired the coin and asked the prime minister if he could have it as a souvenir. Lloyd George refused, the story goes, saying, "This is the only one we have left. All the others are in New York."

8. Cambridge University economist Zara Steiner has summarized the new revisionist view of the reparations controversy by noting that the 124 million gold marks finally demanded by the Reparations Commission set up after the Paris conference in 1921 "were within the German capacity to pay if successive governments had not decided that they would try to postpone or avoid payment altogether. . . . Reparations ended in July 1932; the [Weimar] Republic collapsed six months later. If there were no foreigners to blame, the domestic quarrels became insoluble. If hyperinflation wiped out the German domestic debt, the Hoover Moratorium in 1931 when Germany still owed $77 billion effectively cancelled the reparation debt. There is abundant evidence that Germany covered all its obligation to the allies between 1919 and 1923 through imports of foreign capital, and that from 1924 through 1931 she received more in capital inflows, either through investment or loans, mainly from the United States, than she paid in reparations." The conclusion is that Wall Street, not Weimar, was the big loser. Zara Steiner, "The Treaty of Versailles Revisited," *The Paris Peace Conference, 1919* (Studies in Military and Strategic History) (London: Palgrave, 2001), 20–22.

9. Hoover to Wilson, March 20, 1919. House Papers.

10. Bullitt to Wilson, May 17, 1919. William C. Bullitt Papers, Group 112, Box 10. Sterling Library, Yale University. Also Will Brownell and Richard N. Billings, *So Close to Greatness: A Biography of William C. Bullitt* (New York: MacMillan & Company, 1987) 90–97.

CHAPTER SIX

1. William Stanley Braithwaite, *Anthology of Magazine Verse for 1920* (New York: Small, Maynard & Co., 1921).

2. Harold G. Nicolson, *Peacemaking: 1919* (London: Simon Publishing, 1933), 363.

3. World War I casualty data is subject to controversy to this day. The sources for the data here come from the *Historical Series: American Military History* (Washington, DC: U.S. Army Center of Military History, 2005), chapters 15–19, and *The Twentieth Century Atlas of World History* (New York: Collins, 1991). France: 1.3 million military killed, 4.2 million wounded; Britain: 885,000 military killed, 1.6 million wounded, Australia: 61,928 killed; Canada: 64,944 killed; India 74,187 killed; New Zealand: 18,000 killed. As a rule of thumb, battle wounds ranged between twice to three times the number of deaths. The United States: 116,700 killed, 205,600 wounded. Germany: 2.0 million killed, 4.2 million wounded; Austria-Hungary: 1.1 million killed, 3.6 million wounded.

4. Margaret MacMillan, *Peacemakers: The Paris Conference of 1919 and Its Attempt to End War* (London: Alex Murray, 2001). Also published as *Paris 1919: Six Months that Changed the World* (New York: Random House, 2003).

5. MacMillan, *Peacemakers,* 500.

6. Mooney was head of the Industrial Workers of the World union (known popularly as the "Wobblies"). The union was founded in 1905, and members advocated replacing wages with worker ownership of factories.

7. Inderjeet Parmar, *Think Tanks and Power in Foreign Policy* (London: Palgrave MacMillan, 2004), 24–29. Also, Michael Wala, *American Foreign Relations and the Council on Foreign Relations* (Oxford: Berghahn Books, 2004).

CHAPTER SEVEN

1. Warren G. Harding, "Readjustment," May 14, 1920 campaign speech recording. Washington, D.C.: U.S. Library of Congress photograph and recording collection. Accessible online at www.lcweb2.loc.gov/ammem.

2. Hamilton Holt (1872–1951) was an economist and editor of the liberal weekly magazine *The Independent.* He was a founding member of the National Association for the Advancement of Colored People and of The League to Enforce Peace. He later (1925) served as president of Rollins College. Warren F. Kuehl and Lynne K. Dunn, *Keeping The Covenant: American Internationalists and the League of Nations, 1920–1939* (Kent, Ohio: Kent State University Press, 1997), 48–53.

3. Kenneth Davis, *FDR: The Beckoning of Destiny* (New York: Random House, 2004), 577.

4. Ann Hagedorn, *Savage Peace: Hope and Fear in America, 1919* (New York: Simon & Schuster, 2007), 180–187.

5. Persico, *Franklin & Lucy,* 102–104.

6. *Ibid.,* 125–130. Also, Willis, *FDR and Lucy,* 30–44, and Fenster, *FDR's Shadow,* 101–104.

CHAPTER EIGHT

1. Louis B. Wehle, *Hidden Threads of History* (New York: MacMillan & Co., 1953), 81–85.

2. Blum, *Public Philosopher,* 112. Letter to Ellery Sedgwick, April 7, 1919.

3. *Ibid.,* 132–133. Letter of Oliver Wendell Holmes, Jr. November 18, 1919.

4. Richard Hofstadter, *The American Political Tradition* (New York: Vintage, 1989), 283.

5. Papers of Breckinridge Long. Diaries 1916–1944. Box Three.

Folder Six, Memo. Saturday, February 7, 1920. U.S. Library of Congress, Washington, D.C.

6. WLP. Letter to Felix Frankfurter, April 7, 1920. Also, Blum, *Public Philosopher,* 134–135.

7. Richard Norton Smith, *An Uncommon Man* (New York: Simon & Schuster, 1984), 96–97. Also, Earl Reeves, *This Man Hoover* (New York: A.L. Burt Co., 1924), 146.

8. William Gibbs McAdoo (1863–1941) was Treasury secretary from 1913–1918. His second wife was Wilson's daughter, Eleanor Randolph Wilson. He ran unsuccessfully for the Democratic presidential nomination in 1920 and 1924.

9. After the campaign, Roosevelt gave the members of his 1920 campaign staff gold cufflinks embossed with his initials. In later years, FDR gave other sets to particularly close friends and supporters, and the items became a valued badge of honor among Roosevelt loyalists.

10. Davis, *FDR,* 608–622.

11. WLP. Letter to Graham Wallas, November 4, 1920.

12. WLP. Telegram to FDR, July 8, 1920.

Chapter Nine

1. Harding, "Readjustment."

2. Sumner Welles's sexual proclivities are well documented from a remarkably early date. Among the sources are The Sumner Welles Papers at the Franklin D. Roosevelt Presidential Library, Box 264. Also, Welles, *Sumner Welles,* 52–67. Also, Irwin F. Gellman, *Secret Affairs: Franklin Roosevelt, Cordell Hull and Sumner Welles* (Baltimore: Johns Hopkins Press, 1995), 60–65.

3. In addition to the Treaty of Versailles reached with Germany, the Conference staff negotiated the Treaty of Saint-Germaine-en-Laye with Austria; the Treaty of Neuilly-sur-Seine with Bulgaria

(both in 1919); plus the Treaty of Trianon with Hungary and the Treaty of Sevres with the Ottoman Empire, both in 1920.

4. Ronald W. Pruessen, *John Foster Dulles: The Road to Power.* (New York: The Free Press, 1982), 59–63. Also, Srodes, *Allen Dulles,* 109–126.

5. Schacht's dramatic career is part of the fascinating history of the friendship between the heads of the Bank of England, the Banque de France, and the New York Federal Reserve, which is told in Liaquat Ahmed's authoritative *Lords of Finance: The Bankers Who Broke the World* (New York: The Penguin Press, 2009). Later, the Schacht-Dulles friendship would be an embarrassment to the brothers when he became the architect of the fantasy economic underpinnings of Adolf Hitler's National Socialism, although Hitler would later fire him and put him in a concentration camp. After World War II, Schacht was tried, though acquitted, at the Nuremberg war crimes trials.

6. British Foreign Office Files. The National (U.K.) Archives. Kew. Series FO115. Memos 2785–2866, from Robert Craigie to Sir John Tilley and Lord Balfour, referring to "Mr. Dullas [sic]". Also, Srodes, Allen Dulles, 116–130. Also, Allen W. Dulles Papers. Seeley G. Mudd Manuscript Library, Princeton University. Box 9 (1920), including the correspondence of Clover Dulles. Hereafter, AWD Papers.

7. A retired American diplomat who visited Betty Carp just before her death in 1975 told the author privately that she conceded that her relationship with Allen was platonic but nonetheless genuinely intense. It is also true that when, as CIA director, Dulles would visit Turkey, the first person he insisted on seeing was Betty Carp before he went on with his official tasks.

8. Robert H. Van Meter Jr., "The Washington Conference of 1921–1922," *Pacific Historical Review* 46, no. 4 (1977): 603–624. Van Meter cites a typescript copy of the letter in Box 698 of the collection of Harding's papers held by the Ohio Histori-

cal Society, Columbus, OH. There is no Presidential Library collection of Harding's papers as such.

9. D.C. Watt, "Anglo-American Arms Relationships," *The Review of Politics* 25, no. 2 (April 1963): 280–282. Also Ernest Andrade Jr., "The Cruiser Controversy in Naval Limitations Negotiation, 1922–1936," *Military Affairs* 48, no. 3 (1984): 113–120.

CHAPTER TEN

1. John W. Davis (1873–1955) was a congressman from West Virginia before serving as U.S. Solicitor General and ambassador to Britain during World War I. He was an unsuccessful candidate for the Democratic Party presidential nomination in 1920 and was the party's nominee in 1924.

2. There is some belief now that Roosevelt's illness was Guillain-Barre syndrome, an auto-immune viral infection; while the truth will probably never be known, it is a relevant question since the rigorous massage and exercise regimen to which FDR was subjected might have done more harm than good.

3. Davis, *FDR,* 677–678. Frances Perkins, *The Roosevelt I Knew* (New York: Viking Press, 1946), 29–30, and Eleanor Roosevelt, *This I Remember* (New York: Greenwood Press, 1975), 25.

4. Elliott Roosevelt, ed., *F.D.R., His Personal Letters 1905–1928* (New York: Duell, Sloan & Pearce, 1948), 598.

5. The long-running debate over just how burdensome the financial demands of the Versailles Treaty on the German economy were may never be settled given the vast differences in currency exchange rates, purchasing power, and the nature of Western industrial economies of that day and today. Confusing matters further is the fact that much of the reparations had to be paid in the form of industrial goods and commodities. But a rough rule of thumb applies an eight-marks-per-dollar exchange rate

in 1919 to make the original reparations demand worth about $33.6 billion. By 1921, that exchange rate had become sixty-five marks per dollar, thereby making the new 226- billion-mark demand equal to $3.5 billion. By 1925, when the Dawes Plan was instituted to cut the demand to 132 billion marks, the devaluation of the mark had swollen to nearly 18,000, or roughly $7 billion. For the author's own convenience in judging purchasing power, one can arbitrarily multiply those dollar amounts by thirteen in 2012 purchasing power. Thus, the original Versailles Treaty demand would translate into $437 billion in current dollars. On the face of it, that demand, while not inconsiderable, does not appear to be as fatally draconian as was charged at the time. However, the author admits to the possibility of error.

6. John Foster Dulles, "The Allied Debts," *Foreign Affairs* 1, no. 1 (September 15, 1922): 116–132.

Chapter Eleven

1. Sumner Welles Papers, hereafter SWP. Franklin D. Roosevelt Presidential Library. Hyde Park, NY. Box 264. April 15, 1921, a receipt "for $810 in full settlement of all claims to date from the Capital Taxi Corporation."

2. Welles, *Sumner Welles*, 84.

3. SWP. Box 264. Memos dated February 12 and March 22, 1923 regarding a trip to Virginia Beach, VA, by Mathilde and Sumner, a complaint that "Mrs. Williams, owner of the apartment has had to pay $50 for broken china and for cleaning the apartment."

4. SWP. A note in the files dated March 22, 1923 by Welles states, "I owe Esther Slater Welles $88,900 which I will refund her by installments, beginning at the present date, until the whole debt is cancelled." In Welles, *Sumner Welles*, 389: "Welles finally repaid the debt in full in 1942 after Esther had personally

appealed to Henry L. Stimson, an old family friend and FDR's Secretary of War."

5. Welles, *Sumner Welles,* 100.

6. *Ibid.,* 114.

7. William C. Bullitt, *It's Not Done* (New York: Grosset & Dunlop, 1928).

8. Brownell and Billings, *So Close,* 110–115.

9. Sigmund Freud and William C. Bullitt, *Thomas Woodrow Wilson: A Psychological Study* (Boston: Houghton Mifflin, 1966).

10. William C. Bullitt Papers, hereafter WCBP. Sterling Library, Yale University. New Haven, CT. MS Group 112. Series VI. Box 207. Folder 155. A sixteen-page memo to file titled "1929 Divorce."

11. In 1925, Bullitt had a brief affair on the Riviera with newspaper heiress Eleanor Medill "Cissy" Patterson. They remained friends thereafter. Brownell and Billings, So Close, 115–116.

12. Gwen Le Gallienne was the sister of English poet Richard Le Gallienne. She was one of the set of avant garde artists and authors who frequented the Left Bank of Paris including Jean Cocteau, Man Ray, Sylvia Beach, Gertrude Stein, and others. Among her other reported lovers was Bernice Abbott, the photographer.

13. WCBP. MS Group 112. Series I. Box 3. Folder 53. Correspondence with Nancy Astor, 1919–1959.

14. WCBP. Box 110. Folder 370–374. Correspondence with Colonel Edward M. House. Also, Box 109. Extracts from the House diary.

15. Allyn Abbott Young (1876–1929) was a Harvard economist who in 1927 was recruited by William Beveridge to teach monetary theory at the London School of Economics. He was an important advisor to Benjamin Strong, head of the Federal Reserve Bank of New York during this period.

16. Eleanor Lansing Dulles, *The French Franc, 1914–1928* (New York: MacMillan, 1929).

17. In a conversation with the author, Eleanor stated, "My mother never said a word to me about sex, and I never thought to ask."

18. Allen W. Dulles Papers, hereafter AWDP. Mudd Library. Princeton University. Selected Correspondence E-H, Fox 10–12. Letters from AWD to Clover Dulles, spring 1925 from Geneva. Also, British Foreign Office memorandum. FO371/17356, dated 15 April 1925. United States delegation to the Arms Traffic Conference. Describes delegation as "peculiarly strong."

Chapter Twelve

1. Joseph Maiolo, *Cry Havoc: How the Arms Race Drove the World to War, 1931–1941* (New York: Basic Books, 2010), 41–43.

2. David Carlton, "Great Britain and the Coolidge Naval Disarmament Conference of 1927," *Political Science Quarterly* 83, no. 4 (December 1968): 573–598.

3. Franklin D. Roosevelt, "Our Foreign Policy, A Democratic View," *Foreign Affairs* (July 1928): 573–586.

4. Kenneth S. Davis, *FDR, The New York Years, 1928–1933* (New York: Random House, 1994), 14. This four-volume biography remains the most authoritative literary profile on FDR.

5. Cook, *Eleanor Roosevelt.* Also, Joseph Lash, *Eleanor and Franklin* (New York: W.W. Norton, 2004).

6. Sumner Welles, *Naboth's Vineyard* (New York: Dodd Mead, 1928). Also, Welles, *Sumner Welles,* 125.

7. Joan Hoff Wilson, *Herbert Hoover: Forgotten Progressive* (New York: HarperCollins, 1975), 200–202.

8. Eugene Lyons, *Herbert Hoover: A Biography* (New York: Doubleday & Co., 1964), 212.

CHAPTER THIRTEEN

1. Felix Frankfurter, "The Case of Sacco and Vanzetti," *Atlantic Monthly* (March 1927): 320, 323.

2. Walter Lippmann, *Public Opinion* (New York: The Free Press, 1965), 54.

3. Steel, *Walter Lippmann,* 199.

4. Frankfurter to Roosevelt. November 8, 1928. Max Freedman, ed., *Roosevelt and Frankfurter: Their Correspondence, 1928–1945* (Boston: Little, Brown, 1967), 39. Also, Parrish, *Felix Frankfurter,* 201.

5. Frankfurter to Lippmann. October 23, 1930. Freedman, *Roosevelt and Frankfurter,* 52. Also, Parrish, *Felix Frankfurter,* 202.

6. The Papers of Hamilton Fish Armstrong, hereafter HFAP. Mudd Library, Princeton University. Record Group MC002. Box 35. Folder 15. Correspondence with Colonel Edward M. House, memorandum dated December 31, 1931.

7. HFAP. Box 53. Memorandum dated November 20, 1932. Correspondence with Franklin D. Roosevelt.

8. Edward M. House, "Some Foreign Problems of the Next Administration," *Foreign Affairs* 11, no. 2 (January 1933): 212–219.

9. Office of the Historian, U.S. Department of State. http://history.state.gov.

10. AWDP. Box 13. Norman H. Davis Memorandum of Conversations (written by Dulles), April 8, 1933. Hitler harangued Davis and Dulles about his fears that Poland was poised to invade Germany; their conclusion that he was delusional was confirmed in meetings with British officials who dismissed both Hitler and the threat of Nazism. See also Srodes, *Allen Dulles,* 171–174.

11. Hamilton Fish Armstrong, "Hitler's Reich, The First Phase," *Foreign Affairs* 11, no. 2 (July 1933): 590–608.

12. AWDP. Box 49. Correspondence with Hugh Gibson. Letter, Mallory to Dulles, December 20, 1933.

CHAPTER FOURTEEN

1. Papers of Franklin D. Roosevelt, hereafter FDRP. File 2961. Box 261. Folder 7. FDR Presidential Library, Hyde Park, NY. Horace Greeley Knowles, letter to Louis Howe dated January 1, 1933. Knowles (1862–1937) was a U.S. ambassador to the Dominican Republic and Bolivia for Presidents Taft and Wilson.

2. FDRP. File 2961. Box 263. Folder 1 of 36. Correspondence, Felix Frankfurter, Letter dated February 23, 1933.

3. Norman H. Davis, "Wanted: A Consistent Latin American Policy," *Foreign Affairs* (July 1931).

4. Drew Pearson (1897–1969) had been a foreign correspondent for various newspapers in the 1920s when he married the daughter of *Washington Times-Herald* publisher Cissy Patterson about the same time Welles married Mathilde Townsend. The two men became friends and shared an interest in Maryland state politics since both had large farm estates outside of Washington. Pearson also aided Welles in drafting a number of early foreign policy documents for FDR.

5. Tim Tzouliadis, *The Forsaken* (New York: The Penguin Press, 2008), 2. There is no accurate estimate of how many thousand Americans actually went to Russia during the early 1930s. But Tzouliadis documents that most ultimately were either executed or died in Soviet gulags during Stalin's purges; only a handful returned to America after their imprisonment.

6. *Ibid.*, 10. Tzouliadis quotes a radio address Shaw made on American national radio in which he compared the Russian Revolution with the American War of Independence, stating "That Jefferson is Lenin, that Franklin is Litvinov, . . . that Hamilton is Stalin . . . Today there is a statue of Washington in Leningrad; and tomorrow there will no doubt be a statue of Lenin in New York."

7. The British-born Duranty won a Pulitzer Prize for his now discredited denials of the widespread famine induced by Stalin's repressions. There have been charges that if he were not a paid Soviet agent, he was demonstrably partisan in his reporting. In 2003, the Pulitzer Prize Board reviewed the Duranty articles that earned him the award in 1932 and conceded that the reporting "falls seriously short" of professional standards of accuracy but that it could not find clear evidence of deliberate deception.

8. WCBP. Correspondence with Marguerite Alice "Missy" LeHand. Group 112. Series 1. Box 49. Folders 1181–1193.

9. *Ibid.* LeHand to Bullitt. Letter dated December 30, 1934.

10. Beatrice Farnsworth, *William C. Bullitt and the Soviet Union* (Bloomington, IN: University of Indiana Press, 1967), 109. She notes, "The hurt of his long, political exclusion made it especially important that he be on the inside now. Few documents are more revealing of a man's temperament than are Bullitt's letters to the President. While Roosevelt maintained his breezy, cordial tone, Bullitt's communications were often intense. From aboard the ship on which he sailed to Russia in December, 1933 . . . 'I think you know what a joy it is to me to be able to work with you and under your orders. I know you refuse to admit it—especially to yourself—but the fact is you are a very great human being and a great President. It has just occurred to me that I have never thanked you properly for this assignment to Russia. The reason is, I think, that I feel myself so completely at your disposal and am so entirely ready to do anything anywhere that you may wish that I have the feeling of carrying out a job for you rather than any feeling of personal success.'" Also, Bullitt to Roosevelt. December 6, 1933. FDRP. Presidential Secretary Files, Box 15.

11. Michael Casella-Blackburn, *The Donkey, the Carrot, and the Club: William C. Bullitt and Soviet-American Relations 1917–1945* (Westport, CT: Praeger, 2004), 147–170. Also, Farnsworth, *William C. Bullitt,* 107–110. Also, Brownell and Billings, *So Close,* 140–170.

CHAPTER FIFTEEN

1. Allen W. Dulles, "The Cost of Peace," *Foreign Affairs* (July 1934).

2. Lippmann's favorite was a *New Yorker* cartoon of two stout matrons in a railroad dining car, with one stating, "Of course, I only take a cup of coffee in the morning. A cup of coffee and Walter Lippmann is all I need." Steel, *Walter Lippmann,* 281.

3. Steel, *Walter Lippmann,* 280.

4. WLP. MS Group 326. Series VI. Manuscripts and Typescripts, 1917–1967, "Journalism and the Liberal Spirit." Speech to American Academy of Political Science. March 25, 1931.

5. WLP. MS Group 326. Series III. Correspondence 1931–1981. Letter to Newton Baker. November 24, 1931.

6. WLP. MS Group 326. Series III. Correspondence 1931–1967. Folder 105. Letter to Hamilton Fish Armstrong. March 30, 1935.

7. WLP. Letter from Hamilton Fish Armstrong. March 25, 1935.

8. John Foster Dulles, "The Power of International Finance," address to the Foreign Policy Association. New York. March 24, 1928.

9. John Foster Dulles, "The Road to Peace," *Atlantic Monthly* (October 1935), 492–499. Also, John Foster Dulles, *War, Peace and Change* (New York: Harper and Brothers, 1939). Also, Anthony Clark Arend, *Pursuing a Just and Durable Peace: John Foster Dulles and International Organization* (New York: Greenwood Press, 1988), 21–25.

10. Allen W. Dulles, "Germany and the Crisis in Disarmament," *Foreign Affairs* (January 1934).

11. Drew Pearson, "Washington Merry-Go-Round," *The Washington Post,* October 10, 1934.

12. Ronald W. Pruessen, *John Foster Dulles: The Road to Power* (New York: The Free Press, 1982), 125. "What should be made of the

charges against John Foster Dulles? In some ways, it is tempting to deny them outright. It is clear, for example, that the heavy direct involvement of Dulles and Sullivan & Cromwell in German business and banking during the 1920s and early 1930s was not continued into the Hitler era. There is no reason to doubt the closing of the Sullivan & Cromwell office in Berlin. There is no clear evidence indicating legal work for I.G. Farben, no definitive proof linking the London or New York Schroeders to their German namesakes, no proof at all linking Dulles to Spain's Franco." Note the difference in spelling. The London banking house of J. Henry Schroder was founded in 1804 to finance cotton and tobacco trade with the United States. Its New York branch was opened in 1923. Sullivan & Cromwell represented both branches on legal matters. Neither bank had any ties with the Hamburg-based Schroeder Bank seized by a Nazi official in the 1930s.

13. Allen W. Dulles, *John Foster Dulles Oral History Project*. Mudd Library. Princeton University. Also, Srodes, *Allen Dulles*, 183.

14. Dulles, "The Cost of Peace."

15. Hamilton Fish Armstrong and Allen W. Dulles, *Can We Be Neutral?* (New York: Council on Foreign Relations, 1936), 177–118. See also, Armstrong and Dulles, *Can America Stay Neutral?* (New York: Harper & Brothers, 1939).

16. The Lippmann "Today & Tomorrow column" of May 19, 1933 had appeared after the start of attacks on German Jews by the Nazis and was an analysis of a seemingly conciliatory speech given by Hitler to assuage world opinion. Lippmann termed the speech, "The authentic voice of a genuinely civilized people." He argued that to judge a nation only by its crimes was intolerance. "Who that has studied history and cares for the truth would judge the French people by what went on during the Terror? Or the British people by what happened in Ireland? Or the American people by the hideous record of lynchings? Or the Catholic Church by the Spanish Inquisition? Or Protestantism by the Ku Klux Klan? Or the Jews by their parvenus?"

CHAPTER SIXTEEN

1. Sumner Welles, *Seven Decisions That Shaped History* (New York: Harper & Brothers,1950), 182.

2. The most detailed account of the incident is a memorandum dictated by William C. Bullitt based on a copy of the Southern Railway investigations and interviews with the Pullman Company staff involved. WCBP. MS Group 112. Series VI. Box 210. Folder 217. A more heavily redacted document involving the FBI's investigation of the case—"Memorandum for the Director," January 26, 1941—can be obtained through FOIA requests along with the Bureau's extensive file on Sumner Welles. Also, the Papers of Irwin F. Gellman, housed at the FDR Presidential Library, contain other redacted copies of the FBI's internal memos on the case. Filed under The Papers of Sumner Welles in Box 3. See also, Welles, *Sumner Welles,* 1–3.

3. Christopher D. O'Sullivan, *Sumner Welles, Postwar Planning, and the Quest for a New World Order, 1937–1943* (New York: Columbia University Press, 2008), xiv.

4. Gellman, *Secret Affairs,* 138–150. Also, O'Sullivan, *Sumner Welles,* 20–25. Hull went to great lengths to keep secret his recurring bouts of tuberculosis, which was publicly feared because of its contagious threat. Drew Pearson and other journalists unfairly charged that his frequent convalescence absences were due to laziness.

5. Philip Kerr. Letter, Lord Lothian to Sir John Simon. January 30, 1935. The Papers of Lord Lothian. GD40/17/201. Folios 70–72. Scottish National Archives, Edinburgh. Also, David P. Billington, *Lothian: Philip Kerr and the Quest for World Order* (London: Praeger, 2006), 101–139. Also, J.R.M. Butler, *Lord Lothian* (New York: St. Martin's Press, 1960), 212–237.

6. FDRP. Box 32. Letter, FDR to Roger Merriman. February 15, 1939. Correspondence. Also, Billington, Lothian, 135.

7. HFAP. Unpublished draft by Allen Dulles for *Foreign Affairs.*

October 1938. Box 25. Also, Armstrong and Dulles, "Legislating Peace," *Foreign Affairs* 17, no. 1 (October 1938). Also, Dulles, "Cash and Carry Neutrality," *Foreign Affairs* 18, no. 2 (January 1940).

8. HFAP. Walter H. Mallory, Council on Foreign Relations Report of the Executive Director, 1938–1939.

9. HFAP. Council on Foreign Relations Project for a Study of the Effects of the War on the United States and of the American Interest in the Peace Settlement. Dated December 1939.

10. *Ibid.* Also, *The Council on Foreign Relations: A Record of Twenty-five Years* (New York: CFR, 1947), 15–23.

Chapter Seventeen

1. WCBP. Group 112. Series VI. Box 210. Folder 219, subject Sumner Welles. Memo dated Easter Sunday, April 25, 1943, a conversation at the Hull's home.

2. Wendell Wilkie polled nearly 45 percent of the popular vote (22.3 million) to Roosevelt's 27.3 million), but FDR carried 38 states and 449 electoral college votes to 82 for the GOP. The president had directed a purge of Congressional Democrats who had opposed him with the result that his majority of New Deal supporters in both chambers actually increased.

3. Leo Pasvolsky (1893–1953) was a Russia-born economist and journalist who joined the Brookings Institution staff in 1922 and maintained his ties there until his death. He was recruited by Cordell Hull to advise on trade policy in 1933 and held a number of staff posts at State until February 1941 when he was made director of the new Division of Special Research with the rank of assistant secretary. The Papers of Leo Pasvolsky, a collection of his public papers, is housed at the U.S. Library of Congress Manuscript Room. His papers concerning his work at the Brookings Institution are archived there.

4. Gellman, *Secret Affairs,* 238.

5. WCBP. Box 210 contains what purports to be a handwritten note from Moore to Bullitt referring to the affidavit provided him by Thomas, a summary of which Bullitt dictated in a memo in Folder 219.

6. Carmel Offie (1909–1972) deserves a biography of his own. He was born in Sharon, Pennsylvania, to Italian immigrants; his father worked as a railroad track hand. After working his way through secretarial school, Offie worked first for the Interstate Commerce Commission before being sent to the U.S. Embassy in Honduras. He was sent to Bullitt's staff in 1934. While he kept a life-long relationship with Bullitt, Offie later joined the staff of Robert Murphy, State's representative to Allied forces in Italy and, later, Germany. After the war, he held posts in the early forerunners of the Central Intelligence Agency in a variety of clandestine operations as the Cold War was getting underway. Offie was highly successful in a number of these covert operations, especially in Italy and Eastern Europe. He was finally fired from the CIA in 1950 when Senator Joseph McCarthy's committee began to probe his 1943 arrest record and other reports of his homosexuality. The FBI Official/Confidential file on his various sexual escapades obtained through FOIA runs to 335 pages.

7. FBI Official/Confidential File on Carmel Offie. Obtained through FOIA request.

8. Brownell and Billings, *So Close,* 267.

9. Paul H. Nitze, later a Navy secretary, ambassador, and key foreign policy adviser to a succession of presidents, recounted in conversations with the author about his being part of "a group of young staff who would sneak in the back door of the White House "whenever Eleanor was away" to amuse FDR in the evening.

10. Persico, *Franklin & Lucy,* 216–222.

11. *Ibid.,* 251–255. The FDR Library's Pare Loretz Chronology, a detailed compilation of FDR's private meetings based on

White House logs, records thirty-two visits between Roosevelt and Princess Martha in the first year of her stay in Washington, most of them at her home in Pook's Hill, Maryland.

12. WCBP. Box 210. Folder 217. Sumner Welles. Memo, "Conversation with the President," April 23, 1941.

13. Originally set up as the Committee on Information, Donovan convinced Dulles at the 1940 Republican convention after having secured FDR's approval. The first COI offices were in Rockefeller Center near the suite occupied by British intelligence services, which were being directed by William Stephenson and his mentor, the venerable William Wiseman.

14. Dulles family members have speculated to the author that Blondheim had grown depressed over his estrangement from his Orthodox Jewish parents as well as the couple's financial problems. The couple had been forced to keep separate residences while he taught at Johns Hopkins and she taught at Bryn Mawr.

15. Alger Hiss (1904–1996) had been both a student of Frankfurter and a law clerk to Justice Oliver Wendell Holmes. At Frankfurter's suggestion, Secretary Hull had hired him away from a New Deal agricultural aid agency in 1936 and later appointed him to the Office of Special Political Affairs (OSPA) which drafted the actual architecture of the United Nations plan; Hiss later became the OSPA director. Hiss was the secretary of the Dumbarton Oaks conference that concluded the UN pact in 1944. He travelled with FDR to the Yalta Conference in 1945, and he was the secretary-general of the United Nations organizational meeting in San Francisco. Hiss was supposed to be the UN's first permanent secretary-general, but persisting rumors of his Communist Party membership and charges he had provided classified State documents to Soviet intelligence operatives forced his resignation from State. John Foster Dulles, who had become chairman of the Carnegie Endowment for International Peace, secured the presidency for Hiss, which he held until 1949. His 1950 conviction and imprisonment for

perjury were among the most contentious issues—along with similar charges against Harry Dexter White and the Rosenberg atomic secrets trial—of the McCarthy era prosecutions aimed at countering Soviet subversion of the U.S. government. Hiss remained a polarizing symbol and maintained his innocence the rest of his life. Both Foster and Allen Dulles had initially refused to believe the charges but changed their minds as evidence emerged. Srodes, *Allen Dulles,* 408–412.

16. Italics by Lippmann.

17. Blum, *Public Philosopher,* 434. Letter to Henry A. Wallace, January 27, 1943.

18. WCBP. Folder 210. Box 219. Sumner Welles.

19. The Pare Loretz Chronology records twenty-three visits by Welles to the Oval Office during 1944 alone. FDRP Library.

CONCLUSIONS

1. Arthur Kirsch, *W. H. Auden: Lectures on Shakespeare* (Princeton, NJ: Princeton University Press, 2000), 216.

Acknowledgments

$\mathcal{W}$RITING CAN BE A SOLITARY CRAFT. But no biographer is ever truly alone, and I am no exception. One first stands on the shoulders of historians who have worked the field before, and in the bibliography, I have singled out just a few of the men and women whose previous efforts helped me and can be recommended to the reader who seeks to learn more about the story.

But I would be remiss if I did not also pay special thanks to the scores of professional archivists who collect, preserve, and organize the trove of personal papers of our characters that were my primary sources. I was lucky to have close at hand two treasure houses of history. The District of Columbia's Martin Luther King Library is the repository of so much Washington history. And I owe special thanks to Thomas Mann of the U.S. Library of Congress Main Reading Room and the fine Manuscript Room staff for their cooperation.

One of the pleasures of this project was renewing my friendship with the always-helpful librarians of the Seeley G. Mudd Manuscript Library at Princeton University and the Yale University's Sterling Library Manuscript Room. Equally helpful were the National Archive and Records Administration archivists who made research work so enjoyable at the Presidential Libraries of Franklin

D. Roosevelt in Hyde Park, New York; Dwight D. Eisenhower in Abilene, Kansas; and Lyndon B. Johnson in Austin, Texas.

The task of sifting through the lives of twelve individuals would have been impossible in the time allotted if it had not been for the generous help of friend Diana Fortescue, who braved the Scottish National Archives in Edinburgh where Philip Kerr's papers are housed and did an exhaustive document search of other important British source material. Thanks also to Jacob Roberts and Julien Crochet, who did the initial photograph scouting.

Even if one can manage to get the research and writing done, actually getting a project like this one published requires acts of faith and understanding from a number of other people. Ronald Goldfarb, my agent and friend, merits my everlasting gratitude for his shrewd advice and commitment to finding a home for this book. So too, Charles Winton of Counterpoint Press buoyed my spirits with his enthusiasm for the project and his prescience in bringing me into the orbit of Eric Brandt, one of the finest literary editors in the craft. Thanks also to Jodi Hammerwold of Counterpoint, who has remained cheerfully supportive and efficient throughout.

Finally, let me thank the most meticulous copyeditor, supportive companion, and best wife a man could have, Cecile Srodes.

Index

Acheson, Dean, 213

ACLU. *See* American Civil Liberties Union (ACLU)

African Americans, 23, 29, 104–105, 188, 267

Albertson, Faye, 54–55, 57, 60, 64, 83, 115, 196, 228–229, 239–241

Albertson, Ralph, 44

Allen, Robert S., 214; "Washington Merry-Go-Round," 215, 237; *Washington Merry-Go-Round,* 214

American Civil Liberties Union (ACLU), 196

American Geographic Society, 79

American Jewish Committee, 95, 96

Armstrong, Hamilton Fish, 9, 91, 97–99, 153, 183, 185–186, 198–202, 205–207, 214, 231–233, 238–242, 256–259, 262, 264, 276, 285

Armstrong, Helen. *See* Byrne, Helen MacGregor

Astor, Nancy, 108, 158, 174, 254, 256

Astor, Waldorf, 50, 97, 108, 174

Atlantic Charter, 14, 272–273

Atlantic Monthly, 116, 196

Auden, W.H., 288

Baker, Newton, 52, 55, 56, 57, 59, 64, 199–200, 206, 230

Baker, Ray Stannard, 99

Balfour, Arthur, 71, 95

Bank for International Settlements, 193

Bankhead, Tallulah, 246

Bankhead, William Brockman, 245–248

Baruch, Bernard, 28, 29, 53, 83, 118

Batista, Fulgencio, 216

Bay of Pigs, 284–285

Bell, Alexander Graham, 21–22

Bell, Gertrude, 68

Berle, Adolf A., 88, 198, 253

Bern Legation, 61, 77, 84, 142

Beveridge, Sir William, 175

BEW. *See* Bureau of Economic Warfare (BEW)

Big Four, 74, 93

BIIA. *See* Chatham House

Bliss, Gen. Tasker, 99

Blondheim, David, 176, 275

Blum, Leon, 173

Bolsheviks, 43, 71, 86, 87, 88, 92, 105–107, 136, 144, 220

Borah, William, 64, 102–103

Borglum, Gutzon, 65

Boston Common, 44

Bowman, Isaiah, 79, 82, 259, 264

Brandeis, Louis, 28, 29, 39, 42, 44, 50, 58, 64, 95–96, 213

Bretton Woods, 15, 285

Brewster, Owen, 266

Britain, 11, 12, 14, 23, 34, 38, 41, 46, 49, 51, 58, 66, 68, 79, 83–84, 94, 102, 108, 138–141, 146–148, 153, 161–162, 174–175, 180–183, 189, 193, 203, 231, 246–247, 254–257, 261, 263, 265, 272–273, 275

British Institute of International Affairs (BIIA). *See* Chatham House

Brookings, Robert S., 53

Brookings Institution, 53

Broun, Heywood, 197

Brown v. Board of Education, 286

Bruening, Heinrich, 183

Bryan, William Jennings, 35, 39, 160

Bryant, Louise, 54, 171–173

Buchan, John, 50

Bullitt, Ernesta, 88, 89, 171

Bullitt, William C., 8, 13, 64, 85–89, 94, 97, 102, 123, 170–174, 199, 207–208, 213, 217–225, 250–251, 255, 261–268, 271–272, 276–278, 284–285; *It's Not Done,* 171–172

Bureau of Economic Warfare (BEW), 274, 275

Byrne, Helen MacGregor, 98, 201, 240–241

Campobello Island, 36, 38, 39, 107, 128, 154

Carmody, John M., 249

Carnegie, Andrew, 25

Carp, Betty, 141–143

Castro, Fidel, 216, 285

Cecil, Robert, 99

Central Intelligence Agency (CIA), 275, 284

CFR. *See* Council on Foreign Relations (CFR)

Chamberlain, Neville, 254, 256

Chatham House, 152, 183, 255–256, 258, 286

Childs, James Rives, 70

Churchill, Winston, 14, 173, 261, 272–273

CIA. *See* Central Intelligence Agency (CIA)

Civil War, 19, 20, 25, 26, 121, 168, 190

Clayton Antitrust Act, 30

Clemenceau, Georges, 59, 62, 69, 71–72, 74, 82, 87, 92–93, 183

Cleveland, Grover, 76

Cohen, Ben, 213

Cold War, 279, 283, 284

Committee for Relief of Belgium (CRB), 67

Committee on Public Information (CPI), 81, 116

Communists, 44, 221, 224

Confidential, 284

Congress of Vienna, 72

conservatives, 18, 41, 51, 119, 121, 132, 160, 228, 247, 286

Cook, Nancy, 189, 268

Coolidge, Archibald Cary, 99

Coolidge, Calvin, 123, 129, 131, 159, 160–162, 165, 170, 177, 179, 181–182, 185, 187, 215

Corcoran, Thomas (Tommy the Cork), 212–213

Council on Foreign Relations (CFR), 12, 14, 150, 151–153, 183–184, 193, 205, 209, 214, 233, 241, 242, 258, 259, 284–286

Cox, James M., 127, 129

CPI. *See* Committee on Public Information (CPI)

Craigie, Robert, 78, 141, 143

Cravath, Paul D., 153

CRB. *See* Committee for Relief of Belgium (CRB)

Creel, George, 57, 81, 116

Cromwell, William, 137

Cufflinks Gang, 128, 154, 199, 209, 212. *See also* Early, Stephen; Howe, Louis; LeHand, Marguerite (Missy); McIntyre, Marvin

Curtis, Lionel, 99

Daniels, Josephus, 35, 107, 110, 124, 125, 208, 212

Davis, John W., 153, 199, 206

Davis, Kenneth S., 186–187, 198

Davis, Livingston, 110–111, 158

Davis, Norman, 83, 177, 193, 205–206, 214, 229, 236, 252, 264

Debs, Eugene, 57

Declaration of United Nations, 273

Democrats, 3, 12, 18, 19, 21, 27, 39, 56, 113, 115, 118–123, 126–127, 137, 154–160, 169, 184–189, 198–204, 230–231, 245, 247, 278

Denman, Marion, 55, 97, 196

Depression. *See* Great Depression

Dewey, John, 19, 27

Dewey, Thomas, 247, 285

Dickerman, Marion, 189, 269

disarmament, 12, 25, 146, 149, 166, 176–177, 181, 185, 193, 199, 202, 206, 214, 236–237, 259

Dodge, Mabel, 24, 53

Donovan, William, 275

Drift and Mastery (Lippmann), 51

Dubois, W.E.B., 104

Dulles, Allen Macy, 31, 141

Dulles, Allen W., 2, 8, 31, 61, 75–78, 84, 88, 97–98, 132, 137–143, 175–177, 182–184, 193, 205–206, 227, 236–239, 241, 257–259, 275, 284, 285

Dulles, Edith Foster, 75

Dulles, Eleanor Lansing, 2, 8, 32, 75–78, 175–176, 275, 285

Dulles, John Foster, 2, 8, 26, 31, 61, 75, 83–84, 136–137, 162, 233, 235, 238, 274, 276, 284

Dulles, Mary, 75

Dulles, Nataline, 75

Dulles Clause, 182

Duranty, Walter, 220–221

Early, Stephen, 127, 209, 212

Economic Consequences of the Peace, The (Keynes), 83, 116

Eddy, Mary Baker, 108

Eden, Anthony, 236

Edison, Thomas, 22, 35

Eisenhower, Dwight D., 284, 286

Eliot, T.S., 43, 235

Emmitt, Grenville, 212

eugenicists, 3, 68, 144

Fabians, 41, 46, 51, 97, 108, 174

Farley, James, 246

Farnsworth, Beatrice, 222–223

Fascists, 3, 12, 72, 158, 172, 174, 258, 262

FCC. *See* Federal Council of Churches (FCC)

FDR. *See* Roosevelt, Franklin D.

Federal Council of Churches (FCC), 103, 232–233, 235

Federal Reserve System, 30, 42, 192

Federal Trade Commission, 30

Federal Works Administration, 249

Ferber, Edna, 197

Fitzgerald, F. Scott, 170

Five-Year Plan, 220

Food Administration, 67

Ford, Henry, 22, 35, 64, 97, 220

Foreign Affairs, 153, 162, 183, 185, 201, 202, 203, 205, 214, 215, 227, 236, 240, 242, 255, 257, 285

Forsaken, The (Tzouliadis), 220

Fosdick, Harry Emerson, 234–235

Fosdick, Raymond, 98, 234

Foster, Gen. John Watson, 24, 26, 76

Fourteen Points speech, 51, 71, 79–80, 82

France, 11, 14, 25–26, 38, 56–59, 63, 66, 71–73, 75, 77, 79–80, 83–84,

91–92, 98, 102, 104, 107–108,
117–118, 138–139, 146–148, 155,
161–162, 170, 174–175, 180–183,
193–194, 206, 218, 224–225, 231,
241, 246–247, 250–251, 256,
261–263, 266, 268, 273–274
Frank, Leo, 96
Frankfurter, Felix, 2, 8, 17, 23, 27, 28,
32, 40–47, 50, 52, 54–59, 64, 68,
95–96, 107, 115, 119, 122, 132, 159,
169, 185, 191, 195–199, 212–213,
228, 230, 239, 255, 275, 286
Frankfurter, Marion. *See* Denman,
Marion
Freud, Sigmund, 172, 285

Galleani, Luigi, 106
Garden Suburb, 50, 59, 60, 99
Garner, John Nance, 217, 246
Gay, Edwin F., 153
Geneva Disarmament Conference, 177,
182, 193
George, David Lloyd, 9, 50, 58, 70–72,
80, 82, 86–88, 92–94, 96, 98–99,
147, 183, 255
George V, King, 107
Germany, 11, 12, 13, 14, 15, 26, 28,
41, 62, 71, 75, 82–84, 138, 146–147,
161, 180–181, 183, 202, 205–206,
220, 223–225, 233–238, 246,
253–255, 258, 263, 272, 274–275,
283, 286
Gerry, Mathilde Townsend, 168–170,
208, 215, 262–263, 283
Gerry, Peter, 168, 169, 170
G.I. Bill of Rights, 276
Gibson, Hugh, 207
Glasworthy, John, 64
Goering, Hermann, 205
Good Neighbor policy, 190, 214, 216,
256
Great Crash. *See* Wall Street Crash of
1929
Great Depression, 1, 192, 213, 220,
230, 246
Great War. *See* World War I

Harding, Warren G., 12, 94, 101, 123,
126, 128–129, 131, 135, 143–148,
154, 156, 159–160, 162, 167,
179–181, 185
Hearst, William Randolph, 156, 197
Hemingway, Ernest, 170
Herter, Christian, 88, 97
Hickock, Lorena, 269
Hiss, Alger, 213, 275–276
Hiss, Donald, 213, 275
Hitler, Adolf, 13, 14, 83–84, 93,
205–207, 220, 225, 236, 238–239,
249, 253–257, 261, 263
HMS Prince of Wales, 272
Holmes, Oliver Wendell, 17, 23, 27, 29,
41, 50, 54, 64, 105, 117, 212–213
Holt, Hamilton, 102–103
homosexuality, 189, 266–267
Hoover, Herbert, 2, 7, 13, 65–67,
87, 97, 115, 117–123, 145–146,
148, 161–162, 178–181, 183–195,
200–203, 206, 211–212, 214, 219,
230, 275, 286
Hoover, J. Edgar, 250, 266
Hoover, Lou Henry, 65–66
House, Col. Edward, 31, 38, 49, 50,
51, 52, 59, 60, 61, 62, 79, 80, 81,
82, 85, 86, 99, 119, 121, 122, 186,
199–202, 207, 214, 217, 274; *Philip
Dru: Administrator,* 50; "Some Foreign
Problems of the Next Administration,"
202–203
House of Truth, 7, 8, 9, 17, 19, 21,
23–34, 40, 42, 46–47, 49, 52, 55, 57,
60, 62, 64–66, 96, 117, 131, 174,
178, 184, 208, 229, 255, 281–282
Howe, Louis, 36, 37, 113, 127, 128,
154–157, 160, 185, 189, 209,
211–213, 215, 217
Hughes, Charles Evans, 132, 143,
145–149, 167, 183

Hull, Cordell, 203–204, 215–219, 237, 248, 250–254, 258–259, 261–267, 273–274, 276–278
Hull, Frances Whitney, 261

IMF. *See* International Monetary Fund (IMF)
industrialization, 2, 20, 21
Industrial Workers of the World, 104
Inquiry, The, 59–61, 64, 78–80, 82, 84, 98–99, 153, 252
International Monetary Fund (IMF), 15, 275, 278, 286
isolationism, 101, 144, 206, 211, 231, 236, 242, 246, 247, 250, 260, 266, 273
It's Not Done (Bullitt), 171–172

James, William, 19, 27
Japan, 13, 14, 15, 25–26, 93, 133, 144, 146–149, 166, 181–182, 186, 194, 202, 206, 219, 223–224, 235, 272, 284
Johnson, Mrs. Paul. *See* Mercer, Lucy
Jordan, John M., 21
Joyce, James, 145; *Ulysses,* 145

Karp, Bertha. *See* Carp, Betty
Kaufman, George S., 197
Kellogg, Frank, 170, 177, 182, 183
Kellogg-Briand Pact, 13, 182, 200, 203, 235
Kennedy, John F., 132, 283, 284–285
Kennedy, Joseph, 254
Kerr, Phillip, 2, 9, 46–50, 65, 71, 87, 92, 96, 99, 108, 152, 183, 255–257, 263, 272
Keynes, John Maynard, 83, 116–117, 137, 175, 274; *The Economic Consequences of the Peace,* 83, 116
KKK. *See* Ku Klux Klan
Knowles, Horace G., 211, 215
Knox, Frank, 264
Krock, Arthur, 266

Ku Klux Klan (KKK), 105, 144, 160

labor, 29, 30, 34, 47, 51, 56, 74, 104, 106, 107, 115, 144, 160, 186, 195, 196
Lamont, Thomas, 151, 152, 153, 229, 241
Landon, Alf, 231, 261
Lansing, Robert, 8, 9, 24, 31, 32, 38–40, 57, 61–62, 75–77, 79, 85–89, 123–124, 132
Lardner, Ring, 197
Latin America, 59, 62, 84, 87, 96, 106, 118, 133, 135–136, 149, 167, 170, 186–187, 190–191, 195, 199, 208, 214–215, 216, 217, 252, 254, 258, 278, 285, 287
Law, Nigel, 109, 110
Lawrence, T.E., 68, 96
League of Nations, 1, 12, 13, 14, 15, 34, 72, 74, 82, 88–89, 93–95, 97–99, 102–103, 112, 127, 129, 132, 144, 146–149, 152, 161, 165–166, 176, 182, 186, 203, 206, 224, 225, 231–236, 251, 259, 265, 273, 276, 287
League to Enforce Peace, 34, 97, 102
Le Gallienne, Gwen, 173
LeHand, Marguerite (Missy), 128–129, 154, 157–159, 209, 212–213, 218, 221–222, 266–268, 270, 277
Lenin, Vladimir, 78, 86–88, 171, 173
liberals, 119, 122, 145, 155, 197, 228–230, 251
Liberty and the News (Lippmann), 116–117, 197
Lincoln, Abraham, 18, 253
Lippmann, Faye. *See* Albertson, Faye
Lippmann, Walter, 2, 7, 9, 20–21, 26–28, 32–34, 38, 41, 43–46, 50–60, 64, 79–83, 95, 97–98, 102, 107, 115–120, 122, 129, 131–132, 159, 184–187, 195–200, 227–232, 235, 239–242, 255, 276, 283; *Drift and Mastery,* 51; *Liberty and the News,*

116–117, 197; *A Preface to Politics,* 45,
51; *Public Opinion,* 197; *The Stakes of
Diplomacy,* 51, 53
Little Review, 144–145
Litvinov, Maxim, 183, 219–220, 223,
224
Lodge, Henry Cabot, 89, 102
Lodge Committee, 89, 94
London Daily Mail, 88
London Naval Conference, 193–194
Long, Breckinridge, 39, 47, 120, 208,
212
Longworth, Alice Roosevelt, 33, 64, 85,
109
Longworth, Nicholas, 64
Lothian, Lord. *See* Kerr, Phillip
Lowell, A. Lawrence, 196

MacDonald, Ramsay, 183, 193
Machado, Gerardo, 216
MacMillan, Margaret, 93–94;
Peacemakers, 93–94
Mallory, Walter, 206, 258–259
Martha, Princess of Norway. *See* Thyra,
Märtha Sofia Lovisa Dagmar
Masaryk, Thomas, 78, 173
McAdoo, William, 125, 160
McIntyre, Marvin, 127, 212
McKinley, William, 27, 34
Mercer, Lucy, 33, 36–37, 109–111, 157,
208, 269–270, 283
Messersmith, George S., 258–259
Mesta, Pearl, 69
Metropolitan, 50
Meyer, Eugene, 53
Minh, Ho Chi, 73
Mississippi River floods, 188
Moley, Raymond, 198
Monnet, Jean, 98
Monroe Doctrine, 135, 191, 200
Mooney, Tom, 95
Moore, R. Walton, 219, 250–251, 265,
271, 277
Morgan, J.P., 105, 229

Morgenthau, Henry, 28, 57–59, 96,
142, 158, 274–275
Morrison, Samuel Eliot, 88
Moskowitz, Belle, 156
Mosley, Cynthia, 158
Mosley, Sir Oswald, 158
muckrakers, 28, 42, 99
Murphy, Gerald, 170
Murphy, Sara, 170
Mussolini, Benito, 12, 14, 72, 171, 174,
202, 205–207, 220, 249, 253, 255,
263

Naboth's Vineyard (Welles), 190
National Recovery Act, 213, 230
National Security Act of 1947, 284
Nazis, 13, 15, 202, 205, 225, 238,
253–254, 256, 261–264, 270, 275
neutrality, 133, 135, 206, 224, 239,
242, 246, 247, 257
Neutrality Act of 1935, 224–225, 231
New Deal, 13, 192, 198, 202, 211, 224,
230–231, 237, 246–247, 250, 266
New Republic, 8, 9, 21, 23, 34, 38, 45,
47, 52, 53, 81, 107, 115–116, 119, 197
New York Evening Post, 91, 153
New York Herald Tribune, 195, 228
New York Times, 220, 228, 266, 283
New York World, 197–198, 228
Nicolson, Harold, 92, 99, 141
Niebuhr, Reinhold, 235
Nixon, Richard, 285
Nobel, Alfred, 24–25
Nobel Prize, 12, 24–25, 26, 278

Observer, 108
Office of Strategic Services (OSS), 275,
284
Offie, Carmel, 267, 284
Okrent, Daniel, 3
O'Neill, Eugene, 54
Orlando, Vittorio, 72, 93
OSS. *See* Office of Strategic Services
(OSS)

O'Sullivan, Christopher D., 251–252

Palmer, A. Mitchell, 106, 115
Palmer Raids, 106–107
Paris Peace Conference, 11, 67, 75, 84, 91, 93, 136, 161, 166, 259
Pasvolsky, Leo, 264–265, 274–275
Patterson, Cissy, 266, 277
Peacemakers (MacMillan), 93–94
Peace Ship, 35, 64, 98
Pearl Harbor, 14, 274, 275
Pearson, Drew, 200, 214–215, 217, 237, 253, 266, 278; "Washington Merry-Go-Round," 215, 237; *Washington Merry-Go-Round,* 214
Pennsylvania Railroad, 249, 271
Percy, Eustace, 2, 9, 23, 40–41, 46–49, 52, 65, 71, 80–82, 92, 96, 99, 108–109, 152, 183, 255, 285
Perkins, Frances, 155, 156
Pershing, Gen. John J., 56, 58, 59, 69, 75, 79, 80, 148
Persico, Joseph, 269–270
Philadelphia Public Ledger, 85
Philip Dru: Administrator (House), 50
Philips, William, 215, 255
Porter, Cole, 170
Preface to Politics, A (Lippmann), 45, 51
Progressives, 3, 4, 17, 19, 20, 25–30, 34–35, 40, 44–45, 52, 54, 55, 63, 67, 75, 85, 89, 108, 113, 117, 120–123, 126, 129, 131–132, 143–144, 149, 151, 153, 156, 159–160, 173–177, 181, 184, 186–187, 190, 194, 199, 203, 205–206, 211, 229, 231, 242, 281, 287
Prohibition, 3, 12, 19, 34, 68, 103, 159, 161, 184
Pruessen, Ronald W., 238
Public Opinion (Lippmann), 197
Pulitzer, Joseph, 197, 228

radicals, 2, 30, 43, 44, 51, 53–54, 80, 87, 95, 104, 105, 120, 171, 180, 191, 229

Reed, John, 43, 53–54, 107, 171, 172, 174, 220; *Ten Days That Shook the World,* 171
reparations, 12, 71, 84, 120, 136, 138, 146, 161–162, 193–194, 233
Republicans, 3, 11, 18, 19, 27, 28, 42, 52, 73, 115, 119–129, 132, 144, 146, 159, 160, 177, 180, 184–187, 191, 211, 228, 231, 247, 264, 266, 278
Reston, James, 266
Rhodes, Cecil, 255
Rhodes Scholarships, 255, 256
Rhodes Trust, 255
Robinson, Joseph Taylor, 185
Rockefeller, John D., 43, 105
Rockefeller, John D., Jr., 235
Rockefeller Foundation, 152, 234, 259
Roosevelt, Eleanor, 2, 7, 8, 9, 36, 37, 38, 106–112, 119, 128, 155–158, 188–189, 203, 208, 214, 253, 268–270, 281, 283
Roosevelt, Franklin D., 2, 4, 7, 9, 12, 13, 15, 20–21, 26, 33, 35–38, 57, 65, 85, 105–115, 118–119, 122–132, 151–169, 174, 185–190, 194–195, 198–201, 205, 208–209, 214, 217–218, 221, 223, 225, 230, 242, 245–246, 251–252, 261–262, 268–270, 278–279, 281, 283, 285–286
Roosevelt, Theodore, 4, 8, 11, 21, 25–26, 27, 33, 35–37, 42, 50, 65, 113, 120–122, 191, 199, 229, 231
Roosevelt Corollary, 191
Root, Elihu, 26, 152, 206
Round Table, 9, 49, 183
Royal Institute of International Affairs. *See* Chatham House
Russia, 11, 24–26, 43, 54, 64–65, 69, 78, 85–89, 92, 102, 105, 107, 139, 141, 147, 171, 173–174, 219–224, 252, 265–266, 276, 279
Rutherfurd, Lucy Mercer. *See* Mercer, Lucy
Rutherfurd, Winthrop, 111, 270

Sacco, Nicola, 196
Santayana, George, 19, 27, 44
Schacht, Hjalmar Horace Greeley, 137–138
Schiff, Jacob, 28, 50
Sedgwick, Ellery, 116
Shaw, George Bernard, 51, 108, 174, 220
Shepardson, Whitney, 259
Sims, Adm. William S., 124–125
Sinclair, Upton, 42–43
Slater, Nelson, 40
Smith, Alfred E. (Al), 119, 126–127, 156, 157, 159–161, 170, 184, 185–190, 199, 214
Smoot-Hawley Tariff, 194
Smuts, Jan Christian, 88
Socialists, 3, 43–45, 51, 57, 173, 206, 247
Social Security Act, 224
Social Security Administration, 275
"Some Foreign Problems of the Next Administration" (House), 202–203
Southern Railway, 249–250, 265
Soviet Union. *See* Russia
Stakes of Diplomacy, The (Lippmann), 51, 53
Stalin, Joseph, 174, 219–224
State Department, 9, 14, 31–32, 38–39, 57, 61, 76, 135–136, 139, 143, 170, 176–177, 183, 215, 221, 237, 242, 250–252, 258–259, 262, 264–265, 267, 283
Steffens, Lincoln, 28, 43–44, 86–87
Stimson, Henry, 28, 42, 43, 45, 191, 264
suffrage, 11, 23, 31, 68
Sullivan, William, 69
Sullivan & Cromwell, 8, 31, 61, 69, 77, 84, 137–138, 177, 207, 233–234, 237, 238
Swope, Herbert Bayard, 197

Taft, Robert, 247

Taft, William Howard, 11, 21, 30, 34, 45–46
Tammany Hall, 7, 28, 35, 51, 119, 122, 126, 156, 184
Tarbell, Ida, 43
Ten Days That Shook the World (Reed), 171
Thomas, Luther, 265, 271, 277
Thyra, Märtha Sofia Lovisa Dagmar, 270
Tilley, Sir John, 141
Tillich, Paul, 235
Time, 220
Times (London), 108
Todd, Martha Clover, 140–144, 176–177, 206, 237
Truman, Harry S., 73, 266, 284, 286
Tugwell, Rexford, 198
Tyrrell, Sir William, 80–81
Tzouliadis, Tim, 220; *The Forsaken,* 220

Ulysses (Joyce), 145
UN. *See* United Nations
UNESCO. *See* United Nations Education, Scientific, and Cultural Organization (UNESCO)
United Nations (UN), 14, 15, 236, 245, 251, 260, 262, 264, 276, 278, 282–283, 286
United Nations Education, Scientific, and Cultural Organization (UNESCO), 286
U.S. Department of State. *See* State Department

Valentine, Robert Grosvenor, 21–23
Vanity Fair, 116
Vanzetti, Bartolomeo, 196
Versailles Treaty, 12, 67, 83–84, 88, 89, 93–94, 97, 100, 112–113, 136, 161, 181, 183, 217–218, 225, 232–233, 254, 276
Villa, Pancho, 46, 53

Wagner, Robert F., 189

Wallace, Henry, 247, 249, 274–276

Wall Street, 8, 29, 31, 61–62, 83–84, 119, 137, 146, 152–153, 161, 177, 192, 200, 202, 206, 218, 228, 233–234, 247

Wall Street Crash of 1929, 13, 192

War and Peace Studies, 259, 262, 264

War Industries Board, 53, 77

Warm Springs (GA), 159, 185, 187, 209, 251, 283

Warren Commission, 285

Washington Arms Conference, 147–149

"Washington Merry-Go-Round" (Allen, Pearson), 215, 237

Washington Merry-Go-Round (Allen, Pearson), 214

Washington Post, 53

Washington Times-Herald, 266

Webb, Beatrice, 51, 174

Webb, Sidney, 51, 174

Wehle, Louis, 39, 118–122, 217

Weizmann, Chaim, 58, 68, 95

Welles, Esther Slater, 40, 132–135, 166–169

Welles, Sumner, 9, 14, 38–40, 132–136, 149, 166–170, 186, 190, 195, 199–200, 208, 211, 213–217, 245, 248–279, 283–285; *Naboth's Vineyard,* 190

Wells, H.G., 51, 108

West, Rebecca, 237

Wharton, Edith, 97

White, Harry Dexter, 274, 275

WHO. *See* World Health Organization (WHO)

Willert, Arthur, 64

Willkie, Wendell, 247, 249, 261

Wilson, Woodrow, 4, 7, 8, 11, 12, 21, 24, 27–39, 47, 49–62, 65, 67, 71–74, 79–89, 93–94, 98–99, 102–103, 106–107, 112–113, 116–119, 122–128, 132–133, 135, 139, 153–156, 160, 165–166, 171–172, 186, 199–200, 203, 217, 223, 229, 232–233, 242, 251–252, 263, 268, 282, 285

Wiseman, William, 60, 80

Wobblies. *See* Industrial Workers of the World

World Bank, 15, 278, 285, 286

World Health Organization (WHO), 287

World Trade Organization (WTO), 287

World War I, 1, 11, 13, 26, 51, 57, 96, 102, 108, 124, 129, 131–133, 135, 138, 144, 147, 162, 166, 179, 193, 207, 213, 242, 252, 260

World War II, 14, 148, 149, 216, 250, 284

WTO. *See* World Trade Organization (WTO)

Yardley, Herbert, 70, 148

Young, Allen, 175

Young, Owen D., 193

Zapata, Emiliano, 46

Zionists, 28, 58, 61, 95, 253